BRITAIN'S WAR ON POVERTY

BRITAIN'S WAR ON POVERTY

Jane Waldfogel

Russell Sage Foundation • New York

The Russell Sage Foundation

The Russell Sage Foundation, one of the oldest of America's general purpose foundations, was established in 1907 by Mrs. Margaret Olivia Sage for "the improvement of social and living conditions in the United States." The Foundation seeks to fulfill this mandate by fostering the development and dissemination of knowledge about the country's political, social, and economic problems. While the Foundation endeavors to assure the accuracy and objectivity of each book it publishes, the conclusions and interpretations in Russell Sage Foundation publications are those of the authors and not of the Foundation, its Trustees, or its staff. Publication by Russell Sage, therefore, does not imply Foundation endorsement.

Library of Congress Cataloging-in-Publication Data
Waldfogel, Jane.
Britain's war on poverty / Jane Waldfogel.
    p. cm.
    Includes bibliographical references and index.
    ISBN 978-0-87154-897-9 (alk. paper)
    1.   Child welfare—Great Britain.   2.   Poor children—Services for—Great
Britain.   3.   Poverty—Government policy—Great Britain.   4.   Public welfare—Great Britain.   I. Title.
HV751.A6W34 2010
362.7--dc22   2010003235

Text design by Suzanne Nichols.

RUSSELL SAGE FOUNDATION
112 East 64th Street, New York, New York 10065
10 9 8 7 6 5 4 3 2 1

Contents

About the Author

Jane Waldfogel is professor of social work and public affairs at the Columbia University School of Social Work and visiting professor at the Centre for Analysis of Social Exclusion at the London School of Economics and Political Science.

Acknowledgments

Although primarily based in the United States, I have spent a substantial portion of my time in Britain over the past twenty years. This book benefited greatly from the time I spent there and from the helpful advice and counsel I received. In particular, I owe an enormous debt to the Centre for Analysis of Social Exclusion (CASE) at the London School of Economics, where I have been a frequent visitor throughout the period of reforms covered in this book. John Hills, the director of CASE, has been a superb colleague and guide to the reforms. I draw heavily in chapter 1 on the early article we co-authored on the reforms, and I continued to draw on his wisdom throughout the process of writing this book. John kindly read an early draft and provided many helpful comments. Other colleagues at CASE also provided extremely helpful input. I am particularly grateful to Howard Glenerster and Kitty Stewart and to the wonderful CASE staff, especially Jane Dickson and Nic Warner. I would also like to thank Daniel Sage, my very able research assistant at CASE during the summer of 2009, who helped track down statistics and produced some terrific tables and graphs. I also benefited from many helpful conversations with other colleagues and policymakers in Britain. Paul Gregg was a constant source of information and inspiration. I'd also like to thank: Francine Bates, Alex Beer, Mike Brewer, Simon Burgess, Naomi Eisenstadt, Alexandra Frean, Richard Freeman, Alison Garnham, Lisa Harker, Margaret Hodge, Beverly Hughes, Heather Joshi, Caroline Kelham, Steve Machin, Lee Elliot Major, Sandra McNally, Jane Millar, Carey Oppenheim, David Piachaud, Gillian Pugh, Ray Shostak, Kathy Sylva, Polly Toynbee, Martina Viarengo, and Elizabeth Washbrook.

Most of this book was written during the 2008 to 2009 academic year, when I had the good fortune to be the Marian Cabot Putnam Fellow at the Radcliffe Institute for Advanced Study at Harvard University. The Radcliffe staff and my fellow fellows offered both material and intellectual support, for which I am very grateful. I would particularly like to thank the staff who made my stay so pleasant and productive: Dean Barbara Grosz, Sharon Lin-Hing, Melissa Synnott, Judy Vichniac, and Marlon Cummings. I would also like to thank my Radcliffe research partner, Upasana Unni, who located an impressive array of European statistics, made a terrific set of graphs, and also helped with the references. I also benefited from the generosity and advice of Radcliffe's Harvard neighbors. Participants in Harvard's Social Inequality Program provided extremely helpful early feedback on the book, as well as ongoing stimulation and nurture through the seminar and other programs. I'm particularly grateful to program director Bruce Western and Pam Metz. At the Harvard Graduate School of Education, Dean Kathleen McCartney offered a warm welcome, and I also benefited from attending many excellent Askwith Forums. I'm also grateful to staff at the Gutman Library, in particular Jason DeWaard and Carla Lillvik, who helped with everything from videoconferencing to endnotes. I'd also like to thank colleagues at the Kennedy School, in particular Mary Jo Bane, Kathy Edin, David Ellwood, Ronald Ferguson, and Christopher Jencks.

I would be remiss if I did not also thank my friends and colleagues at Columbia University School of Social Work, where I have been on faculty for the last fifteen years. I could not ask for better guides to the welfare state than my senior colleagues Irv Garfinkel and Sheila Kamerman. I'd also like to thank Dean Jeanette Takamura, as well as M. K. Babcock and Liana Fox. I also had many helpful conversations with American colleagues. I especially would like to thank Sheldon Danziger, who read the complete manuscript and provided detailed comments. His suggestions greatly strengthened the book and also saved me from some errors. I would also like to thank Rebecca Blank, Mark Greenberg, Ron Haskins, and Tim Smeeding. In addition I'm grateful to Bruce Bradbury and Miles Corak for helping to orient me to the antipoverty reforms in Australia and Canada. And I owe a big note of thanks to two anonymous reviewers whose helpful comments strengthened this book.

But the greatest thank-you must go to my family. Katie was unfailingly enthusiastic and supportive. And David, as always, was the perfect sounding board and resource. I could not have done it without them.

Introduction

In March 1999, British prime minister Tony Blair made a dramatic pledge to end child poverty in the next twenty years. The announcement startled the journalists, advocates, and academics he had invited to hear him address child poverty at Toynbee Hall, a settlement house in the East End of London. None among them would have dared imagine he would make such a bold pledge or commit his government to such an ambitious agenda of reform.

Yet, once the pledge was made, it took on a life of its own. Overnight it seemed only right that the government should be aiming to reduce child poverty significantly and to promote more equal life chances for children. And this was not just the view of Blair's Labour Party and its supporters. Even the tabloid press got on board, agreeing with the prime minister that "the child born on a run-down housing estate should have the same chance to be healthy and well-educated as the child born in the leafy suburbs."[1]

What did Blair mean when he pledged to eliminate child poverty, and where did this remarkable pledge come from? What did the government do to reduce child poverty, and what success has it had? Has child poverty been significantly reduced in Britain, as the government pledged, and if so, how has this been accomplished? After a decade of reform, what are the next steps for Britain? And what can the United States and other countries learn from Britain's experience?

This book answers these questions, telling the story of Britain's war on child poverty and drawing out lessons for future antipoverty efforts, both in Britain and elsewhere. The story is a timely one: the ten years that have elapsed since Britain's war on poverty began give us enough time to see the scope of the effort and begin to gauge its effects.

When Britain declared its war on child poverty in 1999, 3.4 million children—one in four—lived in poverty. Within five years, the child poverty rate (measured in relative terms, as is customary in Britain) fell from 26 percent of all children to 22 percent as half a million children moved out of poverty.[2] This was no mean achievement given that a relative poverty line moves up as average incomes rise (as they did quite rapidly in Britain during this period).

On an absolute poverty line, like the one used in the United States, British progress was even greater. Child poverty measured with an absolute line fell by nearly half in the first five years of the British antipoverty effort, from 26 percent to 14 percent, as the number of children in poverty fell by 1.6 million.

So, on both measures, Britain made substantial progress in reducing child poverty in the first five years of its initiative. Although progress slowed after those first five years as public finances were strained and other spending priorities came to the fore, the record nevertheless continues to be impressive. Data from 1999 to 2007 (the most recent year for which figures are available) indicate that 500,000 children have been moved out of poverty defined in relative terms, a reduction of about 15 percent, while 1.7 million have been moved out of poverty defined in absolute terms, a reduction of 50 percent. The relative child poverty rate has fallen from 26 to 22 percent; if measured in absolute terms, child poverty was reduced from 26 to 13 percent.

As of late 2009, the Labour government was still holding to the target of cutting child poverty in half in ten years and ending it in twenty. And the government had filed legislation to enshrine this commitment in law so that future governments would be bound by it.

While Britain was tackling child poverty, the United States was focusing on "ending welfare as we know it."[3] Beginning with "waivers" that allowed states to alter their welfare programs in the early 1990s and culminating with the passage of the federal Personal Responsibility and Work Opportunity Reconciliation Act (PRWORA) in 1996, the United States drastically reformed its approach to cash assistance for low-income families. Under PRWORA, no family could claim federal welfare benefits for more than five years (in their lifetime), and states were free to impose even shorter limits. At the same time, a number of measures, including substantial increases in the Earned Income Tax Credit (EITC), were passed in an effort to make work pay. These reforms were primarily aimed at altering the employment behavior of single mothers, and they were largely successful in doing so. The measures moved thousands of single mothers into work, and for many of them work did pay enough to keep them out of poverty. Others struggled, however, to make ends meet on low-wage work, and some were not able to make the transition from welfare to work. The reforms also affected low-income two-parent families, who were net gainers: they benefited from the reforms to make work pay, while not losing too much in welfare benefits (which they were unlikely to have been eligible for in the first place).

In 1992, when these reforms began, the child poverty rate in the United States was 19 percent measured in absolute terms on the official U.S. poverty line, and 38 percent measured in relative terms, as the Europeans do. By 2001, nearly a decade into the reforms, child poverty measured in absolute terms had fallen to 13 percent (which turned out to be a record low;

child poverty rose again after 2001). The decline in absolute child poverty from 1992 to 2001 amounted to a reduction of about one-third from its starting level; this was good progress, but not as good as the British progress in cutting absolute poverty in half over a shorter time period. Child poverty measured in relative terms remained high, at 35 percent, a reduction of less than one tenth from its starting level, versus the one-sixth reduction in Britain.[4]

Although the British reforms had much in common with U.S. reforms, the British initiatives were much more sweeping. Besides reforms to promote work and make work pay that were similar to the welfare-to-work initiatives emphasized in the United States, the British measures also included increased unconditional financial support for families and a host of investments in children that were aimed at tackling poverty in this generation and the next one. There is much for the United States to learn from these wider-ranging efforts. Not all of them worked as planned, but taken together, the British package was successful in reducing poverty and improving children's life chances.

This book tells the story of those reforms. Before getting under way, I believe that a word of explanation is in order about the unit of analysis and the terminology. My focus is on the reforms at the national level implemented by the New Labour government that came into office in 1997. Over the ensuing decade, responsibility for some aspects of policy was increasingly devolved to the regional level, but most of the policies discussed here remained nationally led. Thus, my focus is on the national level. I refer to the country as "Britain" because that is the term that will be most familiar to U.S. readers. As many readers will know, however, "Britain" technically refers to three regions—England, Scotland, and Wales—while the term "United Kingdom (U.K.)" refers to four—England, Scotland, Wales, and Northern Ireland. To the extent possible, I present data on income, poverty, and inequality at the national level. (Where this is not the case and data either refer specifically to just one region or differ sharply by region, this is noted.)

THE BACKGROUND TO THE REFORMS

The first chapter takes us back to the period leading up to March 1999, when Prime Minister Blair surprised the nation with his pledge to end child poverty. The 1990s had seen unprecedented levels of poverty and inequality in Britain, and it was growing recognition of and concern about these trends that spurred Blair into action and generated such a strong public mandate for change. By the mid-1990s, one in four British children were poor using the most commonly accepted measure of child poverty (up from fewer than one in ten in the 1960s), and Britain had a higher child poverty rate than any other peer country except the United States. Britain (along with the United States) also had a higher level of income inequality than peer nations.

The British statistics also showed that one in five children were growing up in "workless" households (households with no adult in the labor force), a much higher share than in other countries. Contributing to this was the high share of children in lone-parent (primarily single-mother) families, which had risen from 13 percent of all families with children to 23 percent between 1979 and 1997.[5] Most of these lone mothers were not working at all, and only about one in five worked full-time.[6] A further concern was that a growing share—40 percent—of lone-mother families were headed by women who had never been married, meaning that their children were likely to spend more years in lone-parent families and were less likely to receive child support from their fathers than children whose mothers had previously been married.

In addition to these disturbing statistics, two other types of evidence set the stage for the British reforms. The first was a body of work showing that poverty had lasting effects on children's life chances. The second was research, much of it conducted in the United States, showing that well-designed programs could be effective in redressing those effects and improving children's life chances.

British public attitudes toward welfare and poverty also helped set the stage for reform. Survey data pointed to widespread support for the idea that government should do something about poverty, but also indicated that the public favored a nuanced strategy. The Labour Party would in fact implement such a strategy, one that stressed "work for those who can and security for those who cannot."

Taken together, this evidence convinced British policymakers that they could, and should, do something about child poverty. But not even his closest advisers expected Blair to make his remarkable pledge in March 1999 to end child poverty: "Our historic aim will be for ours to be the first generation to end child poverty. It will take a generation. It is a 20-year mission. But I believe that it can be done if we reform the welfare state and build it around the needs of families and children."[7]

As mentioned, the pledge immediately took on a life of its own. The commitment to end child poverty in twenty years and to cut it in half in ten was enthusiastically taken up by members of the government. In particular, Gordon Brown, who was then chancellor of the Exchequer (and later prime minister), put real money into the antipoverty initiative and also set specific targets for reform. Over the next decade the Treasury and other departments implemented a wide-ranging strategy to tackle child poverty and monitored its success.

TACKLING CHILD POVERTY: THE ELEMENTS
OF THE REFORM STRATEGY

The British antipoverty strategy has three distinct parts: promoting work and making work pay; increasing financial support for families with children; and investing in children. The three components are interrelated, but it is useful to consider them separately, since each had its own rationale and distinctive features.

Promoting Work and Making Work Pay

The first strand of the British reform package—a set of measures to promote work and make work pay, described in chapter 2—had much in common with U.S. welfare reforms and in fact drew heavily on U.S. research. At the center of the British work-focused reforms were a series of welfare-to-work programs, collectively known as the New Deal. These programs were strongly influenced by evidence from U.S. welfare-to-work experiments and, again, had many elements in common with them.[8] However, unlike the approach taken in the U.S. welfare reforms aimed at single mothers, the New Deal for Lone Parents (NDLP) at its inception in 1997, was an essentially voluntary scheme that reflected more traditional attitudes about the question of whether mothers should work, particularly when their children are young. It was not until 2001 that lone parents began to be required to attend work-focused interviews, although even then they were not required to actually work or look for work. And it was not until 2008 that some lone parents—those whose youngest child had reached the age of twelve—were required to actually work or look for work as a condition of receiving benefits.

To help make work pay, the New Labour government also brought in Britain's first national minimum wage (NMW) in April 1999. The minimum wage also drew on evidence from the United States, but was implemented at a higher level. Its initial value was 45 percent of median British hourly earnings, whereas the U.S. minimum wage was worth about 38 percent of median U.S. hourly earnings that year. The value of the British minimum wage was adjusted upward every year thereafter, with the result that by 2009 it was considerably more generous than the U.S. minimum wage: it was set at a value of about 50 percent of median British hourly earnings as opposed to about 40 percent in the United States. Taxes were also reduced for low-income workers and their employers.

A further measure to make work pay was the government's introduction of a new tax credit in October 1999, then known as the Working Families Tax Credit (WFTC), for couples with children or for lone parents who were working sixteen or more hours per week (with higher benefits if they worked thirty or more hours). The WFTC replaced an earlier in-work benefit program in Britain but was considerably more generous and also included more support for child care costs. It went to twice as many families as the prior program, and its total cost more than doubled (because benefits per family were higher). In 2003 the WFTC was replaced by the Working Tax Credit (WTC), which was even more generous and included even more support for child care costs. The expansions in the WFTC (and its successor, WTC) were inspired by evidence on the U.S. Earned Income Tax Credit, which had been expanded several times since its introduction in 1975, but most substantially in the mid-1990s as part of the U.S. efforts to make work pay. However, unlike the EITC, which is mainly claimed annually, the WFTC (and WTC) are paid regularly throughout the year.

Did the British reforms succeed in promoting work? The answer is certainly yes. Lone-parent employment increased by twelve percentage points—from 45 percent to 57 percent—from 1997 to 2008.[9] This is an impressive increase, particularly considering that most of the reforms in this period consisted of carrots rather than sticks. It is also impressive relative to the United States, where single-mother employment during welfare reform rose by a comparable amount (about thirteen percentage points) from 1990 to 2000, but under a more punitive set of reforms.[10] As in the United States, it is difficult to separate the causal effects of the reforms from the effects of the strong economy that prevailed throughout most of the decade, but evidence from careful analyses suggests that the British reform programs were responsible for at least half of the growth in employment among lone parents, with the strongest effect on increasing the share of lone parents working at least sixteen hours per week.[11]

The reforms also reduced the number of lone parents on welfare. Overall, the number of lone parents receiving benefits through the means-tested welfare program for nonworking families fell from 1,030,000 in 1997 to 740,000 in 2008, a reduction of over 25 percent. These are, of course, much lower caseload declines than those seen in the United States after welfare reform, but this makes sense given the more drastic nature of the U.S. reforms.[12]

The reforms were also successful in making work pay. Taken together, the minimum wage and the more generous in-work supports (in particular, the increased tax credits and reduced taxes) substantially increased the income that the most disadvantaged families could expect from work, with particularly large gains for lone-parent families. For example, a lone parent working thirty hours per week at the minimum wage and claiming the available benefits and tax credits would have had a net income of £163.73 per week in 1998, equivalent to 101 percent of the poverty line (for a family of her type in that year). By 2008 her net income under the same scenario would have risen to £348.04 per week, or 123 percent of the now higher poverty line.

Increasing Financial Support for Families with Children

The second strand of the British reforms, detailed in chapter 3, was a set of changes to the tax and benefit system to increase the incomes of families with children, even those in which parents were not working. Thus, the British reformers made an explicit decision to not focus solely on reforms to promote work and make work pay, but also to invest substantial resources in increasing financial support for all families with children, whether or not the parents worked. This stands in sharp contrast to the position adopted by the United States, which over the period of welfare reform increasingly made support for children contingent on parental employment As a result, the British reforms included more universal provision (because supports were intended to reach all children whether or not their parents worked).

The reforms in this area included significant real increases in the value of the universal child allowance; known as Child Benefit, this is a very popular program for which all families with children are eligible. Child Benefit is paid to the mother on a regular basis throughout the year and is understood to be intended to help parents cover the costs of children.

In addition to the expansions in the universal Child Benefit, the reforms also included a new, quasi-universal child tax credit, which reaches all but the highest-income families and, unlike the WFTC (and its successor WTC), is not conditioned on parental employment. Like the WFTC and the WTC, this new credit was phased in over time; beginning with a new Children's Tax Credit in 2001, it was replaced with the integrated Child Tax Credit (CTC) in 2003. Since all but the highest-income families are eligible for it, the CTC reaches about 80 percent of families with children. Like the WTC, it is paid on a regular basis throughout the year. And like Child Benefit, it is paid to the mother.

Reflecting increased attention to the importance of early childhood, several of the benefit reforms were targeted to young children. For instance, families with infants received an extra amount of Child Tax Credit (known as "the baby tax credit"). And families with young children received larger increases in the value of their means-tested welfare benefits than did families with older children. These benefits had historically provided higher amounts to families with older children, on the grounds that the costs associated with older children are higher. The reforms in this period equalized benefits upward, so that families with younger children received as much as those with older children.

Taken together, these reforms have substantially raised the amount of support that families with children receive. And although some increases are delivered through universal or quasi-universal programs, nevertheless the largest gains have gone to the lowest-income families. By 2010 the average family with children will have gained £2,000 per year in real terms, while the bottom 20 percent will have gained £4,500—an amount equivalent to about 24 percent of the poverty line for a two-parent family with two children.[13]

The expansions in financial support for families, regardless of employment status, stand in sharp contrast to the approach taken in the United States. Although benefits for low-income families with working parents did increase substantially over the period of welfare reform, the same was not true of benefits for nonworking families. Welfare benefits in the United States continue to lose value in real terms. And even if one takes into account the recent expansions in in-kind programs—such as child care, nutrition, and child health insurance—these do not match the increased direct financial support provided in Britain to low-income families in which parents do not work.

Investing in Children

The third component of the British antipoverty agenda was a set of increased investments in programs and services for children. These investments had the goal of improving outcomes for the current generation of children in low-income families as well as the next generation.

As discussed in chapter 4, programs for preschool-age children were particularly emphasized.[14] In May 1997, shortly after coming into office, the Labour government announced Britain's first national child care strategy. The signature element of the strategy was a commitment to provide universal—and free—preschool for all four-year-olds by September 1998, a commitment that was extended to three-year-olds in 2004. This new entitlement, which was enthusiastically taken up by parents, moved Britain from having one of the lowest preschool enrollment rates in Europe to being on a par with its European peers, most of whom had universal or near-universal participation in publicly provided preschool in the year or two prior to school entry.[15]

For families with younger children, the government expanded not only support for child care provision but also parental leave rights. In common with most other advanced industrialized nations (although not the United States), Britain already had a system of paid maternity leave, but the leave it provided (eighteen weeks) was relatively short by European standards.[16] The Employment Act of 2002 increased the period of statutory maternity leave to six months of paid leave followed by up to six months of unpaid leave, and it established two weeks of paid paternity leave. The act also introduced the right of parents of children under the age of six to request part-time or flexible work hours, to go into effect in April 2003. This policy brought Britain into compliance with a European Union (EU) directive requiring member countries to provide a right for parents of young children to have the opportunity to switch to part-time or flexible hours. The policy proved to be so successful that, following a review in 2008, it was extended to cover parents with older children (up to the age of sixteen), effective April 2009.[17] Parents also benefited from Britain's parental leave program (established in 1999), which provides three months of job-protected parental leave that mothers or fathers can use to meet child care responsibilities or to address a family emergency.

Britain's ten-year child care strategy, released in 2004, extended these child care reforms in several ways. Paid maternity leave was extended to nine months, with a promise to later extend it to twelve months. Free child care for disadvantaged two-year-olds was piloted. And the hours of preschool provision were increased for three- and four-year-olds. In addition, the ten-year child care strategy included a number of measures aimed at raising child care quality. Child care facilities have come under the inspection of Ofsted (Office for Standards in Education), the same agency that inspects schools, and the government is working to raise teacher qualifications in the child care sector. The government has also taken steps to ensure sufficient provision of good-quality care. This goal was enshrined in legislation in the Child Care Act of 2006, which makes local areas responsible for providing adequate child care for all working parents who want it.

For disadvantaged children ages zero to three, the government established Sure Start, a community-based program for families living in the lowest-income areas.[18] Sure Start programs had to offer a core set of services (such as additional home visiting for families with newborns and the offer of a child care place for three-year-olds) but were otherwise free to develop and implement their own distinctive programs. Evaluating this diverse set of programs proved challenging. An early (2005) evaluation found few significant positive effects of the programs on children and families, and some adverse effects for some disadvantaged groups. However, a later (2008) evaluation of the more mature Sure Start programs then in existence found improvements in seven of the fourteen outcomes measured: children in Sure Start areas scored better than their peers in non–Sure Start areas on three measures of behavior, two measures of child health, and two measures of parenting. Moreover, there were no negative effects for disadvantaged subgroups, as there had been in the first evaluation.

The investments in children also included a series of initiatives to improve outcomes for school-age children, described in chapter 5. A major emphasis was improving schools and closing gaps in achievement. In this respect, the British reforms were somewhat similar in spirit to the U.S. reforms under the 2001 No Child Left Behind Act. However, the British reforms differed in being more directly led by the central government, which plays a much larger role in education than does the federal government in the United States.

An early initiative—fulfilling a promise made in the 1997 election manifesto—reduced primary school class sizes to not more than thirty pupils. Another early initiative was the literacy hour, which required primary school teachers to spend an hour each day on literacy instruction and provided guidelines as to how that hour was to be spent.[19] This program was found to produce small but persistent gains in reading (and to a lesser extent, math), at a very low cost (just £25 per pupil). A similar initiative—the numeracy hour—required primary school teachers to spend an hour a day on math instruction. This too was found to be cost-effective in raising student achievement.[20]

Improving secondary school achievement received less attention initially, but that effort grew in importance over time and in particular took on more emphasis in Labour's second and third terms in office.[21] A challenge in the British context was not just to increase the quality of secondary schooling but also to induce more young people to stay in school beyond the minimum school-leaving age (age sixteen). To provide an incentive for low-income youth to complete more education, the government began a pilot program of educational maintenance allowances (EMAs) in the fall of 1999.[22] The EMA gave sixteen- to nineteen-year-olds from low-income families a payment of between £5 and £40 per week (depending on their family income) so long as they were enrolled in school; the program also provided some bonuses for those who satisfied certain attendance and achievement goals. Evaluators found that the EMA raised the share of youth staying in school after the school-leaving age by nearly six percentage points, with 71.3 percent of youth in EMA areas staying on versus 65.5 percent in control areas.

Nevertheless, Britain still had relatively low rates of young people staying in school compared to other peer countries. So in 2008, the government announced its intention to raise the school-leaving age to seventeen in 2013 and to eighteen in 2015, the first increases in the minimum school-leaving age since it was raised from fourteen to sixteen in 1973. This commitment was enacted in the 2008 Education and Skills Act. That same year, the government introduced the "September guarantee"—a promise of a place at a school or work-based training or education program for every sixteen-year-old leaving secondary school. This program was later extended to cover seventeen-year-olds as well,[23] and in spite of severe budget constraints the 2009 budget restated this commitment and included funds for the initiative.

Another thrust of reform was a set of measures to improve secondary schools, with particular attention to raising quality in the worst-performing schools. Several initiatives directed more funding to secondary schools in the most disadvantaged urban areas. There were also initiatives to partner low-performing schools with leaders from higher-performing ones.

The government invested substantial resources in these education reforms. Per capita spending on education doubled in real terms between 1997 and 2007.[24] How successful were these reforms? The pupil test score data, which I review in chapter 5, provide a fair amount of evidence that the early primary school reforms were successful in raising achievement for seven- and eleven-year-olds, and further gains—as well as progress in gap closing—were evident for eleven-year-olds in the later years. The data also indicate that progress was made in raising achievement and closing income-related gaps at the secondary school level and that the government largely succeeded in fulfilling its aspiration of doing away with failing secondary schools.

Programs were also implemented to improve the conditions experienced by children outside of school. The New Deal for Communities invested £2 billion over ten years in thirty-nine very deprived neighborhoods, with the goal of promoting local employment as well as improving housing and the physical environment.[25] Nutrition, health, and recreation programs for children were also expanded.

ONE PERCENT FOR THE KIDS

Taken together, these antipoverty initiatives amounted to a sizable expansion in benefits and services for children. In 2003, in a paper prepared for the Brookings Roundtable on Children, John Hills estimated that the average family with children gained £1,200 per year (comparing actual tax and benefit rates in 2002–2003 with what was in effect in 1996–1997, adjusting only for inflation) and that families in the bottom quintile gained twice as much.[26] In aggregate, this amounted to nearly £9 billion per year, an amount equivalent to nearly 1 percent of Britain's gross domestic product (GDP).[27] To put this figure in perspective, if Washington committed an additional 1 percent of the U.S. GDP to eliminate child poverty, this would amount to about $130 billion.[28] The U.S. audience was so struck by this figure that *One Percent for the Kids* became the title of the resulting conference volume.

Where did the money for the reforms come from? Part of the answer lies in the fact that the reforms were focused on *child* poverty rather than poverty in general. Thus, while benefits and services for children increased sharply over the decade, spending was reduced for programs for working-age adults without children. The government also benefited from the strong economy and low unemployment rates of the late 1990s and early 2000s, which reduced the demand for adult means-tested and unemployment benefits and led to further savings as well as increased tax revenues that could be spent on children. As a consequence, overall spending on the British welfare state as a percentage of GDP did not change much over the decade; what changed was the portion of that spending directed to children rather than working-age adults. The only source of revenue dedicated to spending on social welfare programs that increased substantially over this period was windfall profits taxes on utility companies, which since privatization had yielded substantial profits to their new owners.[29]

However, as we shall see in subsequent chapters, midway through the reforms the rate of increase in spending for the child poverty initiative slowed. In 2001, facing reelection, Prime Minister Blair came under increasing political pressure to deliver improved public services for the middle class, particularly in sectors such as health and education.[30] Accordingly, he shifted some discretionary spending toward those sectors. Although some health and education programs (such as Sure Start) disproportionately benefited low-income children, many (such as programs to reduce waiting times in the National Health Service [NHS]) did not. Later, around 2003, the economy started to slow and the government saw fewer savings in adult benefits and unemployment claims. As a result, benefits were not expanded as generously that year and in subsequent years as they had been in the initial years of the reform. After the first antipoverty target was narrowly missed in 2004, and with the next target not due until 2009 or 2010, the government's attention shifted to other priorities.

Although the pace of the reforms had slowed, nevertheless by 2009 the additional amount invested in children amounted to over 1 percent of GDP per year. And each of the initiatives begun in those first few years of the Labour government had expanded and evolved over the decade of reform. (For a chronology of the major reforms, see appendix 1).

WHAT DID THE REFORMS ACCOMPLISH?

Chapter 6 returns to the core goal of the reforms—reducing child poverty—and presents the latest evidence on the success of the reforms in attaining that goal, using data on the British government's three official measures of child poverty.

The first measure, and the one considered the preferred measure in

Britain, is a relative one under which a child is poor if his or her family has income below 60 percent of median income for a family of their size and composition in that year. This is a tough measure to make progress on because, if median incomes rise, relative poverty also rises unless incomes at the bottom are rising too.

The second official measure is an absolute one under which a child is poor if his or her family income is below a fixed threshold (which is up-dated only for inflation over time). This measure is conceptually very similar to the official U.S. poverty line, which is also set as a fixed thresh-old, and so is particularly useful for a British-U.S. comparison.

The third official measure is material deprivation. This measure does not have a counterpart in the United States but is similar to newer mea-sures being used in Europe. I provide a fuller description of it in chapter 6; here I will briefly note that this measure defines a child as materially deprived if his or her family has a relatively low income and if they do not have certain items—items that most families with children do have—be-cause they cannot afford them.

As detailed in chapter 6, the British record on all three measures is im-pressive. When Blair declared war on child poverty in 1999, 3.4 million children—one in four—were in poverty, whether defined in relative terms or absolute terms. But how much poverty changed over the ensuing de-cade depends very much on whether a relative or absolute definition is used.

Using the government's preferred relative measure of child poverty, the child poverty rate fell from 26.7 percent in 1998–1999 to 22.5 percent in 2007–2008 (the most recent year for which data are available), a 16 percent reduction from the 1998–1999 base.[31] As discussed earlier, using a relative measure imposes a tough standard because, if median income is rising, more low-income children are counted as poor even if their incomes have not fallen in real terms.[32] This was in fact the case in Britain, where over the decade from 1996–1997 to 2006–2007, median income rose 20 percent.[33]

If we look at Britain's progress using its second official measure, an ab-solute poverty line—measured as the share of children below 60 percent of the median income as it was in 1998–1999, with the poverty line in-dexed only for inflation, as it is in the United States—we see a very sub-stantial reduction in child poverty, from a rate of 26 percent of children in 1998–1999 to a rate of 13 percent in 2007–2008, a remarkable reduction of 50 percent from the 1998–1999 rate and a fall from 3.4 million poor chil-dren to 1.7 million.

How can we reconcile the two sets of results? Britain's dramatic prog-ress in halving child poverty as measured in absolute terms confirms that incomes have been rising for families at the bottom. But the slower prog-ress in reducing relative poverty suggests that incomes at the bottom did not rise enough to counteract the fact that incomes have also been rising for middle- and higher-income families. This is not surprising since British policies during the period were focused on raising the incomes of those at the bottom, not on raising taxes or constraining labor market returns for middle- or higher-income workers. So, in a period when overall income inequality was continuing to rise, the improvement in poverty in relative terms was less than the improvement in absolute terms. It is also important to note, however, that with median incomes rising over this period, relative child poverty rates would have risen had the government not undertaken its antipoverty initiative.[34] Thus, the poverty-reducing impact of the reforms is larger than the government gets credit for if we simply compare relative poverty rates before and after the reforms.

Because the United States uses an absolute poverty line, it is straightforward to compare the progress of the United States and Britain in reducing child poverty in absolute terms.[35] The results (presented in figure 6.1) show that the reduction in child poverty in Britain has been larger and more sustained than in the United States. The child poverty rate fell by about one-third between 1992 and 2001 in the United States in response to welfare reforms and the strong economy, in contrast to the 50 percent reduction in Britain over a shorter time period. Data since 2001 show that absolute child poverty has risen in the United States, while holding roughly constant in Britain.

Results for material deprivation are also impressive. In the baseline year—1998–1999—20.8 percent of British children were materially deprived on the government's official deprivation measure; this rate had fallen to 15.6 percent in 2006–2007 before rising to 17.1 percent in 2007–2008, a higher rate than the prior year but still an improvement over the rate a decade earlier. This improvement in living conditions for low-income families is confirmed by data showing reductions in financial distress over the same period, especially for lone-parent families.[36]

We lack a comparable material deprivation measure for the United States, but data on trends for food insecurity are consistent with what we saw earlier in trends for child poverty, with children's living conditions improving in the mid- to late 1990s when the welfare reforms were first implemented and the economy was strong, but then plateauing or slightly deteriorating thereafter.[37] Data on other types of deprivation, available for selected years from the Survey of Income and Program Participation (SIPP), tell a similar story.[38]

Data on family expenditures also point to divergence across the two countries. My research, reported in chapter 6, suggests that in Britain low-income families affected by the reforms are spending more money on items related to children, while in the United States low-income single-mother families, who were the main target of the welfare reforms, are primarily spending more money on items related to employment. This pattern of results makes sense, given the greater emphasis in the British reforms on increasing benefits for children versus the greater emphasis in the United States on boosting single parents' employment.

We can also compare the British record over the decade with the record of other European countries. This comparison provides an important counterfactual as to what might have happened in Britain had the reforms not occurred. Here too Britain compares favorably, both in terms of trends in poverty and inequality and in terms of trends in associated measures of deprivation and well-being. In particular, it is striking that while child poverty defined in relative terms was falling in Britain, it was rising or at best flat in most of Europe over the period.

NEXT STEPS FOR BRITAIN

After a decade of reform, what is the current status of the British antipoverty initiative? And what are the next steps for Britain? As I discuss in chapter 7, the answers to these questions must take into account both the political and economic contexts. As I complete this book in late 2009, Britain is preparing for a national election that must take place by May 2010. So we do not know who will be carrying the reforms forward into the next decade, although at this point the Conservative Party is leading in the polls and looking likely to win. The economic context is also uncertain as the world continues to face the most severe economic crisis since the Great Depression. But certainly public finances will be strained for the foreseeable future, and the demands on the social safety net will continue to be high.

Nevertheless, both major parties in Britain say that they are committed to meeting the child poverty goal, and legislation to make this commitment law is now pending in Parliament. So now is an important time to take stock and think about next steps for the antipoverty strategy.

Fundamental to any effort to further reduce child poverty (whether under a Labour or Conservative government) is the need to understand which children are poor and which specific factors place children at elevated risk of poverty. In chapter 7, I present data on the demographics of poverty and discuss the policies that Britain should adopt to address the challenges suggested by those demographics.

The demographic data indicate that fully half of poor children in Britain live in families where at least one parent is already working in the labor market. Most of these poor children (42 percent) live in two-parent families in which at least one parent is working (often full-time), and a further 8 percent live in one-parent families in which the parent is working (typically part-time). The next largest share of poor children (30 percent) live in one-parent families in which the parent is not working. The remainder (about one-fifth of poor children) live in two-parent families with no parent working.

The demographic data also point to some cross-cutting factors—such as parental disability and large family size—that increase the risk of poverty among children. Child poverty rates are also much higher for some ethnic groups—in particular, children in Pakistani and Bangladeshi families—than they are for white British families.

These demographics of poverty create five challenges that British policymakers must address if they are to succeed in making further reductions in child poverty. The first challenge is to do more to raise incomes in working families. I recommend several measures in chapter 7, including expanding child care and other in-work supports for the lowest-income workers; raising the value of the minimum wage; improving incentives to work additional hours; and expanding measures to improve the skills and qualifications of low-skilled workers, through preschool and school initiatives but also through training and education programs for adults, which thus far have received relatively little attention.

The second challenge is to move more lone parents into work. Here, in addition to the measures just discussed, which would also help this group, I recommend providing more child care and in-work supports for single parents even if they work fewer than the sixteen hours per week currently required for eligibility for such supports. Future reformers might also usefully revisit Britain's policies regarding child support from absent parents, which played little role in the reforms of the past decade but could usefully contribute to poverty reductions in the future.

The third challenge is to address poverty in workless two-parent families. This is a difficult group to move into employment, given their high rates of disability and other work-limiting conditions. Here I recommend a personal advising model, along the lines of what Paul Gregg recommended in his December 2008 review for the government. I also emphasize the importance of child care for this group. Policy for two-parent families has all too often assumed that one parent can work while the other cares for the children. But the high rates of parental disability and other limiting conditions among these families call that assumption into question.

A fourth challenge is to address the disproportionate risk of poverty among particular racial or ethnic groups. Children in Pakistani and Bangladeshi families have a poverty risk three times as high as the risk for white British children. Although some of the factors underlying this difference have been identified—mothers in these families have low employment rates, fathers' earnings are low, family size tends to be large, and the household often includes nonworking extended family members—it is not clear what the policy response should be. So here I recommend more ethnographic research to better understand the situation and views of these families, as well as more local efforts like the antipoverty strategy under way in the Tower Hamlets section of London.

The fifth challenge is to respond to the underlying trends in income inequality, which are of concern both for their implications for relative poverty and for their implications for overall social cohesion and social inequality. In Britain, as in the United States, income inequality has been rising owing to a complex set of factors that are difficult for government policy to alter. But there are some steps that government can take to try to reduce the growth in income inequality or to moderate its effects. One is to continue to work to raise skills at the bottom of the income distribution so as to promote more social mobility and to narrow gaps between the bottom and the middle of the income distribution (which would in turn affect relative poverty). Another is to attempt to rein in income gains at the top of the income distribution through measures such as executive pay caps and tax increases for the wealthy. These latter measures would not affect relative poverty (as it is not affected by income changes at the top) but could be important in promoting more social cohesion and combating aspects of social inequality.

However, the underlying trends in inequality, and the links between those trends and relative poverty, also raise questions about how the government should measure poverty and what targets it should hold itself accountable for. In Britain it is generally assumed that poverty should be measured mainly in relative terms, as it is in Europe. Thus, although official British poverty statistics throughout the past decade have included a relative, absolute, and material deprivation measure, the relative measure is seen as the primary one. However, I would argue that if the government is going to continue to be committed to a goal of ending child poverty— and I certainly think it should—then all three measures should be viewed as important. A progressive government should aspire to reduce child poverty on all three measures, but they are distinct constructs and should also have distinct targets. This is precisely why the British government has used three official measures of poverty, and I think this is a sound decision and one that should be carried forward.

LESSONS FOR REFORMS IN THE UNITED STATES AND OTHER COUNTRIES

After a decade of British reform, now is an opportune time to pause and consider the lessons it may present for antipoverty reforms in the United

States and other countries. The time is also right in that ambitious anti-poverty initiatives are now on the public agenda in the United States and several other countries in a way that they have not been for quite some time.

What lessons can the United States and other nations draw from the British experience over the past decade? Britain's success in reducing child poverty over the past decade provides at least one very clear lesson: where there is a serious public intention and effort to tackle child poverty, substantial reductions can in fact be achieved. If we think that there is nothing government can do to reduce child poverty—defined in American terms—the British example clearly provides strong evidence to the contrary. Child poverty is not an intractable problem, nor are high child poverty rates an inevitable feature of our advanced industrialized economies. If Britain can cut absolute child poverty in half in ten years, the United States and other wealthy nations can too.

A related lesson is that it is not necessary to work out all the details of an antipoverty policy in advance. Stating a goal and setting targets—as Blair and Brown did in 1999—can mobilize government and drive the development of specific strategies. Targets, of course, are not a cure-all, and they do carry risks. But if chosen well and prioritized, targets can be a very effective way of mobilizing government.

Mayor Michael Bloomberg's antipoverty initiative in New York City provides a striking illustration of what a British-style antipoverty campaign might look like in the U.S. context. New York City's Commission on Economic Opportunity, led by Geoffrey Canada (the founder of the Harlem Children's Zone) and Richard Parsons (then chairman of Time Warner), brought together individuals from various sectors of the city to brainstorm on how the city could meet the mayor's goal of making a substantial reduction in poverty.[39] The result has been a plethora of innovative antipoverty reforms that are now being implemented—some citywide, others on a pilot basis.[40] Not all of these reforms will be successful, but in all likelihood some will be. And all of them are being evaluated, so there will be opportunities for other cities and jurisdictions to learn from New York City's efforts.

At the national level, the report of the Center for American Progress Task Force on Poverty provides another example of what a British-style antipoverty effort might look like in the U.S. context.[41] Led by Angela Blackwell (the director of Policy/Link) and Peter Edelman (professor of law at Georgetown University) and directed by Mark Greenberg (then a senior fellow at the Center for American Progress), this task force endorsed a goal of reducing poverty in the United States by half and identified a set of twelve specific policies to achieve that goal. Since the task force report was issued in 2007, its goal of cutting poverty in half has been picked up and endorsed by several other groups. A national campaign called "Half in Ten" has been formed to advocate for this goal, and a resolution endorsing the goal has been introduced—and passed—in Congress.

Yet other examples come from Canada (where the province of Ontario in 2008 embarked on an ambitious British-style antipoverty initiative), Australia (where the Senate in 2004 released a report calling on the government to launch a comprehensive poverty reduction strategy), and New Zealand (where the children's commissioner released a report in 2008 calling on the government to establish a child poverty strategy).

If the United States and other countries are to launch antipoverty campaigns, what other lessons can they draw from the British experience of the past decade? Chapter 8 highlights three types. The first set of lessons has to do with specific aspects of the reforms that Britain enacted, the second involves the process of reform, and the third concerns the politics.

With regard to specific aspects of the British reform package, there are several elements from which the United States could usefully glean some lessons. Contrasting the British approach to the approach the United States took under the 1990s welfare reform initiatives and subsequent reforms, and highlighting the elements that seem to have been most successful in the British antipoverty effort, I would recommend the following for the United States:

- Drawing on Britain's success in introducing a national minimum wage—one that is set at a higher level than in the United States and updated annually—the United States should set an appropriate level for the minimum wage and ensure that it is updated annually.

- Drawing on Britain's model of having in-work tax credits paid weekly or monthly, rather than at the end of the year, and with no charge to the family, the United States should experiment with programs to increase the take-up of the advanced payment option for the EITC and also to help families claim the credit without paying exorbitant fees to tax preparers.

- Drawing on the example of the British Child Tax Credit, which reaches all low- and middle-income families whether or not parents are working, the United States should make its federal child tax credit fully refundable so that it reaches all poor children.

- Drawing on the British efforts to shift resources to the youngest children and ensure that they receive equal or even higher benefits, the United States should explore ways to target additional benefits to families with the youngest children.

- Drawing on the British expansions of paid maternity leave and establishment of paid paternity leave, the United States should enact paid parental leave to allow parents to stay home with newborns.

- Drawing on Britain's successful implementation of the "right to request," the United States should enact a right for working parents of young children to request part-time or flexible hours to help them better balance their work and family responsibilities.

- Drawing on Britain's decisive move to universal preschool for three- and four-year-olds, the United States should make a commitment to provide universal preschool for three- and four-year-olds, but should draw on evidence from U.S. preschool and prekindergarten programs in deciding what type of provision to support.

- Drawing on Britain's ambitious Sure Start program for children ages zero to three, the United States should commit to directing more investments to the youngest disadvantaged children, but should draw on evidence from U.S. early intervention programs in deciding which programs to support.

- Drawing on Britain's success in improving its primary and secondary schools, the United States should consider whether some of the British education reforms—in particular, curriculum initiatives such as the literacy hour and numeracy hour and accountability initiatives such as the inspection system—might work in the U.S. context.

There are also some lessons having to do with the process of reform. First, to promote more evidence-based policymaking, it would be useful to emulate the British practice of writing or commissioning background papers to review the evidence before enacting major new social policies. Second, to address the tension between the need for large-scale initiatives and the role of smaller pilots, the British experience over the past decade suggests the merits of a dual-track strategy: mounting comprehensive initiatives in key priority areas where the mandate for change and evidence about what works is strong, while at the same time experimenting in areas where the support for change or the evidence base is weaker. Third, the British case makes clear that having an appropriate and up-to-date measure of poverty is critical. To this end, the United States should revise its official poverty measure, along the lines of what was recommended by the National Academy of Sciences in its report on measuring poverty in 1995, and should set up a mechanism to review and update that measure on an ongoing basis.

Finally, the British case offers a cautionary tale with regard to the politics of reform, suggesting that reformers must carefully nurture public support, making the case for tackling child poverty, framing the issue in a way that elicits rather than undermines public support, publicizing the actions they are taking, and also making sure the public knows when reform efforts have been successful.

CONCLUDING THOUGHTS

As I conclude this book in late 2009, the continuing worldwide financial crisis and recession raise serious questions about the ability of Britain, the United States, and other nations to fund expanded antipoverty programs. At the same time, however, the downturn in the economy makes the demand for such programs greater than ever. Moreover, as U.S. president Barack Obama has argued, investments in such programs not only provide a safety net for those out of work but also help to stimulate the economy and create jobs. Thus, tough economic times do not allow us to turn our backs on the war on poverty but make it all the more urgent for governments to spend public money wisely—and give us all the more reason to learn from Britain's war on poverty.

Chapter 1

One in Four Children

W hen Tony Blair and the Labour Party came into office in May 1997, there was mounting evidence that the position of children in Britain was growing worse. More children were living in poverty, and more were living in one of two situations associated with increased risk of long-term poverty—in one-parent families or with parents who were out of work and reliant on government benefits. At the same time, evidence was accumulating that poverty has lasting effects on children's outcomes but that programs to improve children's life chances can be effective in redressing those effects. This evidence base set the stage for the Labour Party's pledge to end child poverty.[1]

THE GROWTH OF CHILD POVERTY

In Britain, as in the rest of Europe, child poverty is mainly defined in relative terms—that is, as the share of children whose family income is below a certain percentage of the national mean or median family income. Under this kind of relative definition, when income inequality rises, as it did in the 1980s and 1990s, poverty rises as well. Indeed, Britain (and the United States) experienced an unprecedented increase in income inequality over that period. One commonly used measure of income inequality is the ratio of the income of families in the top tenth (decile group) of the income distribution to the income of those in the bottom tenth, known as the 90/10 ratio. In 1979 the 90/10 ratio in Britain stood at about five-to-one, but by the mid-1990s it had doubled to ten-to-one.[2]

Another commonly used measure of inequality, the Gini coefficient (which can range from zero, indicating perfect equality, to one, indicating complete inequality), rose from about 0.25 in 1979 to about 0.35 in 1997; this was a larger percentage increase than occurred in any other advanced industrialized country except the United States, and an increase to a higher level.[3]

As in the United States, the increase in income inequality in Britain was driven mainly by an increase in the inequality of earnings, which in turn

Figure 1.1   Share of British Population in Relative Poverty, 1961 to 1997–1998

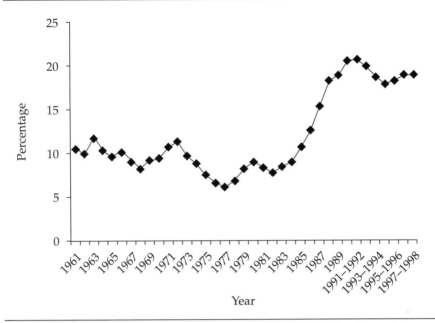

Source: Author's compilation based on data from Goodman and Webb (1994) and Department for Work and Pensions (2004).
Note: Relative poverty is defined as income below half of average income, before housing costs.

was driven by an increased demand for high-skilled workers as more advanced technology was adopted in the workplace; a decline in the influence of unions and other labor market institutions, which played a particularly important role in protecting incomes at the bottom in Britain, given the absence of a national minimum wage; and an increase in trade in the global economy. Since earnings are the largest component of income for most people and families, as earnings inequality widened, income inequality widened too.

As mentioned, when poverty is measured in relative terms, rising income inequality leads to an increasing proportion of people in poverty. In the 1990s the most commonly used measure of poverty in Britain and in the rest of Europe was the share of people with incomes below 50 percent of average income for their country. This measure is a relative one, in that it defines poverty with reference to other people's income, rather than an absolute standard. Figure 1.1 shows that the relative poverty rate in Brit-

Figure 1.2   Share of British Children in Relative Poverty, 1961 to 1997–1998

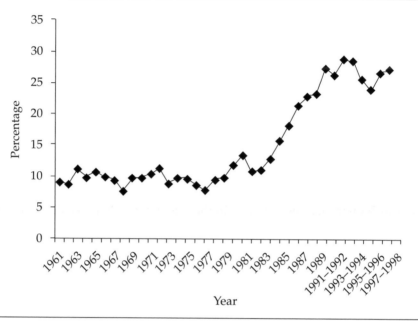

Source: Author's compilation based on data from Institute for Fiscal Studies (2009).
Note: Relative poverty is defined as income below half of average income, before housing costs.

ain using this measure rose to above 20 percent in the early 1990s, compared to around 10 percent in the 1960s.[4]

The increase in poverty was even steeper for children (see figure 1.2). Using the same type of relative measure (the share of children in families with incomes below 50 percent of average income), the child poverty rate rose from 8 percent in 1968 to around 25 percent in the 1990s. Thus, by the 1990s one in four British children were poor using the most widely accepted measure.[5]

If the government had used an absolute standard, analogous to the way the United States defines its poverty line, the trends over time would have been more favorable.[6] However, even using that absolute standard, one in four children were in poverty in 1997.

The concern about child poverty was aggravated by statistics comparing the situation in Britain with that of fellow members of the Organization for Economic Cooperation and Development (OECD), a group made up of the world's advanced industrialized countries. OECD statistics showed Britain moving from being a country with an income distribution that was one of the most equal in the 1970s to having a distribution that was one of the most unequal in the mid-1990s.[7] As a result, comparative studies found that Britain had one of the highest child poverty rates in the OECD in the mid-1990s. For instance, a fifteen-country study, in which poverty was defined as income below half of the country's median income, found that Britain had nearly the highest child poverty rate (20 percent)—surpassed only by the United States (22 percent) and Italy (21 percent)—while other European countries had much lower rates—11 percent in Germany, 8 percent in France, and 3 to 4 percent in the Scandinavian countries (see figure 1.3).[8]

Britain's position in international terms was not much better when defined with reference to the U.S. poverty line. In analyses using an absolute poverty line based on the U.S. poverty line (with income defined consistently across countries and converted into dollars), Britain's child poverty rate was higher than the U.S. rate in the mid-1990s—29 percent versus 19 percent—and again, other European countries had much lower levels of child poverty—12 percent in Germany, for instance.[9]

The mounting evidence about growing income inequality and poverty was well publicized. Particularly influential was the 1995 report of the Inquiry into Income and Wealth, a blue-ribbon panel sponsored by the Joseph Rowntree Foundation. The report, drafted by John Hills from the London School of Economics (LSE), documented how much inequality had grown and what it meant for Britain.[10] The report included a striking "income parade" in which each quintile (one-fifth) of the population was represented by ten illustrative people whose individual height was shown as proportional to his or her relative income. Thus, on the left of the income parade were tiny folks with low incomes, in the middle were average-sized people with average incomes, and on the right stood giants whose growing incomes left them towering over not just those at the bottom but the vast bulk of the population in the middle as well.

Also influential were reports showing that a growing number of children were growing up in households that were at risk of long-term or persistent poverty because they were headed by parents who were out of work or were lone parents. The economists Paul Gregg and Jonathan Wadsworth at the Centre for Economic Performance (CEP) at the LSE were the first to document the growing phenomenon of "workless households"—households in which no adult had a job.[11] In 1968 only 4 percent of working-age households in Britain were workless, but by 1996 over 17 percent were.[12] Moreover, in contrast to continental Europe, where workless households typically were made up of older adults, in Britain a majority of workless households had children. By 1996, 20 percent of children were living in workless families, compared to 4 percent in 1968.[13]

Figure 1.3   Child Poverty Rate in Britain Versus Other Countries in the Mid-1990s

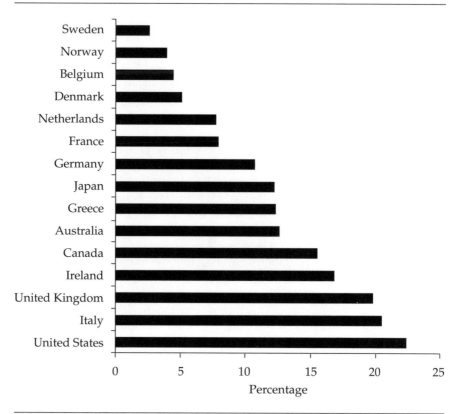

Percentage

Source: Author's compilation based on data from UNICEF Innocenti Research Centre (2000).
Note: Poverty is defined as income below half of national median income.

And in some parts of Britain, rates of worklessness were much higher: in inner London, 36 percent of children were living in workless families in 1996, while in the northeast region 28 percent were.[14] Although worklessness was a growing concern in other European countries, a study of fifteen OECD countries found that Britain had by far the highest rate of worklessness among families with children: nearly 20 percent of British families with children did not include a working adult in 1996, compared to fewer than 10 percent on average across the fifteen countries.[15]

Lacking labor market income and often relying on income from government benefits, workless households were at high risk of poverty. An analysis by Paul Gregg and Jonathan Wadsworth found that in 1996, nine out of every ten workless households with children were poor.[16] More- over, workless households were at elevated risk of persistent poverty, ow- ing to the tendency for workless adults to remain out of the labor market for extended periods of time or to cycle between periods of no pay and low pay.[17]

Part of the increase in worklessness was due to the increase in lone- parent families. In Britain the term "lone parent" is used to refer to a mother (or more rarely a father) who is not married or cohabiting. While similar to the U.S. term "single parent," it differs in that single parents in the United States include parents who are unmarried but cohabiting, whereas in Britain a parent who is unmarried but cohabiting is viewed as living in a couple rather than as a lone parent. The proportion of families with children headed by lone parents (mostly lone mothers) rose from 13 to 23 percent between 1979 and 1997.[18] Most of these lone mothers were not working at all; only about one in five worked full-time.[19] A further concern was that a growing share of lone-mother families—40 percent— were headed by women who had never been married; their children were thus more likely to spend more years in lone-parent families and less likely to receive child support from their fathers than children with di- vorced mothers.

Lone-mother families were much more likely to be in poverty than two-parent families. In 1997, although they represented only 23 percent of families with children, they were about 40 percent of families with chil- dren in poverty. And they were much more likely than two-parent fami- lies to rely on means-tested welfare. About three-fifths of lone-mother families received Income Support, the means-tested cash assistance pro- gram for people who have low incomes and are not working or who are working less than sixteen hours per week (see figure 1.4); this is a higher proportion than those who received that type of assistance in other coun- tries in Europe.[20] In contrast, while 60 percent of British children in pov- erty were in two-parent families in 1997, two-parent families were less likely than lone-parent families to be workless and were much less likely to be on Income Support (see figure 1.5). Relatively few in either group participated in the Family Credit program, which required an adult to be working sixteen or more hours per week (see figures 1.4 and 1.5).

It is worth noting that lone-parent families represented a much smaller share of poor families in Britain than was the case in the United States, where in 1997, 68 percent of poor families with children were single-par- ent families and only 32 percent were married-couple families.[21] Although it is true that cohabiting couples would typically be counted as single par- ents in the United States and as two-parent families in Britain, the num-

Figure 1.4   Share of Lone Parents in Britain on Income Support and Family Credit, 1990 to 1997

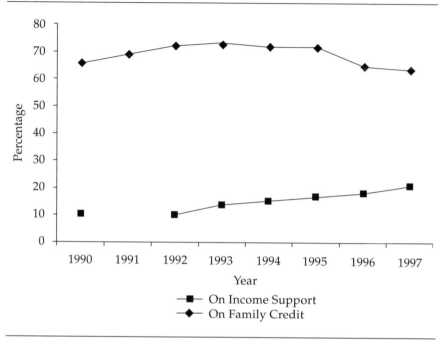

Source: Author's compilation. Numbers of lone parents on Income Support and Family Credit from *Social Security Statistics* (Department for Social Security, various years); number of lone parents from Millar and Ridge (2001).
Note: No data available for "On Income Support" for 1991.

bers in this group are relatively small, and this alone does not explain the higher representation of two-parent families among poor families in Britain. Child poverty in Britain, though linked with lone parenthood, is not identified with it in the same way that it has been in the United States, and thus low-income two-parent families, even if not as reliant on benefits as lone-parent families, were definitely a target of the reforms.

Although benefit levels for those on means-tested cash assistance were low, the rising number of workless households dependent on benefits led to rapid escalation in caseloads, as well as expenditures. By 1997 there were a record 5.5 million workless people on benefits, including some 1 million lone parents on Income Support (about four times the number who had been on such benefits in 1979), and nearly 3 million other workless people receiving benefits because of sickness or disability (about two times the number on such benefits in 1979); in addition, about 1.5 million were on unemployment benefits (one and a half times the number on such

Figure 1.5   Share of Couple Parents on Income Support and Family Credit in Britain, 1990 to 1997

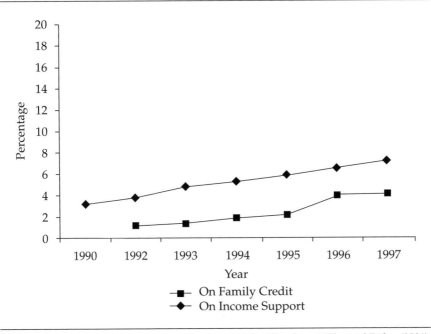

Source: Author's compilation. Number of two-parent families from Millar and Ridge (2001); number of two-parent families in receipt of Family Credit from *Social Security Statistics* (Department for Social Security [DSS], various years).
Note: Number of two-parent families in receipt of Income Support calculated by subtracting the number of lone parents in receipt of Income Support (available from *Social Security Statistics* [DSS, various years]) from the total number of Income Support recipients with dependent children (available for 1992 to 1997 from *Social Security Statistics* [DSS 1998]).

benefits in 1979).[22] Total government expenditures on social insurance and social assistance benefits rose to £92 billion in 1997, nearly twice the level (in real terms) of what had been spent in 1979.[23]

Paralleling the concern about worklessness at the individual level was a concern about what happens "when work disappears" at the neighborhood level.[24] With industrial restructuring, differences in rates of employment and unemployment had grown not just across regions but also across local areas, and these disparities were accompanied by disparities in outcomes such as reliance on means-tested benefits, crime, school achievement, health and mortality, and housing conditions.[25] Community-level analyses showed that many of the poor and workless were concentrated in areas characterized by multiple types of deprivation, and there was concern that living in a poor area could impede the prospects of poor children.[26] As Blair had highlighted in his Toynbee Hall speech, children's life chances were becoming less equal as a result of not only growing disparities in the position of families but also growing disparities between neighborhoods.

There was also growing concern about the risk of what in Britain (and the rest of Europe) was called "social exclusion."[27] The concept of social exclusion, first introduced in France in the late 1980s, differs from poverty in two main ways. First, it emphasizes the dynamic aspects of poverty, placing special weight on the risks associated with long-term or persistent poverty. Hence, individuals with low skills or problems with addiction or a criminal record are seen as being at risk of social exclusion not just because they have had low incomes at some point in time but because they are at risk for persistent poverty. Second, the concept of social exclusion adds a focus on dimensions of disadvantage other than income. For instance, homeless or workless individuals are seen as being at risk of social exclusion not just because of their low incomes but also because of their lack of connection to stable housing and employment. Examples of groups seen as being at risk of social exclusion, in addition to those experiencing problems related to drug addiction, crime, illiteracy, and innumeracy, include young people leaving foster care, people living on the streets, teenage mothers, and workless households.[28]

EVIDENCE ON LONG-RUN EFFECTS
OF POVERTY AND THE EFFECTIVENESS
OF PROGRAMS

Besides the evidence on the extent of poverty and inequality, the British government was influenced by two other kinds of evidence: evidence on the long-term impact of childhood poverty and disadvantage and evidence on the effectiveness of interventions.[29] Analysts in the Treasury made use of a wide range of academic evidence on the long-term impacts of childhood disadvantage and persistent poverty, drawing in particular on longitudinal analyses of Britain's rich birth cohort data.[30] As the Treasury noted at a conference on "Persistent Poverty and Lifetime Inequality: The Evidence," held in November 1998 (four months before Blair's speech),

> these datasets make it possible to move from a static analysis of poverty and inequality to a dynamic focus. Looking at the dynamics of poverty and inequality of opportunity enables us to pinpoint the processes and events which lead people to be at greater risk of low income and poorer life chances. These data provide a firmer underpinning for policies which aim to tackle these problems at source.[31]

In particular, the studies reviewed by the Treasury showed that childhood poverty, particularly if persistent, was linked to poorer adult outcomes and thus led to the transmission of poverty across the life course and across generations. Together, this evidence contributed to a view among policymakers that reducing child poverty, particularly persistent child poverty, would improve outcomes in the long run.

At the same November 1998 conference, the Treasury also heard evidence that programs could be effective in improving child outcomes, particularly in early childhood. Much of this evidence came from the United States. For instance, research from experimental studies in the United States on the long-run benefits of early childhood interventions such as the Perry Preschool Program and the Abecedarian Program was heavily cited, along with evidence from the United States on the impact of the Head Start program and from studies of the effects of child care and maternal employment.[32] This research showed that high-quality early childhood programs could substantially improve outcomes for disadvantaged children, but it also raised concerns about possible adverse effects of early and extensive maternal employment and nonparental child care.

Britain also drew on the extensive U.S. literature on welfare-to-work experiments, in particular the many studies carried out by the Manpower Demonstration Research Corporation (MDRC). British policy advisers closely followed the U.S. welfare-to-work experiments and also visited reforming states to observe model programs, such as New Hope in Wisconsin and Riverside in California. This evidence from the United States suggested that a combination of carrots (more generous work incentives) and sticks (stricter work requirements) could be effective in dramatically boosting the employment of lone parents. Although British policymakers did not endorse all the goals of the U.S. reforms (in particular, they did not agree that mothers of young children should be required to work), they did accept that the U.S. reforms demonstrated what was possible and what types of reforms could be most effective. They were also influenced by evidence from Sweden and other Nordic countries showing the effectiveness of active labor market policies and the potential to encourage high rates of lone-parent employment through the provision of parental leave, child care, and other family-friendly benefits.

PUBLIC OPINION AND VOTER PREFERENCES

John Hills has documented that public opinion surveys in the mid- to late-1990s showed strong support for the government to do something about poverty and inequality. According to Hills, the British public started out with a higher level of concern about inequality than was evident in the United States, and this concern grew over time as inequality increased.[33]

For instance, the share in favor of increased taxes and spending on health, education, and social benefits (as opposed to no change or reduced taxes and spending) rose from 32 percent in 1983 to 61 percent in 1995.[34] Over the same time period, the share saying the gap between those with high incomes and those with low incomes was too large grew from 72 percent to 87 percent.[35]

The public also expressed support for the notion that government should do something about poverty and inequality. In 1998, 73 percent said it was definitely or probably the government's responsibility to reduce income differences. However, the public also expressed a great deal of concern about the existing welfare system. Although nearly half (in 1996) felt that benefits for the unemployed were too low and caused hardship, one-third agreed that if welfare benefits were not so generous, people would learn to stand on their own two feet.[36] Thus, although a solid majority supported the government increasing taxes and spending more on health, education, and social benefits, a declining share (43 percent in 1996 versus 55 percent in 1987) thought that government should spend more money on welfare benefits for the poor.[37]

Public opinion data also revealed sharp differences in how various groups of the poor were viewed. Respondents drew a distinction between those seen as able to work and those seen as not able to work. In particular, in contrast to the United States, there was a good deal of public support for the idea that mothers with young children should not be required to work. This is perhaps not surprising given that a lower share of mothers work in Britain than in the United States, particularly when children are young. In 1996, 77 percent of women with school-age children were in the labor force in the United States, versus about 69 percent in Britain; among those with preschool-age children, the corresponding figures were 62 percent in the United States versus 51 percent in Britain.[38] Among women who did work, part-time work was much more common in Britain than in the United States. In 1996, 39 percent of British women who worked were working less than thirty hours per week, in contrast to only 19 percent of U.S. women.[39] And as noted earlier, rates of lone-parent employment were particularly low (see figure 1.6).

This may explain why, when asked what specific actions government should take to combat poverty and inequality, the British public indicated support for a nuanced strategy. For those who could work—for example, young people or single adults—public opinion favored work-based programs rather than unrestricted cash benefits. However, public opinion also indicated support for more generous cash benefits, without strict work requirements, for those seen as not able to work—such as those caring for young children or for disabled dependents—while sup-

Figure 1.6   Lone-Parent Employment Rates, by Age of Youngest Child, 1978 to 1998

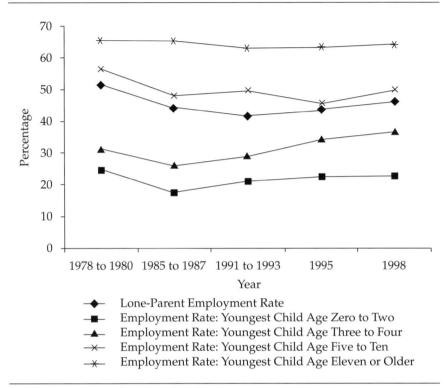

Source: Author's compilation based on data from Gregg and Harkness (2003, table 1).

porting a combination of work and cash benefits for parents of older children.[40]

Children, of course, were not expected to work, and thus, consistent with the attitudes discussed earlier, they were seen as being particularly deserving of support. Public support for providing resources to children was long-standing and robust and was also maintained by advocates such as the Child Poverty Action Group. Whatever reservations the British public had about the merits of welfare for adults, there was widespread support for maintaining and even strengthening benefits for children.

As John Hills and I pointed out in our 2004 analysis of the reforms, Prime Minister Tony Blair and Chancellor Gordon Brown implemented exactly this kind of strategy in their antipoverty campaign. In contrast to

Bill Clinton's campaign promise to "end welfare as we know it," Blair pledged in his March 1999 speech to make welfare popular again:

> Today I want to talk to you about a great challenge: how we make the welfare state popular again. How we restore public trust and confidence in a welfare state that 50 years ago was acclaimed but today has so many people wanting to bury it. I will argue that the only road to a "popular welfare state" is radical welfare reform.[41]

But the radical welfare reform that Blair had in mind was not ending welfare. Rather, he went on to make a remarkable pledge to end child poverty: "Our historic aim will be for ours to be the first generation to end child poverty. It will take a generation. It is a 20-year mission. But I believe that it can be done if we reform the welfare state and build it around the needs of families and children."[42]

THE PLEDGE TO END CHILD POVERTY

As we have seen, there are sound reasons why the Labour government felt it should do something about child poverty. But where did the audacious idea of pledging to *end* child poverty come from?

The short answer is that no one really knows. Blair's speech in the spring of 1999 was preceded by an extensive consultation process, with leading poverty researchers meeting with his staff at 10 Downing Street and submitting their ideas about how the government should tackle poverty. These consultation papers (and his speech) were published after the speech, but there is no record in them of anyone suggesting that the government should pledge to eliminate child poverty.[43]

The closest thing to such a suggestion that I have been able to locate is in a piece written by Tony Atkinson, an economist at Nuffield College, Oxford. In an address delivered at the Institute for Public Policy Research (IPPR) (a London think tank with close links to the Labour government) and published in 1998, Atkinson called for Britain to set an official poverty target and to assess annual progress toward it using one or more official poverty measures:

> My proposal is that the U.K. should set an official poverty target. While it is too late to abolish poverty for the Millennium, this may be a reasonable aspiration for 2015 when the children born today will become adults. Moreover, we should introduce a regular *Poverty Report* on the extent and nature of poverty.[44]

Atkinson had been developing this proposal for some time, noting that similar ideas were gaining momentum in Europe.[45] In particular, he pointed out that the Copenhagen Summit on Social Development held in 1995 had committed European Union member countries to establish "strategies and affordable time-bound goals and targets for the substantial reduction of overall poverty and the eradication of absolute poverty."[46] Atkinson also pointed out that Ireland had already made a commitment to this goal, setting a specific poverty reduction target (although not pledging to eliminate poverty altogether).

So perhaps the idea for the pledge came from Atkinson. But how did it make its way into Blair's speech? Most likely the pledge was added at the last minute by a speechwriter looking to jazz up what otherwise could have been a speech long on depressing statistics and short on sound bites.[47] According to Polly Toynbee, a journalist for *The Guardian*, not even Blair's cabinet knew in advance that he intended to make the pledge.[48]

Wherever the pledge came from, it met with an enthusiastic response among members of Blair and Brown's government, who were frustrated at having spent their first two years in office living under spending limits set by the previous Conservative government. The Labour Party had pledged to live under those spending limits as a way of demonstrating its fiscal restraint and dispelling fears that it would tax and spend.[49] But that decision was unpopular. Government staffers were also aware of the unpopularity of their decision to implement a Conservative Party proposal to eliminate a special welfare benefit that one-parent families received. Although this change was meant to balance how the welfare system treated one- and two-parent families, the proposal was taken as an attack on one-parent families and a step backward in combating child poverty.[50] The poverty pledge committed the Labour government to take a more progressive stand.[51]

Once the pledge to end child poverty was made, it took on a life of its own. Politicians often set lofty goals, but they do not always live up to them. Why did this pledge prove to be so powerful? One reason is that it was consistent with the values of the Labour Party. As Blair stressed in his speech, the commitment to end child poverty was grounded in a commitment to social justice. He made an impassioned case that "the child born on a run-down housing estate should have the same chance to be healthy and well-educated as the child born in the leafy suburbs."[52]

A second reason for the pledge's forceful impact was that government staffers and poverty advocates were keen to see it carried forward. They had waited nearly twenty years for the Labour Party to come back into office, and they were eager to see a more progressive agenda put in place.

They also felt that the situation inherited from the Conservative government demanded drastic action. As David Piachaud from the Centre for Analysis of Social Exclusion at the London School of Economics had pointed out in his briefing paper for Blair:

> After 18 years of Conservative government there was
> . . . more poverty.
> . . . more inequality between rich and poor.
> . . . more dependent on benefits, especially means-tested benefits.
> . . . more homeless on the streets. [53]

But another reason for the impact of the pledge was that the man controlling the purse strings—Chancellor of the Exchequer Gordon Brown at the Treasury (and Blair's eventual successor as prime minister)—was even more committed to eliminating child poverty than was Blair. As Brown pointed out to Blair, "children are 20 percent of the population but they are 100 percent of the future."[54] In Britain, the chancellor can exert a lot of influence over the level of government spending and how that money is allocated, and Brown played a particularly consequential role, given the power-sharing agreement that he and Blair had made upon taking over leadership of the Labour Party in 1994, as discussed in the next section. Rather than putting on the brakes, as might have occurred under another chancellor, Brown instead took a number of steps that made the commitment more concrete and more lasting. Early on, Brown assumed leadership of the antipoverty initiative. A few months after Blair's speech, when Brown convened a meeting at Downing Street to discuss his plans for ending child poverty, he told the assembled group: "Many important meetings have been held in this room but none more important than this."[55]

Over the next decade, as we shall see, Brown put real money into the initiative, set specific antipoverty targets, and also set in motion a series of annual reports documenting the government's progress toward the targets. After he had succeeded Blair as prime minister in 2007, Brown maintained a focus on child poverty and continued to commit resources to the antipoverty effort. In 2009 he filed legislation enshrining the commitment to end child poverty in law so that future governments would be committed to it.

NEW LABOUR AND THE "THIRD WAY"

The antipoverty strategy that the New Labour government adopted was grounded in a larger rethinking of government called the "Third Way," to distinguish it from traditional approaches taken by those on the left or the right.[56] Third Way thinking incorporates concepts traditionally emphasized by the Labour Party and the left—such as social justice—alongside concepts more traditionally identified with the Conservative Party and the right—such as mutual responsibility. Emphasizing its status as New Labour and its Third Way positions allowed the Labour Party to distinguish itself from Old Labour—which had not been able to win a national election for nearly two decades—while reassuring its constituents that it was not entirely abandoning Labour principles.

In this respect, New Labour's Third Way strategy resembled the approach taken by the "New Democrats" in the United States in the years leading up to President Bill Clinton's election in 1992. New Democrats tried to stake out positions more moderate than those taken by traditional Democrats as a way to regain the support of middle-of-the-road Democrats and independents. New Labour too tried to stake out a middle ground. However, what constituted a middle-ground position on issues such as the reform of the welfare state differed in the two countries.

The development of the Third Way vision for the welfare state in Britain began in the early 1990s, with the Institute for Public Policy Research playing a leading role. In the early 1990s, IPPR sponsored the Commission on Social Justice, chaired by Labour Party leader John Smith. When Smith died suddenly at the age of fifty-five in May 1994, he left a leadership vacuum that would be filled two months later by Tony Blair, who reached an agreement with Gordon Brown, the other contender, whereby, if Labour was elected, Blair would become prime minister and Brown would become chancellor with extensive authority over social welfare policy.

The report of the Commission on Social Justice emphasized that for a nation that prided itself on its social cohesion, it was not right to have such vast gaps in income and wealth.[57] The report also called for a more intelligent approach to the welfare state.

As applied to the welfare state, Third Way thinking implied "not to dismantle it, or to protect it unchanged, but to reform it radically."[58] As Blair explained in his March 1999 speech, a Third Way welfare state would have six defining characteristics:

> First, it will tackle social exclusion, child poverty, community decay in an active way; and tackle it through tackling the fundamental causes: structural unemployment; poor education; poor housing; the crime and drugs culture. . . .
>
> Second, welfare will be a hand-up not a hand out. Mutual responsibility. . . .

Third, where people really need security, the most help should go to those with the most need. . . .

Fourth, we must root out fraud and abuse in any way we can. . . .

Fifth, the welfare state need no longer be delivered only through the state or through traditional methods of government. . . .

Sixth, welfare is not just about benefits. Active welfare is about services too—schools, hospitals, the whole infrastructure of community support.[59]

These Third Way principles help explain why the British reforms focused on a broader set of programs than the U.S. welfare reforms, which focused mainly on meeting Clinton's campaign pledge to "end welfare as we know it" by converting the traditional cash assistance program, Aid to Families with Dependent Children (AFDC), into a time-limited and work-oriented program, Temporary Assistance to Needy Families (TANF). These principles also help explain why the British reforms blended measures such as expanded supports for some groups (such as mothers with young children) with tightened rules for eligibility for others (such as single young adults). But to fully understand the similarity and difference in approach across the two countries, some background about the development and orientation of their respective welfare states is helpful.

THE BRITISH VERSUS U.S.
WELFARE STATES

Following the typology of the political scientist Gøsta Esping-Anderson,[60] comparative scholars identify three main types of welfare states among the advanced industrialized countries: the Anglo-American group, Continental Europe, and the Nordic group. Britain and the United States— along with Australia, Canada, and New Zealand—belong to the Anglo-American group. Although, as we shall see, there are important differences between the Anglo-American countries, they are grouped together because they share a common heritage—in Britain's Poor Laws—and because several features of their welfare states, as discussed later, distinguish them from the other two groups.[61]

Britain's Poor Laws, dating from the Act for the Relief of the Poor of 1597 and the Elizabethan Poor Law of 1601 (and subsequently amended several times thereafter), were designed to address the challenge of providing needed assistance to poor individuals and families without at the same time undermining the work ethic and other strongly held social values—in particular, the integrity of the family unit and the importance of the local community.[62] To that end, the Poor Laws established the principle of "less eligibility"—the idea that whatever benefits were provided to the poor should not make them better off than a person who worked for a living. A second principle enshrined in the Poor Laws was that aid should be provided only to "the deserving poor." The definition of "deserving poor" has changed over time (and varies across countries), but basically it has been used to identify those who are unable to work and are therefore poor through no fault of their own, in contrast to the "indolent poor," who are poor because they make little effort to work. A third key principle was the concept of localism: the poor have some right to aid, but only in their area of origin; this principle discourages the poor from moving in search of aid, and localities from shirking their responsibility.

As a result of this legacy, the Anglo-American countries have less generous and less complete welfare states than other advanced countries. Fearful of compromising the work ethic, providing aid to those who are not deserving, or creating incentives for the poor to shop around for aid, the Anglo-American countries have what have been called "residual" or "incomplete" welfare states characterized by fewer overall programs, lower levels of spending, and a heavier reliance on means-tested rather than universal programs.[63] These countries tend to rely to a larger extent than others on the private market and employers for social welfare provision; they also have less-regulated labor markets and more income inequality.

Another factor that has reinforced the resemblance between countries within the Anglo-American group is that they tend to look to each other when it comes to reforming their welfare states, in part because reforms are seen as more readily transferable when they come from a similar country. It probably also helps that materials about the reforms from other Anglo-American countries are available in English—that is not always the case for reforms in Continental Europe or the Nordic countries. In addition, the United States and Britain, owing to the long-held view of their "special relationship," are particularly likely to borrow reforms and ideas from each other.

Within the Anglo-American group, however, there is considerable variation. On most dimensions of welfare state policy, the United States (along with Australia and New Zealand) has traditionally lagged the furthest behind other advanced countries and has been characterized as having one of the most incomplete welfare states.[64] And even though the Anglo-American group has tended to spend less on its welfare states as a share of gross domestic product than have the Continental European and Nordic countries, the United States in particular displays one of the lowest rates of investment (see table 1.1, which shows the United States ranking seventeenth of twenty-one countries while Britain is ranked ninth).[65]

The variation across the Anglo-American countries also reflects the fact that there have been significant changes in policy within the countries over time. In Britain the most important changes to the welfare state (prior

Table 1.1   Government Social Welfare Expenditure As a Percentage
of Gross Domestic Product in OECD Countries, 1960,
1975, and 1990 (Countries Ranked by Percentage in 1990)

Country	1960	1975	1990
1. Sweden	15.6	27.4	39.6
2. Norway	11.0	23.2	35.5
3. Netherlands	12.8	29.3	34.4
4. Denmark	9.0	27.1	33.9
5. Finland	14.9	21.9	33.8
6. France	14.4	26.3	31.9
7. Belgium	n.a.	28.7	30.6
8. Austria	17.4	26.0	29.9
OECD average	12.3	21.9	27.9
9. United Kingdom	12.4	19.6	27.6
10. Germany	17.1	27.8	27.5
11. Italy	13.7	20.6	26.7
12. Canada	11.2	20.1	25.5
13. Ireland	11.3	22.0	25.2
14. Spain	n.a.	n.a.	23.8
15. Portugal	n.a.	n.a.	20.8
16. Switzerland	8.2	19.0	20.5
17. United States	9.9	18.7	20.1
18. Greece	n.a.	10.0	19.5
19. New Zealand	12.7	19.0	19.8
20. Australia	9.5	17.3	17.7
21. Japan	7.6	13.7	15.3

Source: Author's compilation based on data from Kamerman and Kahn (1997, table 4.1).
Note: 1990 figures for Greece, Italy, and New Zealand are from 1985; 1990 figure for Switzerland is from 1984.

to the period of reforms considered here) took place after World War II, when the Poor Laws were repealed and replaced by a new framework for welfare provision.[66] The lead author of the post–World War II reforms was William Beveridge, a civil servant who was asked to chair an interdepartmental commission on social insurance during the war.[67] Delivering his report to the government in December 1942, Beveridge called for a landmark set of reforms, including national health insurance, and this report set the stage for the reforms implemented after the war in July 1948.[68] It was in conjunction with the fiftieth anniversary year of those reforms that Blair delivered his Beveridge Lecture in March 1999, and the site he chose to deliver it—Toynbee Hall—was the East London settlement house where Beveridge had worked as a young man.

Beveridge's reforms rested on an analysis of the major factors that placed individuals and families at risk of poverty.[69] As Howard Glennerster details in his history of the modern British welfare state,[70] the Beveridge reforms addressed those risks in a way that was informed by six key principles: the goal of full employment; the responsibility of the state to set and enforce a national minimum standard of living; the right to equal and free access to health and education (prior to this, there had been no national health service, and only primary education had been free); the need for a greater role for the central government (as opposed to local authorities); the appropriateness of services being provided by the state (rather than private entities); and the importance of continuity (so that the new system built on the old). Taken together, Beveridge's reforms moved the British welfare state away from the limited Poor Law provisions and toward a more complete, and more generous, social welfare system.

In the United States one could point to the 1935 Social Security Act and the 1960s War on Poverty as constituting major extensions of the welfare state. However, even after those changes, the U.S. welfare state remained incomplete compared to the British one (and even more so compared to the Continental European or Nordic countries). In particular, although Title XIX of the Social Security Act enacted in 1965 during the War on Poverty introduced Medicaid for the poor and Medicare for the elderly, the United States still lacked the universal health insurance that Beveridge's reforms had introduced in Britain.

More recently, two other trends have been important in the evolution of the British welfare state. One has been an increased emphasis on personal choice and personal responsibility. From the 1970s forward, and particularly after the election of Margaret Thatcher as prime minister in 1979, there has been a shift toward more personalized service provision and also toward a greater role for markets in service delivery. At the same time, more attention has been paid to addressing problems of dependency.

A similar trend was evident in the United States, particularly under President Ronald Reagan, elected in 1980. However, there is an important difference in the experience of the two countries in the 1980s. In Britain the services being reformed were universal and widely used by the middle class, and several of the reforms improved those mainstream services, with the result that at least some elements of the welfare state were arguably more popular at the end of the Thatcher reforms than before.[71] In the United States, in contrast, Reagan cut spending on means-tested welfare and related programs while criticizing welfare recipients, paving the way for the radical welfare reforms of the 1990s.[72]

The other recent trend of note is that Britain has become increasingly integrated into the European Union, which brings it into closer contact with the welfare states of Continental Europe and the Nordic countries. Inevitably, this has led Britain to consider different models of welfare and social policy provision, either because of the example set by these other countries or because of explicit direction from the European Union. As a result, Britain has moved closer to the Continental European and Nordic models, leaving the United States as even more of an outlier. Already by 1990, as shown in table 1.1, Britain was close to the OECD average in terms of the share of its GDP devoted to social welfare programs, while the United States, as mentioned earlier, ranked seventeenth out of twenty-one countries. A decade later Britain remained close to the OECD average, but the United States rank had fallen further, to nineteenth out of twenty-one.[73] Thus, at the end of the twentieth century the United States, unlike the other advanced industrialized countries, did not have a system of universal health insurance, nor did it have a universal program of income support for families with children. In common with Britain, it had very limited public support for preschool-age child care. And in common with Britain, it had a welfare state that relied very heavily on means-tested benefits, which often produced inadvertent unemployment and poverty traps (since families would lose those benefits if they moved into work and raised their incomes). The welfare reforms of the mid-1990s in the United States and the antipoverty reforms in Britain in the late 1990s thus needed to address some similar shortcoming in their existing systems of support. But those systems, although sharing a common origin in the British Poor Law, had already diverged in important ways.

LOOKING AHEAD

So what did New Labour do to tackle child poverty? And what did those efforts accomplish? Chapters 2 to 5 examine the three main strands of the reforms—the initiatives to promote work and make work pay, to increase financial support for families with children, and to invest in children—and detail what was done and how successful those efforts have been. Chapter 6 returns to the core goal of the reforms—reducing child poverty—and presents the latest evidence on that target. Chapter 7 discusses the next steps for the British reforms. The final chapter concludes by drawing out lessons for the United States and other countries.

Chapter 2

Promoting Work and Making Work Pay

The reforms to promote work and make work pay were far-reaching and included the New Deal welfare-to-work programs, Britain's first national minimum wage, a series of new tax credits for low-income workers, and a set of reforms to income and payroll taxes. These reforms had much in common with the U.S. reforms to promote work and make work pay and in fact drew heavily on the U.S. research. But they also drew on evidence from other Anglo-American countries—in particular, Canada and Australia—as well as Nordic countries, especially Sweden. This chapter details the development of these reforms. It also summarizes the evidence to date on their effects.

THE NEW DEAL

The British welfare-to-work programs are collectively known as the New Deal. The name "New Deal," although reminiscent of the reforms implemented by President Franklin Delano Roosevelt in the United States in the 1930s, was chosen by New Labour to signify the new contract between benefit recipients and the state. Central to the New Deal was the concept of mutual responsibility. The state was seen as having an obligation to provide help and support, but this was contingent on recipients who were able to work meeting their responsibility to participate in activities that would help them find and retain jobs.

Consistent with this concept of mutual responsibility, the New Deal programs include compulsory employment for groups such as young people and long-term unemployed single adults. In this respect, they look similar to U.S. welfare-to-work programs, and in fact, the design of the programs was strongly influenced by evidence from the U.S. welfare-to-work experiments of the 1990s.[1] Recipients meet with personal advisers who help them develop a plan for employment and then monitor their compliance with it.

However, a notable difference is that the New Deal for Lone Parents (NDLP), launched in eight pilot areas in 1997 and then extended nationwide in 1998, was voluntary, in contrast to the U.S. welfare-to-work reforms, which were mandatory for single mothers. Under the NDLP, lone parents receiving Income Support (the means-tested cash welfare program for low-income families with either no adult working or adults working less than sixteen hours per week) were invited to the welfare office for an interview with a personal adviser to discuss job search, training options, and the benefits and tax credits available to those who were working. They were also reminded about the availability of a different means-tested program, the Family Credit program, for those working at least sixteen hours a week. Family Credit had been in place since the late 1980s but was still received by relatively low numbers of lone parents (about 300,000 as of 1997, compared to about 1 million on Income Support).

In its first few years of operation, the New Deal for Lone Parents was offered on a purely voluntary basis and very few lone parents (fewer than 10 percent of those eligible) participated in the program. Starting in 2001, some single mothers on Income Support were required to attend work-focused interviews (starting first with existing clients with children age thirteen or older, as well as new clients with children age five or older), but they were still not required to participate in training or work. Thus, the NDLP included a push toward work, but there were no benefit reductions or other sanctions for lone mothers who chose not to work, as was the case for such single mothers in the United States.

This soft-touch approach to employment for lone mothers reflected the more traditional attitudes toward women's roles that are still common in Britain. Although British attitudes have moved over time toward a more positive view of working mothers, a substantial share of women and an even larger share of men still express reservations about mothers working. These attitudes are reflected in table 2.1, which reports data from the British Social Attitudes Survey administered in 1989 and 1994. As late as 1994, half of British men and women agreed that mothers should stay home when children are under school age, and more than one-third believed that children suffer if mothers work full-time.[2] In contrast, data for the United States for 1996 (the year federal welfare reform was enacted) indicate that two-thirds of men and women agreed with the statement that "the mother working doesn't hurt children," and even when asked about young children, just over half (52 percent) disagreed with the statement that "preschool kids suffer if the mother works."[3]

These attitudes are reflected in maternal employment rates. Data in table 2.2 indicate that prior to the reforms, in 1994, only 26 percent of British lone mothers with children under the age of six were working in the labor market, in contrast to 44 percent of comparable U.S. lone mothers. Moreover, in Britain those who were working were much more likely to be

Table 2.1   British Attitudes Toward Working Mothers, 1989 and 1994

	1989	1994
Women should stay home when a child is under school age (percentage agree)		
Men	67%	60%
Women	64	55
Family life suffers when a woman has a full-time job (percentage agree)		
Men	45	32
Women	39	33

Source: Author's compilation based on Crompton, Brockmann, and Wiggins (2003, tables 8.3 and 8.7).

working part-time, contrary to the pattern seen in the United States. Employment rates for married mothers with young children were closer across the two countries (56 percent in Britain versus 61.5 percent in the United States), but again, with a large gap in the proportion working part-time.

A central component of the New Deal programs was personal advising. As in the United States—where reformers such as the economist David Ellwood from Harvard's John F. Kennedy School of Government had advocated changing welfare offices from places that determined eligibility and wrote welfare checks to places that asked, "What can we do to help?"—the shift to personal advising was designed to provide individu-

Table 2.2   Employment of Mothers with Children under the Age of Six in Britain and the United States, 1994

	Britain	United States
Mothers in couple families		
Working full-time	15.7%	33.7%
Working part-time	33.1	19.2
Not working	46.2	38.5
Lone mothers		
Working full-time	9.1	33.8
Working part-time	16.8	10.3
Not working	74.0	55.9

Source: Author's compilation based on Organization for Economic Cooperation and Development (2001a, table 4.2).

Figure 2.1   Lone-Parent Employment Rate, 1997 to 2008

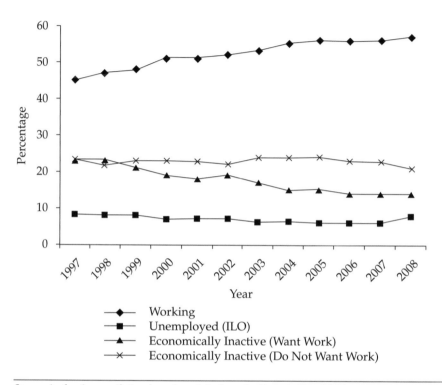

Source: Author's compilation based on data from the Poverty Site (2009).

alized support for recipients to meet their responsibilities and achieve greater financial independence.[4]

This culture change did not come easily. In Britain, welfare and employment services had historically been delivered out of two distinct sets of offices. Benefits Agency offices paid benefits to unemployed people as well as to individuals from groups not typically expected to look for work, such as lone parents; these offices did not see helping with employment as part of their mission. At the same time, Employment Service offices gave advice on job search and employment opportunities, but they did not see lone parents as a group they were supposed to serve; moreover, these offices did not welcome the expansion of employment services to this group. To implement the welfare-to-work agenda, the government combined these separate offices. This effort, which began with pilot programs in

Figure 2.2   Share of Lone Parents on Income Support, 1997 to 2008

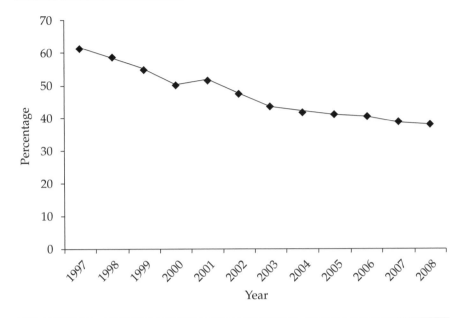

Sources: Author's compilation. Number of lone parents from Department for Social Security (1999b) and Department for Work and Pensions (DWP), *Households Below Average Income* (2004, 2005, 2007a, 2008a, 2009a), available at: http://research.dwp.gov.uk/asd/hbai_arc.asp. Numbers on Income Support from DWP, *DWP Tabulation Tool,* available at: http://research .dwp.gov.uk/asd/tabtool.asp.

1999, took over two years to accomplish and culminated in the introduction of combined "Jobcentre Plus" offices in March 2002.

Over time the push to encourage lone parents to work intensified.[5] The initial soft-touch reforms had been successful in moving some lone mothers into employment, but the numbers who were not working and who remained on Income Support were still high (see figures 2.1 and 2.2). It was clear that many more lone mothers would have to work if child poverty was to be successfully tackled.

Starting in March 2002, all new Income Support claimants were required to attend a work-focused interview. And starting in April 2004, the requirement to participate in a work-focused interview was extended to existing claimants with children under the age of five (a group that had been exempt prior to that date). By the autumn of 2004, some lone parents were required to come in for such interviews every quarter, and the staff they met with were required to develop an action plan for each family (although lone parents were not required to participate in or sign their plan).

Various incentives to work were also offered. For example, lone parents who actually went to work could benefit from an extra "in-work credit" benefit (set at £40 per week in 2004) for the first year of working, or they might receive a flat grant (£250 in 2004) upon moving into work. Lone parents who agreed to search for work in accordance with their action plan could receive a weekly grant (£26 per week in 2004) for up to half a year. Starting in 2005, lone parents entering the labor force could receive a special "child care assist" grant to help with the costs of care in the week before starting work, while another program allowed nonworking lone parents to try out a child care program for five days free of charge (rather than having to make a copayment based on income).

There was also a New Deal for partners program for the non-employed wives or partners of those claiming benefits in couple families. Unlike lone parents, who could claim Income Support simply by virtue of being a low-income lone parent, a couple had to have at least one adult who was sick or disabled in order to qualify for the program. (Those who were not sick or disabled but were unemployed qualified for a different program that had always emphasized job search and employment.) Although not a large group (as we saw in Chapter 1), the couples on Income Support were a group with whom policymakers felt they could make some head-way, since the benefit system had not previously engaged at all with the wives and partners, some of whom might have been interested in moving into work. Like the New Deal for Lone Parents, this program was initially voluntary, again reflecting more traditional attitudes about mothers working, but it evolved over time to involve more compulsion in recognition that increased employment rates were needed to cut child poverty and reduce the numbers of sick and disabled on Income Support, which, if anything, had been rising since 1997 (see figure 2.3). With few wives and partners taking it up on a voluntary basis, the program was relaunched in April 2004 to include the same requirements as for lone parents, including mandatory interviews for new and existing claimants.

Although the primary focus of the New Deal reforms was to move low-income recipients into employment, it was recognized that employment retention and advancement would have to be addressed if poverty was to be reduced in the long run. The "low-pay-no-pay" cycle—the tendency of low-income workers to be stuck in low-paid jobs, alternating with periods of nonwork—had been well documented.[6] To boost skills, the New Deal programs offered mentorship and training to recipients who were out of the labor market. And the Employment Retention and Advancement (ERA) demonstration program, piloted in October 2003, provided support to recipients as they moved into work and also helped them advance beyond their entry-level jobs.

Nevertheless, in 2006, after nearly a decade of effort, the NDLP had still

Figure 2.3   Income Support Caseload Numbers, 1997 to 2008

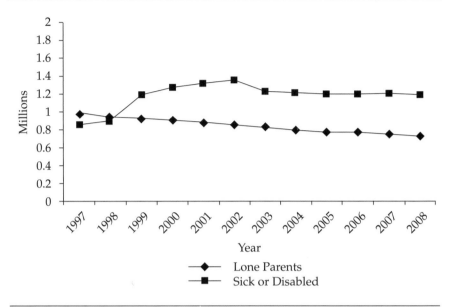

Source: Author's compilation. Data for 1999 to 2008 from Department for Work and Pensions, *DWP Tabulation Tool,* available at: http://research.dwp.gov.uk/asd/tabtool.asp. Data for 1997 and 1998 from *Social Security Statistics* (Department for Social Security, various years).

not been successful in raising lone-parent employment to the levels the government had hoped to attain. The lone-parent employment rate had risen eleven percentage points, from 45 percent in 1997 to 56 percent in 2006 (as shown in figure 2.1), but was still short of the government's target rate of 70 percent. The government began experimenting with a more comprehensive program; called the New Deal Plus for Lone Parents, it included clear guarantees about the financial rewards from work, the availability of child care support, and the provision of ongoing support and personal advice.[7] At the same time, it was broadly agreed that if this kind of package of support was guaranteed, it would be possible to consider "strengthening lone parents' responsibility to look for work as the logical next step."[8]

Thus, starting in 2006 and thereafter, the subject of greater work compulsion for lone parents rose to a more prominent place on the public agenda.[9] The push toward stronger work requirements was led by a series of new employment ministers appointed by Blair as he re-exerted his authority over the welfare-to-work agenda, which previously had been directed by the Treasury.[10] But even then, the government was careful to

49

point out that it did not intend to replicate U.S.-style welfare reform, such as the Wisconsin Works program, which paid no cash assistance to lone mothers who did not work.

> We have found good international practice and will be using that where appropriate. We have also found schemes that we do not see as the way ahead for Britain. "Wisconsin Works" has been cited by some as a ready-made model of welfare reform that could be imposed here. This tough approach on its own does not work, and we will not be adopting it wholesale. . . . In contrast, our radical new approach is a welfare system in which, increasingly, claimants are not passive recipients of benefits, but instead active job-seekers preparing for a return to work, in which they will be better off.[11]

In moving toward stronger work requirements for lone parents, the government was influenced by an independent report that it commissioned from the businessman David Freud in 2007. Not an expert on welfare or social policy, Freud was an odd choice to produce this report, but his selection signaled Blair's intention to move welfare-to-work policy in a different direction. And Freud's report did just that. Emphasizing the difficulty of moving children out of poverty when their parents were not working, Freud called on the government to impose new work requirements on lone parents—a group that, as we have seen, had been largely exempt from such requirements to date. Freud also called for further involvement of the private sector in the delivery of employment and training services.

In 2007, in a move that would have been unthinkable ten years earlier, the government took the Freud review to heart and floated the idea of requiring lone parents to work when their youngest child reached age twelve. After a period of consultation, that requirement went into effect in November 2008, with plans to extend the requirement to families with a youngest child age ten in October 2009 and to families with a youngest child age seven in October 2010. With the expansions in measures to make work pay and the expansions in child care (discussed later in this chapter and in chapter 3), opposition to work requirements for lone mothers had eased. The share of the public agreeing that benefits for a lone parent should be stopped or significantly reduced if she did not attend her work-focused interview increased from 30 percent to over 41 percent between 2000 and 2003, while the share stating that under these circumstances a lone parent's benefits should not be affected or should be reduced only a little fell from 67 percent to 55 percent, with 3 to 4 percent offering no opinion.[12]

Moreover, it was widely recognized that if the aspiration was to end child poverty, most parents would have to work, since public support and public funding could never be sufficient to move all families out of poverty through benefits alone. Comparative statistics on lone-parent employment showed that, in most peer countries, a much higher share worked. As of 2000, 60 to 80 percent of lone parents were working in European Union countries and the United States, in contrast to only about 50 percent in Britain.[13]

Nevertheless, the government remained committed to the model of personal advising and to tailoring work expectations to individual circumstances. This vision was set out in an independent report commissioned by the government from Paul Gregg, a professor at the University of Bristol and a former member of the government's Council of Economic Advisers. Released in late 2008, Gregg's report proposed a system of personalized conditionality and support and argued that virtually all benefit recipients should be helped into employment but that assistance should be tailored to individual circumstances.[14] In particular, Gregg recommended that a distinction be made between three main groups: those who are ready to work, those who should be making progress toward work, and a small group (including parents with children under the age of one) who should not be expected to work. Gregg argued that any parent whose youngest child had reached age seven should be viewed as potentially ready to work, while any parent whose youngest child was age one to six should be expected to make progress toward work, but on a voluntary basis. Gregg emphasized that each lone parent should be treated on an individual basis, with a program designed specifically for her. For some, the plan might involve improving literacy skills, while for others it might involve getting treatment for an underlying medical condition. In this way, Gregg's personalized approach was reminiscent of the "ladder to work" approach of the welfare reformer Toby Herr in Chicago: each individual had her own specific goals to achieve in order to make incremental progress up the rungs of the ladder to work.[15]

The government, in a December 2008 white paper, endorsed the Gregg recommendations, but with the proviso that the government would at least initially treat only parents whose youngest children were ages three to six as potentially ready to progress into work and that it would set lower expectations for parents whose youngest children were one or two years old; the latter parents would be invited for work-focused interviews, but not required to participate in other activities to prepare for work. Thus, even after the changes to increase work requirements for lone parents, the expectations in the British system remained very different from those in the U.S. system—a reflection, as we have seen, of different norms and values.

BRITAIN'S FIRST NATIONAL
MINIMUM WAGE

To help make work pay, the New Labour government brought in Britain's first national minimum wage in April 1999 (the country had previously had minimum wages in some sectors, but those had been abolished by the Conservative government in the 1980s). A nationwide minimum wage had been part of the platform on which Labour campaigned in 1997, and one of its first acts after coming into office was the appointment of a Low Pay Commission in July 1997. The commission was charged with reviewing the likely impact of a national minimum wage and making recommendations for its implementation, including whether a separate minimum wage should be established for youth. The commission completed its review in less than a year and released its first report in June 1998.[16] Legislation was passed in July 1998, and the minimum wage came into effect the following April.[17]

The Low Pay Commission concluded that the implementation of a national minimum wage would not necessarily have adverse employment consequences for most workers. The report cited studies of the minimum wages that had existed in some sectors in Britain in the past. Although early studies had found that higher sectoral minimum wages decreased employment in the affected sector, later studies tended to find that increases in the minimum wage did not affect employment (perhaps because minimum wages had declined relative to average wages and thus did not have much bite). In addition, studies that tracked employment after the abolition of sectoral minimum wages did not provide any evidence that abolishing minimum wages led to employment increases.[18]

The report also cited U.S. research by the Princeton economists David Card and Alan Krueger.[19] This work overturned the conventional wisdom that higher minimum wages inevitably discourage hiring by placing too high a price on low-skilled labor. Instead, Card and Krueger suggested that there can also be an important supply-side effect that leads some individuals who are out of the labor force to seek jobs in response to a higher minimum wage.

Following the recommendations of the Low Pay Commission, a national minimum wage was implemented on April 1, 1999. The rate was set at £3.60 per hour (with a lower rate of £3.00 per hour for those under age twenty-two). This was high compared to the U.S. national minimum wage rate at the time—about 45 percent of median hourly full-time earnings in Britain versus 38 percent in the United States (see table 2.3).[20] And because the British minimum wage has been raised several times during a period when the national minimum wage rate in the United States mostly held

Table 2.3   National Minimum Wage Rates in Britain and the United States, 1999 to 2009

	Britain		United States	
Year	Level	As a Percentage of Median Earnings	Level	As a Percentage of Median Earnings
1999	£3.60	46%	$5.15	38%
2000	3.70	45	5.15	37
2001	4.10	44	5.15	35
2002	4.20	47	5.15	35
2003	4.50	47	5.15	34
2004	4.85	48	5.15	34
2005	5.05	49	5.15	33
2006	5.35	50	5.15	32
2007	5.52	51	5.85	35
2008	5.73	51	6.55	38
2009	5.80	51	7.25	40

Source: Author's compilation. Data for Britain from Cooke and Lawton (2008), HM Treasury (2008), and Low Pay Commission (2008). Data for the United States from Economic Policy Institute (2008) and author's calculations using data from the Current Population Survey (CPS) Outgoing Rotation Groups (ORG).

constant, the value in Britain has gone up relative to the value in the United States. As shown in the table, after an increase to £5.35 per hour in October 2006, the British minimum wage had risen in value to 50 percent of median hourly full-time earnings, whereas the U.S. rate relative to the median had declined to 32 percent. Even after increases in the U.S. national minimum wage in 2007, 2008, and 2009, the British minimum wage, which was also increased each of those years, maintained its higher value, standing at over 50 percent of the median as of 2009, versus only 40 percent in the United States.

Nevertheless, the minimum wage—on its own—is not sufficient to keep families with children out of poverty. In 2008 the relative poverty line for a family with two parents and two children was £361 per week (see appendix 5). If one parent worked forty hours per week at the minimum wage, his or her earnings would have amounted to £229 per week—only 63 percent of that amount. Even with one parent working forty hours per week and the other working twenty hours a week, the family's income from earnings at the minimum wage would not quite reach the poverty line.[21] Of course, these back-of-the-envelope estimates do not take into account the taxes that would be deducted from earnings, the tax credits, and other benefits available to supplement earnings. We consider these aspects of policy next.

WORK-CONDITIONED TAX CREDITS

As a further measure to make work pay, in October 1999 the government introduced a new tax credit, known as the Working Families Tax Credit (WFTC), for couples with children or for lone parents who were working at least sixteen hours per week (with higher benefits if they worked at least thirty hours). A bit of history is helpful in understanding how WFTC fit into the British welfare system. Since 1972, Britain had operated two separate cash assistance programs for low-income families, one for families with no working adults or with adults working less than sixteen hours per week, and the other for families with at least one adult working at least sixteen hours per week. Immediately prior to the Labour government reforms in 1999, the first of these was known as the basic Income Support program (for low-income families with no adult working or working less than sixteen hours per week), while the second was known as Family Credit (for low-income families with one or more adults working at least sixteen hours per week). WFTC, which was conditioned on work, replaced the Family Credit program.

In comparison to the former Family Credit program, WFTC increased work incentives by providing a higher level of benefits and by withdrawing those benefits more slowly as earnings rose. Benefits under the British system are calculated based on an amount per adult and an amount per child, with the amount per child often varying by the age of the child. Under Family Credit, the basic adult rate in 1998 was £48.80 per week, the rate for a child age zero to ten was £12.35 per week, and, to address what were believed to be greater costs associated with raising older children, the rate for a child age eleven to sixteen was £20.45 per week. These rates added up to about 37 percent of the relative poverty line of £222 per week for a couple family with two children in 1998.

Under WFTC, benefits for each child age zero to ten went up by £2.50 per week; this increase of 20 percent from the value of these benefits under Family Credit reflected an emerging view that additional resources should be targeted to young children to the extent possible. In addition, the earnings allowance before benefits were withdrawn was raised by £10 per week, and the rate at which benefits were withdrawn was cut from 70 percent to 55 percent of after-tax earnings.

As a result, benefits increased sharply with the move from Family Credit to WFTC, and the greatest gains were seen by families with young children. For instance, a family with two parents, one of whom worked more than thirty hours per week, earning £200 per week, and with two children between the ages of eleven and sixteen, gained £21.46 per week from the shift to WFTC, an amount equivalent to about 10 percent of the relevant poverty line. A similar family with two children under age ten would have seen their benefit increase by £26.46 per week, equivalent to about 12 percent of the poverty line.[22]

Another important change was that, under WFTC, families could receive 70 percent of child care costs up to a limit of £70 per week for one child and £105 per week for two or more children. These were sizable increases relative to the previous limit of £60 per week per family, which could be disregarded from income under Family Credit.[23]

The central role of the WFTC in the reforms was inspired by evidence on the U.S. Earned Income Tax Credit (EITC). The EITC had been in existence since 1975 and was a relatively minor program until the 1990s, when it was expanded substantially, first in 1990, under the George H. W. Bush administration, and then even more substantially in 1993, under the Clinton administration, at the urging of the Harvard economist David Ellwood and others who argued that it was an essential component of a strategy to make work pay for low-income families.[24]

Essentially, the EITC rewards work by providing a refundable tax credit to low-income families who have worked in the labor market in the prior year. The real (adjusted for inflation) value of the maximum EITC available to a low-income family with one child rose by 90 percent between 1990 and 1998, while the real value of the maximum EITC available to a family with two or more children rose threefold.[25] In combination with the increases in the minimum wage in 1990, 1991, 1996, and 1997, the expansions in the EITC substantially raised the returns to work for low-skilled workers. Analyses by the economists Rebecca Blank and Lucie Schmidt show that a single mother with one child who worked full-time at the minimum wage in 1989 would have had a post-tax income of $10,013, equal to only 89 percent of the poverty line for her family type and size, but that by 1999, with the increased minimum wage and EITC, her post-tax income would have been $12,612, equal to 110 percent of the relevant poverty line (in real 1999 dollars).[26] Gains for a single mother with two children were even greater, owing to the greater increase in the value of the EITC for that group: a single mother working full-time at the minimum wage would have seen her post-tax income rise from 76 percent of the relevant poverty line to 105 percent.[27]

In contrast to the pre–welfare reform period, when it often did not pay for women to move from welfare to work, after the reforms low-skilled women were clearly better off in work than on welfare because of the measures to make work pay. The economist Sheldon Danziger, director of the National Poverty Center at the University of Michigan, and his colleagues document this shift using a sample of low-income women who received welfare in 1997 and were followed over time.[28] Comparing women who were working in 1999 with those who were still on welfare, they found that the women who were working were considerably better off, with annual household incomes averaging 112 percent of the poverty line versus only 56 percent of the poverty line for those relying solely on welfare.

Although estimating the effect of the EITC as distinct from the other welfare reforms (and the strong economy) has been challenging, because the reforms occurred together and also because their effects may have been interactive, studies have found that the EITC expansions during the 1990s were an important factor in increasing single mothers' employment.[29]

A distinctive feature of the EITC is that, unlike traditional welfare programs, it is administered through the tax system. Another point of difference with traditional welfare benefits is that the EITC is typically received as a lump sum, once a year at tax time. (Families can in principle elect to receive their EITC benefits through small payments made on a regular basis throughout the year, but very few take up this option.) Studies have found that families use the EITC to purchase durable goods, such as furniture or cars, as well as to catch up on back bills, set aside some money for savings, or purchase needed items.[30]

At its inception, WFTC was very similar to the EITC. However, there were some differences. Unlike the EITC, which is typically paid once a year at tax time, British tax credits are paid regularly through the year, with eligibility for benefits redetermined every six months (a period later extended to twelve months). Also, as discussed in the next chapter, benefits for parents who are not working were also increased in Britain, so that while gains from work relative to nonwork increased with the expansions in the WFTC, they did not do so nearly as much as in the United States.

The WFTC was subsumed into a new and more generous tax credit system in April 2003. WFTC was replaced by the Working Tax Credit (WTC), which was quite similar to WFTC in design but more generous in its provisions. The basic grant for a couple or lone parent working at least sixteen hours per week was increased, with an additional bonus if the parent (or two parents combined) worked thirty or more hours per week. Child care reimbursement remained at 70 percent, but the maximum allowable costs that could be claimed rose to £135 per week for one child and £200 per week for two or more children. At the same time, the rate at which benefits were reduced as earnings increased was reduced (to 37 percent), and assets and child support payments were no longer considered in determining eligibility.

These changes, along with the introduction of the Child Tax Credit, which also occurred in April 2003 (discussed in the next chapter), resulted in a more generous set of supports for families—as shown in appendices 2 to 4, which present illustrative income packages for a lone-parent family with two children under age eleven, a couple family with two children under age eleven, and a couple family with three children (two under age eleven and one age fourteen). For example, appendix 2 shows that a lone parent working thirty hours per week at the minimum wage saw her net income increase from £248.91 per week in 2002 to £260.79 per week in 2003. Of this increase, only £4 per week was due to the rise in the minimum wage between 2002 and 2003; the remainder was due to the increased generosity of the tax and transfer system. At the same time, however, median incomes were rising, and most of the increased generosity of the tax and benefit changes went to compensate for the resulting increase in the poverty line (which was defined in relative terms as 60 percent of median income). Thus, appendix 2 also shows that the lone mother working thirty hours per week at the minimum wage saw her net income as a proportion of the poverty line increase only slightly, from 124 percent in 2002 to 126 percent in 2003.[31]

The reforms led to a substantial increase in the numbers receiving in-work tax credits (see figure 2.4). The WFTC went to twice as many families as Family Credit (the in-work cash benefit it replaced)—by 2002–2003, 1.4 million families with children had received this benefit, out of a total of 15 million. Because WFTC also provided higher benefits than Family Credit, spending on the program more than doubled over that period, rising from £2.4 billion in 1998–1999 to £6.3 billion in 2002–2003 (an increase of 140 percent in real terms). The April 2003 reforms and subsequent reforms further increased the numbers receiving the WTC. By 2009, about one in four families with children received this benefit, and total spending on the program had risen to nearly £12 billion.[32]

An important challenge with both the WFTC (which used a twice-annual assessment) and its successor WTC (which used an annual assessment) was how to handle the risk of overpayments if a family's circumstances changed after their assessment. Although the Treasury planners were aware of this risk and took it into account in designing the program, they were to have many problems as a result of this feature. When overpayments—inevitably—occurred, the Inland Revenue was understandably keen to recoup them. But this often created hardships for the low-income families involved.

Figure 2.4   Share of Families with Children Receiving Work-Related Tax Credits, 1997 to 2008

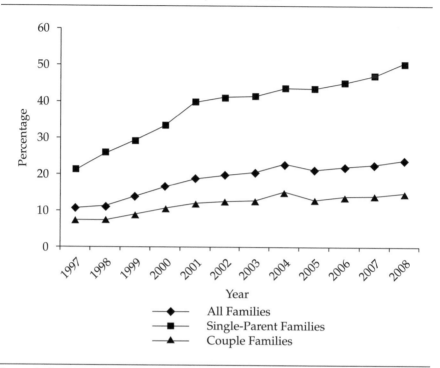

Source: Author's compilation. Total number of lone-parent and couple families from Department for Social Security (1999b) and Department for Work and Pensions, *Households Below Average Income* (2004, 2005, 2007a, 2008a, 2009a), available at: http://research.dwp.gov.uk/ asd/hbai_arc.asp. Tax credit data for 1997 and 1998 are for receipt of Family Credit and come from *Social Security Statistics* (DSS, various years). Tax credit data for 1999 to 2002 are for receipt of Working Families Tax Credit; data for 2003 to 2009 are for receipt of Working Tax Credit; both come from HM Revenue and Customs, "Personal Tax Credits," available at: http://www.hmrc.gov.uk/stats/personal-tax-credits/menu.htm.

REFORMS TO INCOME AND PAYROLL TAXES

The measures to promote work and make work pay also included reforms to income tax and National Insurance Contributions (Britain's social security taxes). The overall thrust of these reforms was to reduce the direct tax burden for low-income workers. In particular, various jumps—or notches—in tax liability were removed. These changes allowed low-income workers to keep more of their pay and also reduced the penalties they incurred if they moved into work or increased their income from work. In addition, the tax burden facing the employers of low-wage work-ers was reduced, a measure that was seen as compensating for any ad-verse impacts of the national minimum wage.[33] As shown in appendix 2, in 2000 a lone parent with two children who worked sixteen hours per week at the minimum wage earned £60 per week, but was exempt from tax and national insurance contributions; by 2008 her earnings at the min-imum wage would have increased to £92 per week, but her tax and na-tional insurance contribution would still be zero.

WHAT EFFECTS DID THE
REFORMS HAVE?

As we have seen, the objective of this set of reforms was twofold: to pro-mote work, and to make work pay. How successful were these reforms in achieving these goals?

The measures to promote work certainly were successful, although their effects varied by group. The reforms had their largest employment effects on lone parents. Prior to the New Deal reforms, no one in the ben-efits system encouraged lone parents to work, and the in-work supports provided to them (child care, for instance) were minimal. This all changed with the New Deal and other welfare-to-work reforms: lone parents were called in for work-focused interviews and were also offered a range of work incentives (expanded child care among them).

As shown in figure 2.1, lone-parent employment increased by twelve percentage points—from 45 percent to 57 percent—from 1997 to 2008.[34] Although not sufficient to meet the government's target of 70 percent em-ployment for this group, this is an impressive increase, particularly con-sidering that most of the reforms in this period consisted of carrots rather than sticks. It is also impressive when considered relative to the United States, where single-mother employment during welfare reform rose by a comparable amount (about thirteen percentage points) from 1990 to 2000, but under a more punitive set of reforms.[35]

Although, as in the United States, it is difficult to separate the causal effects of the reforms from the effects of the strong economy that prevailed throughout most of the decade, my reading of the evidence suggests that the reform programs were responsible for at least half the increase in lone-parent employment over the decade. For instance, analyses conducted in 2002 found that the overall package of reforms had just in the first few years led to a five-percentage-point increase in lone-parent employment.[36] This is nearly half the gain that would be seen over the entire decade, and it is likely that the reforms played a larger role in the second half of the decade as the economy slowed. As might be expected given the design of the reforms—which reward work of at least sixteen hours per week—the most notable effect has been to increase the share of lone parents working at least sixteen hours per week. Studies examining the initial wave of the reforms have found up to a seven-percentage-point increase in the share of lone parents working at least sixteen hours per week.[37]

The reforms also reduced the number of lone parents on welfare. Overall, the number of lone parents receiving Income Support fell from 1,030,000 in 1997 to 740,000 in 2008, a reduction of over 25 percent (see figure 2.2). These are, of course, much lower caseload declines than those seen in the United States after welfare reform, but this makes sense given the more drastic nature of the U.S. reforms. As in the United States, it is difficult to determine what share of the caseload declines is due to policy reforms and what share is due to the strong economy. Early analyses of the New Deal for Lone Parents found that it reduced the share of lone parents relying on Income Support by 2.5 percentage points in the first year and by 3.3 percentage points after eighteen months.[38]

Employment changes for other groups were much more modest: employment for women in couples rose by 3.5 percentage points, and employment for men in couples rose by 2.5 percentage points from 1997 to 2008. In contrast to the results for lone parents, empirical analyses for mothers in couples found only minimal effects of the reforms on their employment, with some studies finding very small increases and others finding small reductions.[39] This result makes sense given that the incentives to work were increased much more for lone mothers than for mothers in couples, who in fact faced reduced incentives to work if their partners were working and receiving increased benefits via WFTC.[40] Nor did analysts find strong employment effects for other groups.[41] This makes the gains in lone-parent employment all the more impressive.

With regard to the second objective, making work pay, the reforms were also successful. Taken together, the minimum wage and the more generous in-work supports (in particular, the increased tax credits and reduced taxes) have substantially increased the income that the most disadvantaged families can expect from work, with particularly large gains for lone-parent families. This is shown in table 2.4, which displays the income that two types of families—a lone-parent family with two children and a two-parent family with two children—could expect if a parent worked thirty hours per week at the minimum wage in 1998 and 2008. (Detailed results for various family types and under various employment and child care scenarios, for the entire 1998 to 2008 period, are provided in appendices 2 to 4.) A lone parent working thirty hours per week at the minimum wage would have had a net income of £163.73 per week in 1998, equivalent to 101 percent of the poverty line (for a family of her type in that year). By 2008 her net income under the same scenario would have risen to £348.04 per week, or 123 percent of the poverty line.

Table 2.4   Net Income from Working Thirty Hours per Week at the Minimum Wage in 1998 and 2008

	1998		2008	
	Net Income	Income As Percentage of Poverty Line	Net Income	Income As Percentage of Poverty Line
Lone-parent family: child care £50 per week	£163.73	101%	£348.04	123%
Couple family: no child care expenses	218.10	98	355.67	99
Couple family: child care £50 per week	177.49	80	345.67	96

Source: Based on author's calculations and sources listed in appendices 2 and 3.
Note: Estimates are for families with two children under the age of eleven. See appendices 2 and 3 for details.

Couple families also gained over the period, although how much they gained depended on whether they were using child care and thus benefiting from the expansions in child care subsidies. Table 2.4 shows that in 1998 couple families with one earner and no child care expenses already had net incomes close to the relative poverty line (working thirty hours per week at the minimum wage); that situation was unchanged in 2008, since the benefit increases for that group merely kept pace with the increases in median incomes. For couple families using child care, however, the reforms made a big difference. In 1998 working full-time at the minimum wage would have earned a couple family with child care costs a net income equal to only 80 percent of the poverty line, or about what they would have received on Income Support. By 2008 the same family would have had a net income equal to 96 percent of the poverty line, a substantial improvement over what they would have received under Income Support.

Throughout the decade, both lone parents and couple parents were clearly better off working than they were on Income Support (or receiving other nonwork benefits), with gains from work ranging from £36 to £94 per week for lone parents (which translates to £2.25 and £2.35 per hour) and from £51 to £76 per week for couple parents (which translates to £1.70 and £1.90 per hour; as shown in appendices 2 to 4). But some parents continued to be apprehensive about forgoing benefits. To drive home the point that families would be better off working, the government in 2008 established a new benefit called the "better off in work credit," which guarantees long-term benefit recipients that they will be at least £25 per week better off working than they would be receiving benefits.[42]

It is important to note that the measures to make work pay benefited not just those who moved off benefits but also those who had been working at low-wage jobs. Low-paid workers saw sizable gains through the increases in the minimum wage and more generous tax credits, and these gains translated into a reduction in child poverty. Analyzing the reduction in child poverty between 1998–1999 and 2004–2005 (a period when the child poverty rate, defined in relative terms, fell from 26 percent to 21 percent), Jonathan Shaw at the Institute for Fiscal Studies found that 80 percent of the reduction was due to the sharply decreased incidence of poverty within groups: there were poverty reductions for children with working parents owing in part to the higher minimum wage and in part to the expanded provisions to make work pay, and expansions in overall child benefits led to reductions in poverty for children with nonworking parents.[43] In contrast, only 13.5 percent of the poverty reduction was due to changes in the composition of families with children, the most important of which was the decline in the share of children living with workless parents. (Changes in other characteristics of the population accounted for the remaining 6 percent.)

WHAT DID THE REFORMS NOT ACCOMPLISH?

As we have seen, the gains in employment, while impressive, have not been sufficient to reach government targets. While the lone-parent employment rate did increase by twelve percentage points, at 57 percent as of 2008 it still falls short of the 70 percent target. The employment rate of women in low-income couples did not increase in any notable way and remains far short of what is needed to reduce poverty in those families. And not all working families have escaped poverty. Although their poverty risk is certainly less than it was before reform, it has not been eliminated.

The government therefore is now considering further measures to promote employment and to make work pay. In doing so, policymakers will have to pay particular attention to the groups for whom employment has not increased. One such group is clearly married or cohabiting mothers in low-income couples, who until now have not been a main target of reform. Another group consists of lone mothers who are not working in spite of the increased incentives that have been offered. What both groups have in common is a tendency to have little attachment to the labor market and little experience in it. As Gregg's report emphasized, such women need a personalized package of advice and support.

Although much of the focus in the first decade of reforms was on getting parents into employment, there is also clearly a need to raise employment continuity and earnings among low-income workers. The reforms to make work pay were a step in that direction but have had limited effects to date. A recent analysis by the economists Richard Dickens and Abigail McKnight at the London School of Economics found that the policy changes led to small increases in employment continuity (a 3 percent increase for men and a nonsignificant 2 percent increase for women) and did not lead to significantly higher wages for either group.[44] Qualitative work by Jane Millar and Tess Ridge at Bath University illustrates the range of challenges (such as ill health, child care problems, family emergencies, or problems getting along with employers) that sometimes lead lone parents to abandon work or keep them from progressing in work.[45] The Employment Retention and Advancement demonstration programs have had some success, but as the government acknowledges, further efforts will be needed:

> We have been very successful at getting people into work . . . but while work remains the most sustainable way out of poverty, helping parents get a job will not always be enough to lift them and their children out of relative poverty. . . . If we are to tackle in-work poverty it is important that we build on our success in getting people into work by helping them to stay in work and progress in their jobs.[46]

A related challenge, which the government also recognizes, is the need to raise the skill levels of low-income workers. As Gordon Brown said on the occasion of the tenth anniversary of the New Deal in 2008:

> Now as we look ahead we need a reformed New Deal to help us face the challenges of the next decades. In the old days the problem may have been unemployment, but in the next decades it will be unemployability. If in the old days lack of jobs demanded priority action, in the new world it is lack of skills. And that means that our whole approach to welfare must move on.[47]

As important as the welfare-to-work reforms were, they were only one component of the British antipoverty strategy. The twin goals of the strategy were "work for those who can" and "security for those who cannot." As we shall see in the next chapter, the latter goal could not be achieved without raising incomes for families with children whether or not the parents were working.

Chapter 3

Increasing Financial Support for Families with Children

The British reformers made an explicit decision to focus not solely on reforms to promote work and to make work pay but also on investments of substantial resources in increasing financial support for all families with children—whether or not the parents worked. As the Treasury stated in 1999: "[The] tax and benefit system needs to provide support for all families with children, both in and out of work. This support recognizes the extra costs and responsibilities that parents face when their children are growing up, and the importance of children for the future of society as a whole."[1]

This commitment to support families "both in and out of work" stands in sharp contrast to the position adopted by the United States, which over the period of welfare reform increasingly made support for children contingent on parental employment. As a result, the British reforms included more universal provision, since supports were intended to reach all children, regardless of their parents' employment status. But within this universal framework, the government also committed itself to "targeting help on those who need it most, when they need it most. This includes families on lower incomes and those with children under [age] one."[2] This approach of targeting within universalism, another distinctive feature of the British reforms, came to be known as "progressive universalism."

Comparing the benefit system in 2007 with the one the Labour government inherited a decade earlier, the key changes in financial support for families include: significant real increases in the value of the universal child allowance, the Child Benefit (received by virtually all children); substantial increases in allowances for younger children in nonworking families receiving benefits through the means-tested welfare program Income Support; and the introduction of a new quasi-universal Child Tax Credit that benefits all but the highest-income families with children. These increases are in addition to those provided through increases in the generosity of in-work benefits and tax credits for low-income working families with children, described in the prior chapter.

THE RATIONALE FOR THE REFORMS

Although government policymakers were strongly committed to the principle that work is—and should be—the best route out of poverty, they also recognized that it was not realistic to expect all low-income parents to take that route. Some low-income parents face serious barriers to work, such as their own disability or mental health problems or simply lack of skills or experience. Others are prevented from working because they have family responsibilities that, whether in the short or long term, make it difficult for them to work in the labor market. This is the case for parents with newborns, disabled children, or other family members needing special care.

To reduce poverty among all children in low-income families would require putting additional resources in the hands of parents, even if they did not work. Of course, this strategy ran the risk of reducing work incentives, and it was also widely recognized that relying on higher income transfers alone was not a sustainable way to reduce poverty. So benefit increases for nonworking families were implemented alongside measures to promote work and make work pay.

Underlying the decision to increase financial support for families with children was fairly widespread agreement among British policymakers—based on long-standing evidence from British birth cohort studies and other longitudinal studies, as we saw in Chapter 1—that poverty was adversely affecting children's life chances and that raising incomes for low-income families with children, in concert with other changes, would improve their outcomes. In the words of Chancellor Gordon Brown during a House of Commons debate on March 17, 1998: "Giving a child the best start in life takes more than money, but it can not be done without money."[3]

At the heart of the British approach was a fundamental assumption: that putting more money in the hands of parents, by boosting their earnings as well as their income from benefits and tax credits, would improve child outcomes. This assumption has been challenged by some researchers in the United States who have suggested that raising parental income does not necessarily improve child outcomes. Even though many studies in both Britain and the United States have shown that children whose families have low incomes fare worse on a host of health and developmental outcomes, researchers have questioned the extent to which these adverse outcomes are due to low income.[4]

In *What Money Can't Buy*, the sociologist Susan Mayer argues that the effects of income have been greatly overstated and that much of the association between low incomes and worse child outcomes is due to other factors, so that giving poor families more money does not necessarily lead to large improvements in child outcomes.[5] Studies by economists have also cast doubt on how large a role income plays in child development.[6]

Lacking experimental evidence on this question (since we do not have studies in which one group was randomly assigned to receive more income while another comparable group was not), social scientists have increasingly turned to evidence from "natural experiments."[7] These natural experiments mimic a randomized controlled trial by exposing one group to a change in income while another group's circumstances are held constant. The advantage of such experiments over simple correlational studies using observational data is that the income change is exogenous—that is, the income change is not associated with other characteristics of the family but rather is determined by factors external to the family.[8] Researchers at MDRC in the United States have used the welfare-to-work reforms as natural experiments to assess the effects of income gains for children. Although it is difficult to separate the effects of the employment increases from the effects of income increases, there is some variation across welfare-to-work experiments that can be used to distinguish the effects of income from those of employment. Such studies suggest that when welfare-to-work programs raised incomes, the income gains were associated with improvements in child health and development.[9]

Also relevant to the question of whether the income gains associated with benefit changes might improve child outcomes are two more recent studies conducted in the United States and Canada. Both were conducted after the British reforms got under way, but they provide support for the assumption underlying those reforms. In both cases researchers found that income gains from benefit changes did lead to improved child outcomes for the affected children. In the U.S. case, increases in the EITC were found to lead to improvements in child cognitive development.[10] In the Canadian case, increases in child benefits led to improvements in child health and development, as well as maternal mental health.[11]

Although grounded in research, the decision to invest resources in raising family incomes was also a pragmatic one. Brown recognized that with more than half of poor children living in workless households—at the start of the reforms—ending child poverty could not rely on income from employment alone. As much as raising employment was a goal, it was clear that raising incomes for families out of work had to be a goal as well.

THE ELEMENTS OF REFORM

Britain's universal child allowance, known as Child Benefit, played an important role in the reform. Universal child allowances provide an income floor for families with children by providing a small cash grant to any family with children, regardless of family income, family structure, or work status. Typically, grants are calculated per child, and thus families with more children receive a higher amount. Britain has had a child allowance program since 1946, when it was established as part of the Beveridge reforms. The original program, called Family Allowance, provided a small cash grant for families with more than one child, the idea being that families with more children faced higher costs and it was not realistic to expect a father's earnings (the main source of family income at that time) to adjust to take that differential into account. Consistent with the idea that the program was supplementing earnings for families with more children, the payment of the allowance was typically made through the father's paycheck.

The Child Benefit program replaced Family Allowance in 1977.[12] The program is very popular, and almost all families apply for the benefit. Application is done by mail, and benefits are paid directly into the family's bank account or account at the post office (so that no visit to a welfare office is required). Benefits are usually paid monthly but can be paid weekly for families who have low incomes or are headed by a single parent. In a shift from the earlier Family Allowance program, Child Benefit is paid directly to the main carer (usually the mother), which is considered to be important in light of evidence that mothers and fathers tend to allocate money differently within the household.[13] In keeping with its name, Child Benefit is widely understood to be a benefit that is to be used for the children. Unlike the prior Family Allowance program, Child Benefit includes a grant for the first child as well as subsequent children.

At the time the Labour Party came into office in 1997, Child Benefit rates were low. After rising sharply in real terms between 1977 and 1979, Child Benefit rates had been flat in real terms since 1979. As of 1997, families received £11.05 per week for the first child and £9 per week for each additional child; families headed by a lone parent received a special supplement (worth £6 per week in 1997) called Lone Parent Benefit, which effectively raised the rate of Child Benefit for the first child.[14]

Low-income families with children could receive additional support through various means-tested programs. Income Support was the main cash assistance program for low-income families in which the parents did not work in the labor market or did not work enough hours to qualify for the work-conditioned Family Credit program. There were also some programs not conditioned on the presence of children. For instance, the Housing Benefit program provided assistance with housing costs for low-income individuals and families, whether or not they had children. Similarly, Council Tax Benefit helped low-income families with the cost of their local council taxes.

The first reform that the New Labour government made to this portion of the safety net—in October 1997—was to implement a measure that had been proposed by the prior Conservative government: eliminating the Lone Parent Benefit program. Determined to stay within the Conservative spending limits, the new government also justified this move on the grounds that families should not receive special benefits simply as a result of having lone parents. Instead, it argued, all needy families, whether headed by one parent or two parents, should receive additional support.

Lone-parent groups and child poverty advocates saw this controversial change as an attack on lone-parent families and a step backward in combating child poverty. Subsequent New Labour reforms, however, more than made up for the elimination of the Lone Parent Benefit. As financial supports for all low-income families with children were raised, lone parents—who had lower incomes and relied on such benefits to a greater extent than married or cohabiting parents—saw substantial gains.

The budget announced in April 1999 saw a dramatic increase in financial support for children. The value of Child Benefit was increased, with the rate for the first child raised by £2.50 per week (beyond what was required to keep pace with inflation); this amounted to a more than 20 percent real increase (from its prior rate of £11.45 per week), the largest increase in the history of the program.[15] A further increase, in April 2000, raised Child Benefit rates to £15 per week for the first child, representing a 35 percent real increase since 1997; at the same time, benefits for each subsequent child were raised to £10 per week.[16]

The Labour government also expanded support for means-tested cash assistance. A key thrust of the government's approach in this area was to focus additional support on families with young children. Historically, the British welfare system had paid higher benefits to families with adolescents, who were thought to incur higher costs for food and clothing. But with a new recognition of the importance of early childhood, the government decided to raise benefits for families with young children to equal those for families with older children. In March 1999 the Treasury announced that "the Government is increasing the amount of support available to children. It is targeting extra support on families when they need it most when their children are young, thereby ensuring that the financial support available for families with children is fairer."[17]

Accordingly, in April 1999, Income Support rates for low-income non-working families with young children (ages zero to ten) were raised by £2.50 per week (beyond what was required to keep pace with inflation). As discussed in the prior chapter, a similar change raising benefits for young children had been implemented in the Family Credit program in October 1998.

Reformers in the Treasury were also keenly interested in making the tax system more supportive of low-income families with children, whether or not the parents worked, and more closely integrating the support offered to such families through the benefit and tax systems. In 1999 they announced the new Children's Tax Credit, to come into effect in April 2001. The new program was based in part on the experiences of Canada and Australia.[18] Both countries had a tax credit program (called the Child Tax Benefit in Canada and the Family Tax Payment in Australia) that provided financial support to low-income families with children.

Britain's Children's Tax Credit replaced the former married couple and related allowances in the tax system, but at a more generous rate (up to £416 per year) and targeted to low- and middle-income families (with the credit withdrawn from higher-income taxpayers). In this sense, Children's Tax Credit is more similar to the U.S. Child Tax Credit (which is phased out for higher-income taxpayers) than to the U.S. personal tax exemption for children (which is available to all taxpayers with children). However, Britain's Children's Tax Credit is available to all low- and middle-income families, whereas in the United States the Child Tax Credit is only partially refundable—that is, families must have a minimum amount of income and tax liability in order to claim the credit.

The introduction of Children's Tax Credit in April 2001, along with the continuing increases in Child Benefit, represented a substantial increase in support for children. Families with incomes below £34,000, who would have received £11 per week in 1997 in Child Benefit for their first child, would receive twice as much (£23 per week) in 2001 in Child Benefit and Children's Tax Credit combined.[19] According to the Treasury, by 2001 the government was spending an additional £6 billion a year on benefits and tax credits for children (compared to 1997) and, of this, nearly one-third—£1.8 billion—was spent on Children's Tax Credit, with another third being spent on increases in Child Benefit and means-tested benefits (such as Income Support). Spending on the work-conditioned tax credit program, Working Families Tax Credit, constituted the other third.[20]

In April 2003, all of the various benefits and tax credits for children (apart from Child Benefit) were amalgamated into a single Child Tax Credit (CTC), which replaced the Children's Tax Credit program. Britain again drew on the example of Canada and Australia, which were well on the way toward combining these tax credits with other programs to create a more integrated child benefit and tax credit (called the Canada Child Tax Benefit and, in Australia, the Family Tax Benefit). The introduction of the CTC brought together all the means-tested tax and benefit programs for families with children. The government called it the biggest reform since Beveridge:

Introduced together with the WTC in 2003, the CTC represents the biggest single change in the way the Government provides financial support for families since the Beveridge reforms in the 1940s. CTC delivers a single, seamless system of income-related support for families with children, integrating the various child elements previously provided through the Working Families' Tax Credit, Disabled Person's Tax Credit, Income Support, Jobseeker's Allowance, and the Children's Tax Credit.[21]

The CTC provides a fully refundable tax credit with equal value to those out of work and in low-paid work. Benefits are also equal across dual-earner and single-earner families, so long as their overall income is the same. As noted earlier, the credit is gradually withdrawn from those with higher incomes, but about 80 percent of families with children (nearly all lone-parent families and about two-thirds of two-parent families) receive at least some payment (see figure 3.1).[22] This system is run by the tax authority (Revenue and Customs, formerly Inland Revenue, comparable to the U.S. Internal Revenue Service) using a system of annual income assessments to establish the size of the credit, but with regular payments of credits through the year (on either a monthly or weekly basis, depending on the family's situation). Payments are made directly to the family's bank account or account at the Post Office. Like Child Benefit, payments are made directly to the mother rather than through an earner's paycheck (as they had been under the prior Children's Tax Credit).

Appendices 2 to 4 show the combined level of support in 2003 for illustrative family types depending on their gross household income, employment, and child care usage. It can be seen that the effect of the April 2003 reforms was to shift upward the financial support being provided to low-income families with children.

After the reforms, a lone parent with two children received £207.52 per week if she did not work, an amount equal to the poverty line. If she worked sixteen hours per week at the minimum wage (£4.50 per hour from October 2003), her net income was £257.34 per week (after allowing for the various tax credits, Child Benefit, income tax, and social insurance payments), an amount equal to 124 percent of the poverty line; if she worked thirty hours per week, it was £260.79 per week, or 126 percent of the poverty line. These amounts are all substantial improvements over the comparable figures for 1998, when a lone parent had income of about 91 percent of the poverty line if she did not work, and income of about 100 percent of the poverty line if she worked sixteen hours per week and also if she worked thirty hours per week (see appendix 2 for details). However, it is also striking that the net gain from moving from working sixteen hours per week to thirty hours per week is negligible. This reflects the fact that the primary aim of the policies was to move low-income parents into part-time work, rather than full-time work.

A nonworking two-parent family with two children and no earnings at

Figure 3.1   Share of Families with Children Receiving Child Tax Credit, 2003 to 2008

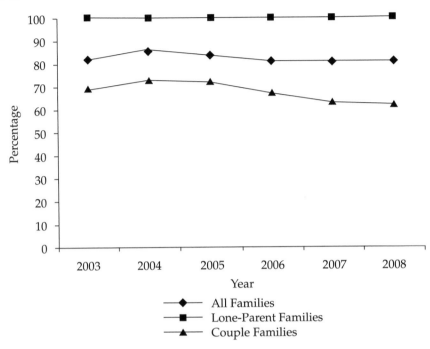

Source: Author's compilation. Number of lone-parent and couple families from Department for Work and Pensions, *Households Below Average Income* (2004, 2005, 2007a, 2008a, 2009a), available at: http://research.dwp.gov.uk/asd/hbai_arc.asp. Tax credit data from HM Revenue and Customs (various years).

all received a total of £238.62 per week in 2003, an amount equal to 84 percent of the relevant poverty line. The same family with one earner working thirty hours per week at the minimum wage had a net income ranging from £275.93 per week to £290.93 per week (depending on whether they had child care expenses), amounts equal to 98 to 103 percent of the poverty line. These amounts also reflect improvement over 1998, when a two-parent family had income of about 79 percent of the poverty line if they did not work and income of between 62 and 80 percent of the poverty line if they worked thirty hours per week (see appendix 3 for details). Having two earners (working a total of sixty hours per week between the two of them) results in only a small additional gain, given the higher child care costs such a family would likely face. Again, this reflects the aim of the

71

policies, which was primarily to create incentives for at least one parent to work full-time, rather than encouraging both parents to work full-time.

OTHER FINANCIAL SUPPORTS FOR FAMILIES WITH CHILDREN

An early theme for the New Labour government was the need to provide extra financial support to families with newborn children. At a 1999 conference jointly convened by the Treasury and the Centre for Analysis of Social Exclusion, researchers presented analyses of longitudinal data showing the extent to which having a new child raised a family's risk of poverty.[23] At a time when the overall child poverty rate was about 25 percent, nearly 40 percent of children were being born into poverty. The longitudinal data revealed that about 15 percent of families with newborns were not poor prior to their birth but instead were pushed into poverty by the birth as family income fell (because mothers cut back on work and were not fully compensated by maternity pay) and family needs rose (because of the addition of the new child to the household). It was also widely agreed that the first year of life represented a particularly crucial period for child development.[24]

The government took a series of steps to address the extra needs of families with newborns.[25] Maternity leave benefits paid to mothers with some previous work record were made more generous and broader in coverage so that they would reach more low earners, and their duration was extended from eighteen weeks to six months in 2003, with a further extension to nine months in 2007. Statutory Maternity Pay, the primary maternity benefit for those with sufficient work and earnings history, is paid at 90 percent of average weekly pay (with no upper limit) for the first six weeks and at a flat rate of up to £123 per week (as of April 2009) for the subsequent thirty-three weeks. Maternity Allowance, for those with some work history but not enough to quality for Statutory Maternity Pay, is paid at a flat rate of up to £123 per week (as of April 2009) for the full thirty-nine weeks. Statutory Maternity Pay is paid by employers, while Maternity Allowance is paid by the Department for Work and Pensions, but, as is customary in Europe, funds for both programs come primarily from social insurance, to which both employees and employers contribute. In addition, paternity leave of two weeks, also funded through social insurance, was instituted in 2003.

For low-income mothers, the government raised the amount of Social Fund Maternity Payments; these onetime grants to help cover the costs of purchasing essential items for a newborn had been frozen at £100 since 1990. In April 1999, the grants were raised to £200, relabeled Sure Start

Maternity Payments, and linked to contact with a health care professional. After several further increases, Sure Start Maternity Payments were worth £500 as of April 2002.

The government also reformed the Welfare Foods program (a program similar to the Special Supplemental Nutrition Program for Women, Infants, and Children [WIC] in the United States), which provided coupons for milk and vitamins for low-income pregnant women, breast-feeding mothers, and infants and children under the age of five. The Welfare Foods program was replaced with the new Healthy Start program in 2004. Healthy Start, which like the Welfare Foods program was targeted to teen mothers as well as any low-income mother receiving benefits, differed from the prior program in providing support for a broader range of healthy foods, including cereals, fruit, and vegetables. It was also tied to attendance at prenatal visits and child health visits. To provide further support for nutrition in pregnancy, in 2008 the government introduced the Health in Pregnancy Grant, a new universal benefit which provides a onetime grant of £190 for any pregnant woman in her third trimester, so long as she has been seen at a prenatal clinic.[26]

The government also ensured that families with infants received more support from the Children's Tax Credit program (and its successor Child Tax Credit), which reaches about 80 percent of families with children (excluding only those with the highest incomes). Starting in April 2002, families with a child under the age of one received an extra payment, known as the "baby tax credit," which doubles the value of the family component of the tax credit. As of April 2009, the baby tax credit was worth an extra £10.50 per week, or £545 per year.[27]

The government also introduced a system of Child Trust Funds, popularly known as "baby bonds." Inspired by the work of the Washington University social work researcher Michael Sherraden, who pioneered asset-based welfare programs in the United States, baby bonds are intended to ensure that all children have some assets and a stake in society.[28] Starting in September 2002, all children receive an initial endowment of £250 at birth from the government, with this amount doubled for children from low-income families. The government invests a further £250 per child (£500 per low-income child) when the child turns seven. Income from the account is tax-free, and parents, friends, and family members can deposit additional amounts in the child's account (up to £1,200 per year). In this way, the trust funds build up over time to produce an asset that children can access when they reach adulthood. Amounts will vary depending on how much parents and others deposit, but even if they make no further investments, children are guaranteed £500 in the account from the government deposits, or £1,000 if they are low-income.

HOW DOES THE U.S. EXPERIENCE COMPARE?

In the prior chapter, we saw that there were close connections between the U.S. welfare-to-work reforms and the British reforms to promote work and make work pay. That similarity is not present here. As noted, to the extent that the British reforms to raise financial support for families with children drew on international examples, these came from Canada and Australia, both countries that were expanding their supports for children over this period.

In the United States, in contrast, the same decade saw very little in the way of increased financial supports for families with children, apart from those provided to working families.[29] As discussed in chapter 2, there were dramatic expansions in the Earned Income Tax Credit, as well as in child care supports for working families. But these expansions benefited only working families, in contrast to the British reforms discussed in this chapter.

The picture in terms of benefits that are not conditioned on parental employment is quite different in the United States. With the important exception of child health insurance, which saw dramatic expansions over the decade (discussed later), other portions of the means-tested safety net for nonworking families either saw little change or actually lost value. In all but a handful of states, the value of welfare benefits declined in real terms between 1996 and 2008 as these were not indexed and were only rarely raised by legislative action. By 2008, Temporary Assistance to Needy Families (TANF) benefits ranged from 12 percent of the poverty line (in Mississippi) to 50 percent (in Alaska); TANF plus food stamp benefits were below 70 percent of the poverty line in every state except Vermont (70 percent), Hawaii (75 percent), and Alaska (79 percent).[30] And with welfare reform, the number of families receiving cash welfare benefits fell sharply.

The federal food stamp program—now called the Supplemental Nutritional Assistance Program (SNAP)—continues to be an important source of non-work-conditioned assistance to families with children. As of 2008, the program served 22 million low-income people each month, about half of whom were children. Low-income young children and their families also benefited from the WIC supplemental nutrition program. But neither food stamps nor WIC were substantially expanded or made more generous over this period.[31]

At the federal level, there was a push to expand the U.S. child tax credit and to make it more refundable (so that it would reach more families with incomes too low to pay income taxes). However, the amounts involved were small relative to the amounts being provided through the British system. The amount of the federal tax credit was raised to $1,000 per child per year in 2003. A low-income family with two children could therefore expect to receive up to $2,000 a year in child tax credits. The child tax credit was made more generous and extended to more low-income families (reaching families with earnings as low as $3,000 per year) as part of economic stimulus packages in 2008 and 2009, and both Congress and the president have budgeted for making these extensions permanent.[32] But even after those reforms, it was still not fully refundable and thus did not reach the lowest-income families.

U.S. policymakers did substantially expand child health insurance coverage over the decade. Given the importance of health care costs in low-income family budgets, the expansions in child health insurance coverage through the establishment of the new Child Health Insurance Program (CHIP) for low-income children in 1997 and growth in the long-standing Medicaid program for low-income children and adults constitute an important form of financial support to families (as well as an investment in children), and support that is not conditioned on parental employment.

CHIP was passed with bipartisan support in 1997, reflecting a shared belief on both sides of the aisle that since tough welfare-to-work reforms had been passed the prior year, Congress could now take this step toward providing more help with health care costs for low-income families.[33] The original CHIP legislation authorized $40 billion in federal matching funds to cover health insurance for low-income children over the first ten years of the program. Over the period 1998 to 2008, annual federal spending on the program grew from $122 million to $7 billion, while the number of children served grew more than tenfold, from 660,000 to 7.4 million (with this latter figure representing about 5 percent of all children).[34] Over the same period, the share of poor and near-poor children who had no insurance coverage was cut in half, from 28 percent to 15 percent.[35]

After being twice vetoed by President George W. Bush in 2007 and 2008, the CHIP reauthorization was signed into law by President Barack Obama in February 2009.[36] The 2009 reauthorization provided funding to cover an additional 4 million children, which would bring the total number of children served to 11 million (nearly 8 percent of all children).[37]

ADDING IT ALL UP

Taken together, the British tax and benefit changes represent a very substantial investment in financial support for low-income children and families. In real terms, the cost of the benefits, tax credits, and tax allowances related to children rose from £14 billion in 1997–1998 to £19 billion in

Figure 3.2   The Impact of the First Five Labour Budgets on Family
Income, by Income Decile

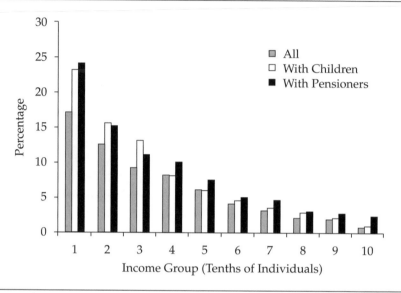

Source: Sutherland (2001).

2002–2003, an increase equivalent to nearly 0.5 percent of GDP.[38] And this
support was strongly targeted to the lowest-income families with children, as we can see in figure 3.2.

By 2004–2005, financial support for families with children—through
tax credits, Child Benefit, and other benefits—had increased by £10.4 billion from the level in 1997, an increase of 72 percent in real terms. The extra spending was targeted to low-income families, with the bottom 20 percent of the income distribution receiving 40 percent of the additional
support. As a result, while the average family with children gained £1,350
per year compared to what they would have received in 1997, the bottom
20 percent gained £3,000 per year. As we have seen, the increase in support was greatest for families with younger children. While support for all
low-income families rose by 72 percent in real terms, support for families
with children ages zero to ten rose by 85 percent in real terms.[39]

By 2006 the average family with children had gained £1,500 per year in
real terms, while the bottom 20 percent had gained £3,400, an amount
equivalent to 20 percent of the poverty line for a two-parent family with
two children.[40] By 2010 the average family will have gained £2,000 per

year in real terms, while the bottom 20 percent will have gained £4,500, an amount equivalent to about 24 percent of the poverty line for a two-parent family with two children.[41]

We will consider how these income gains affected child poverty and other outcomes for children in chapter 6. But first, chapters 4 and 5 provide an overview of the third leg of the reforms, the investments in children. Although designed primarily to reduce poverty in the next generation, some of these reforms (such as the child care expansions) also played a role in helping to reduce poverty in the current generation.

Chapter 4

Investing in Children in the Early Years

The third leg of the British reforms was a set of investments in children. These investments were seen as essential not just in helping to reduce income poverty for children today but also in preventing poverty when the current generation of children becomes adults. If tomorrow's parents were to have a better chance of raising their children on incomes above the poverty line, a key step was to equip low-income children with more of the skills and experiences that middle-class children typically had. In particular, this effort required improving the quality of care that children received in early childhood and the quality of instruction they received in school.

This chapter presents the reforms in services for preschool-age children, and the succeeding chapter reviews the education reforms and other policies for school-age children. What both sets of reforms have in common is the assumption that investing in children—from birth to adulthood—is critical. This component of the British antipoverty program is reminiscent of the U.S. War on Poverty of the 1960s. Breaking the intergenerational cycle of poverty by raising the skills of the next generation was a key goal of that initiative as well, although one that proved difficult to achieve.[1]

THE IMPORTANCE OF THE EARLY YEARS

At the time when New Labour came into office, scientists from a range of disciplines were emphasizing the importance of early experiences in determining children's later trajectory and adult outcomes. In particular, psychologists, pediatricians, and neuroscientists drew attention to the processes of early brain development and the role of early experiences in shaping that development. This evidence was summarized in *Neurons to Neighborhoods*, the report of a commission on the science and ecology of early childhood development convened by the U.S. National Academy of Sciences.[2]

A striking finding from the National Academy of Sciences report and other studies of early child development was that a good deal of inequality in children's health and development already existed before children entered school.[3] At the same time, economists stressed the cumulative nature of learning and the extent to which early learning, and disparities in early learning, laid the foundation for knowledge later in life. As the Chicago economist James Heckman, who would later be awarded the Nobel Prize, argued: "Learning begets learning."[4] Heckman also pointed out that it was generally much more difficult and costly to improve children's position later in childhood: "Like it or not, the most important mental and behavioral patterns, once established, are difficult to change once children enter school."[5]

A further impetus to invest early was evidence that, without early intervention, children from low-income families would fall further behind more-advantaged peers. Using data from Britain's birth cohort studies, Leon Feinstein—in a graph that was later cited repeatedly by policymakers—showed that high-income children with lower initial ability levels had caught up to low-income children with higher initial ability levels by age five and had overtaken them by age ten.[6] Feinstein's graph made it clear that without some intervention to support low-income children in early childhood and the first few years of school, even those with high initial ability were going to be on a trajectory toward a future of low educational attainment and low income. At the same time, evidence from countries such as Denmark that provided more extensive early childhood education suggested that preschool could be a factor in equalizing school readiness and school achievement across social class groups.[7]

Together, the scientific evidence pointed to education as a key factor in tackling poverty and to early childhood as a critical time period in which to invest. These two emphases are reflected in the chronology and nature of the reforms.

THE FIRST NATIONAL CHILD CARE STRATEGY

In May 1997, shortly after coming into office, the Labour government announced Britain's first National Child Care Strategy. The signature element of the strategy was a commitment to provide universal—and free—preschool for all four-year-olds by September 1998 (a commitment that was extended to three-year-olds in April 2004). This new entitlement, which was enthusiastically taken up by parents, moved Britain from having one of the lowest preschool enrollment rates in Europe to being on a par with its European peers, most of whom had universal or near-universal participation in publicly provided preschool in the year or two prior to school entry.[8]

The universal preschool entitlement, in addition to boosting overall levels of enrollment, also narrowed income-related gaps in enrollment. Prior to the policy coming into effect, lower-income children were the least likely to be enrolled in preschool, as is typically the case when child care arrangements are privately funded.[9] In 1997, 82 percent of low-income three- and four-year-olds—but 93 percent of higher-income three- and four-year-olds—were enrolled in care.[10] Although the universal program was taken up by both low- and higher-income families, the gains in enrollment were greater for lower-income families, and thus inequality in attendance narrowed.[11] By 2008, 92 percent of low-income three- and four-year-olds were attending preschool, versus 97 percent of those from higher-income families.[12] However, even after the expansions, low-income children from Asian families were much less likely than others to attend, suggesting that cultural differences might have been playing a role. As of 2006, only 85 percent of three- and four-year-olds from Asian families (many of whom were Pakistani or Bangladeshi) were enrolled in child care, and only 74 percent received free child care, compared to figures of 95 percent and 88 percent, respectively, for white British children.[13]

The first National Child Care Strategy also included some attention to increasing the supply of high-quality care. The Early Excellence Centers initiative, begun in 1997, supported the development and dissemination of model preschool programs. The Neighborhood Nurseries Initiative of 2001 provided funding to support the establishment of preschools in low-income areas.

The provision of universal preschool for three- and four-year-olds did not address the question of what services should be provided for younger children. The existing research, while showing clear benefits to children's school readiness of preschool at age three or four (or even two), was less clear on the benefits (or risks) associated with child care at younger ages.[14] Although high-quality interventions, delivered to very disadvantaged children, had been found to produce strong gains in school readiness, with no ill effects on children's social or emotional adjustment, there were also worrying findings in the literature about possibly harmful effects of early and extensive day care, particularly if the settings were not of good quality. Since child care in Britain (as in the United States) was mainly delivered by private providers, the government had little direct control over its quality, and in fact existing studies had found that child care quality was not particularly high. Putting more infants and toddlers into child care therefore did not seem like a prudent investment, nor one that would be popular with parents.[15] Instead, the government moved to strengthen leave rights.

EXPANSIONS IN LEAVE RIGHTS

Improving leave rights, while mainly justified on the grounds that it would constitute an important investment in child health and development, was also seen as benefiting the child poverty initiative because it would enable more parents to enter and stay in employment. Measures to improve paid leave were also seen as helping to improve financial support for families (as we saw in chapter 3).

The Employment Act of 2002 significantly expanded leave rights and flexibility for working parents with young children. The first policy it addressed was maternity leave. Although, like most other advanced industrialized nations (but not the United States), Britain already had a system of paid maternity leave, the leave it provided was relatively short by European standards.[16] In 2001, at a time when European countries provided an average of ten months of paid maternity leave, Britain provided only about four months (eighteen weeks).[17]

Comparative studies, taking advantage of natural experiments induced by policy variation across countries and over time, indicated that when countries had longer periods of paid leave, infant mortality rates were lower.[18] Research also showed that when mothers took longer periods of leave their mental health was better and children were more likely to receive recommended preventive health care, such as well-baby visits and immunizations.[19] In the Employment Act of 2002, the government increased the period of statutory maternity leave to six months of paid leave, followed by up to six months of unpaid leave. (This was extended again in 2004 as part of the Ten-Year Child Care Strategy, as discussed later).

In addition to the maternity leave expansions, the Employment Act of 2002 established two weeks of paid *paternity* leave, in recognition of the growing consensus that it is important for newborns to have their father home as well as their mother and that even the most important employees can be spared for a week or two of leave. (This perception was helped by the fact that both Prime Minister Blair and Chancellor Brown took paternity leave while in office, in 2000 and 2001, respectively). But with paternity leave rights limited to just two weeks, this remained an area where Britain lagged behind the rest of Europe, and the government was soon put under pressure to provide a longer period of paid leave for fathers. This pressure resulted in a commitment to further extend paid paternity leave rights—as expressed, for example, in the Work and Families Act of 2006—although as of 2009 additional paternity leave had not yet been enacted.

The Employment Act of 2002 also introduced the right of parents of children under the age of six to request part-time or flexible work hours, effective April 2003. This policy brought Britain into compliance with a European Union directive requiring member countries to provide a right for parents of young children to have the opportunity to switch to part-time or flexible hours. The policy proved to be popular among both parents and employers. In the first year alone, 1 million parents came forward with requests for reduced or flexible hours, the vast majority of which were granted, suggesting both that there was a large pent-up demand for more flexible working hours and that firms did not have strong objections to granting those requests.[20] Indeed, the policy was so successful that, following a review in 2008, it was extended in April 2009 to cover parents with older children—up to the age of sixteen.[21]

Parents also benefited from Britain's parental leave program (established in 1999), which provided either mothers or fathers with three months of job-protected parental leave to meet child care responsibilities or to address a family emergency. Although the program was limited in that the leave was unpaid and could be used only once in the life a child, it nevertheless was a welcome source of flexibility for families (just as the Family and Medical Leave Act had been when it was enacted in the United States in 1993).

SURE START

The maternity leave, paternity leave, flexible working hours, and parental leave measures benefited parents across all income groups, but given the evidence on the importance of early experiences and early social gradients in school readiness, the government was determined to do more to address the needs of young children in the lowest-income families and communities. After an interdepartmental review of the international evidence on early intervention programs for disadvantaged young children, led by Norman Glass at the Treasury, in July 1998 the government announced that it would spend £540 million over the next three years on Sure Start—a new community-based program for low-income families with children ages zero to three.[22]

Sure Start was (and remained) an area-based program, with eligibility for funding limited to the most-disadvantaged communities—ones that not only had high poverty rates but also high rates of other indicators of disadvantage, such as low birth weight and teen pregnancy. The areas selected for the first 260 Sure Start local programs were deprived on multiple dimensions, with rates of worklessness and Income Support receipt among families with young children about twice the national average—40 percent in Sure Start areas versus 20 percent nationally.[23] To obtain funding, service providers from various sectors in a local area had to develop a plan for coordinating their efforts to deliver services to families with young children. So service integration, across diverse sectors of provision such as social services and health, was a key element of Sure Start. There were also a few program elements mandated by the central government: each Sure Start program had to offer several home visits to families with newborns (going beyond the limited number of visits offered to all families with newborns through the National Health Service), and programs also had to offer access to a part-time preschool place for three-year-olds whose parents wanted one (a requirement that proved not to be very consequential since the government later rolled out universal preschool for *all* three-year-olds). But beyond these few elements, local areas had a great deal of discretion in how they constructed their Sure Start programs and the services they delivered. This discretionary aspect of Sure Start later created challenges for evaluating the program, since it was not really one national program but rather a collection of varied local programs.[24]

Following the initial announcement in July 1998, Sure Start expanded rapidly. Within a year, some sixty-six "trailblazer" programs were established, and the following year Sure Start's funding was increased by another £500 million, to cover five hundred local programs by 2003–2004, reaching one-third of all poor children in the country. It was becoming clear, however, that an approach that targeted poor areas would, by definition, miss low-income children living in nonpoor areas. At the same time, it was felt that all children could benefit from the voluntary and integrated service delivery model that Sure Start programs exemplified. In the absence of Sure Start, services to children and families were all too often fragmented and uncoordinated, and there was a good deal of interest in creating a more integrated service delivery system for children and families at the community level.

Thus, starting in 2003, the government began rolling out what it called Children's Centers—local area hubs for early education, child care, health, family support, and help with employment. The initial goal (as of early 2004) was to set up seventeen hundred such programs, one in each of the country's 20 percent most-disadvantaged local areas. By early 2005, nearly two hundred Children's Centers had been established, and Sure Start local programs were being folded into them. By mid-2006, one thousand had been established; about half were former Sure Start programs, and many of the others were former Neighborhood Nurseries or Early Excellence Centers. In principle, these centers were now covering a much larger share of the country's poor children, but they were also less sharply focused on serving poor children since the mandate of the Children's Centers was for them to be available to all families with children in the community.

These changes to the Sure Start program were controversial. The program's founder, Norman Glass, argued against the rapid expansion of the program and later criticized what he saw as the government's decision to abolish it by converting it into Children's Centers.[25] But the government was determined to expand its early years policies to reach more children and communities. As even Glass acknowledged, the "fatal flaw" in the original Sure Start program was that it could not reach all disadvantaged children and that it led to some areas having a well-funded program in one neighborhood but no program at all in other neighborhoods.[26] As Kitty Stewart of the London School of Economics observed, Sure Start programs were "a victim in effect of their own popularity."[27]

As Children's Centers were rolled out to expand and coordinate child care provision, they became an important part of the government's child care strategy. By 2009 there were three thousand Children's Centers in place; this was well on the way toward meeting the goal of having thirty-five hundred by 2010—or one in every community. But Children's Centers were not the only element of the government's plan. As discussed earlier, Britain's first National Child Care Strategy introduced universal entitlement to free preschool for four-year-olds and (later) three-year-olds. The government's Ten-Year Child Care Strategy went even further.

THE TEN-YEAR CHILD CARE STRATEGY

The Ten-Year Child Care Strategy was released in December 2004 after an extensive period of review and consultation, including a seminal conference in March of that year on "Life Chances and Social Mobility," organized by the Institute for Public Policy Research and HM Treasury and attended by Chancellor Gordon Brown.[28] The conference heard the latest evidence on life chances and social mobility, including a review of the evidence on the importance of the early years. In that review, I called for three major changes in early years policy: extending parental leave for parents of infants; improving the quality of care and education for the under-threes; and developing a more integrated system of high-quality care and education for three- to five-year-olds.[29] This was in fact the approach adopted in the Ten-Year Child Care Strategy announced in December 2004.

Called "Choice for Parents, the Best Start for Children," the Ten-Year Child Care Strategy emphasized supporting parental choice *and* improving child care. For families with infants, paid maternity leave was extended. The 2002 reforms had instituted six months of paid maternity leave followed by up to six months of unpaid leave. The unpaid leave time was predominantly being used by higher-income women, however, since lower-income families could not afford unpaid time off work. For this reason, as part of the Ten-Year Child Care Strategy, the government announced that it would extend the period of paid maternity leave to nine months, effective April 2007, with a commitment to extend paid maternity leave to twelve months eventually and with a promise of future legislation to allow mothers to transfer a portion of their paid leave time to fathers. Thus, under the reforms both of the paid maternity leave programs were extended to thirty-nine weeks. Statutory Maternity Pay, the employer-based program for those with sufficient work and earnings history, was paid at 90 percent of average weekly earnings (with no upper limit) for the first six weeks and at a flat rate of up to £123 per week (as of April 2009) for the next thirty-three weeks. Maternity Allowance, a benefit paid by the Department for Work and Pensions for those with some work experience but not sufficient to qualify for Statutory Maternity Pay, was paid at a flat rate of up to £123 per week (as of April 2009) for the full thirty-nine weeks. As in other European countries, take-up of paid maternity leave is very high, and it is common for mothers to claim the full thirty-nine weeks available to them.

For the under-threes, pilot programs were introduced extending free publicly funded preschool to some disadvantaged two-year-olds (the goal was to have sufficient provision to reach the 15 percent most-disadvantaged two-year-olds by September 2009), and funding for child care subsidies was expanded through increases in the child care element of the Working Tax Credit. For older preschoolers, measures were taken to increase availability and affordability—including extending the hours of free provision for three- and four-year-olds from the existing twelve and a half hours per week, thirty-three weeks per year, to fifteen hours per week, thirty-eight weeks per year.[30]

In addition, recognizing the still generally low quality of care in the early years sector, the Ten-Year Child Care Strategy introduced a host of measures to improve child care quality. These included steps to further reform and integrate child care regulation and inspections, building on the recent change (under the Children Act of 2004) that gave responsibility for inspecting child care and other children's programs to the Office for Standards in Education (Ofsted), the respected agency that inspects schools. The strategy also included steps to raise the quality of the child care workforce.

The aim of the Ten-Year Child Care Strategy was "to make early years and childcare provision a permanent mainstream part of the welfare state."[31] To that end, the Ten-Year Child Care Strategy was followed by the Child Care Act of 2006, which placed a new duty on local authorities to provide adequate child care for all working parents who wanted it. And certainly, child care provision expanded, with local authorities spending about £4 billion on child care for children under age five in 2007–2008, compared to around £1 billion in 1997.[32] Nevertheless, quality and affordability remained important issues. On the quality front, the government, inspired by research from Britain's Effective Provision of Preschool Education (EPPE) study showing that children learn the most in centers led by staff with a university degree, moved toward a requirement that every child care program have a graduate leader (with programs in disadvantaged areas having at least two graduates) by 2015, and it committed funding (£305 million in 2008) to help programs achieve this goal.[33] This would be a sharp change for this sector, where, as of 2008, only 4 percent of the workforce had a university degree.[34]

EVALUATING THE IMPACT

As is evident in this chapter's discussion, the British government's investments in early childhood were very wide-ranging and extensive. This makes it challenging to evaluate their impact. The strongest evaluation designs compare outcomes for a group that received an intervention (the treatment group) with a group that did not (the control group). But for most of the early childhood reforms, it is not possible to isolate one group of children who were treated by a new policy and compare them to a control group of children who were not. When policies such as universal preschool or maternity leave extensions or the right to request part-time or flexible work were introduced, all the children in the relevant age group were treated. The cohort of treated children can be compared to earlier cohorts, but that is an inherently weaker research design, since other factors—besides the policy of interest—may have changed over time. A further complicating factor is that the cohort of children growing up under New Labour received many different policy inputs because several policy reforms were implemented around the same time. Thus, for the most part, we cannot isolate the effect that specific policy reforms have had on children's outcomes. We can look at evidence on how cohorts of children compare to earlier ones, but for the reasons just discussed, we must be cautious in doing so.

The one exception in the early childhood area, and the only large-scale program that has been the subject of a rigorous evaluation, is Sure Start. Although Sure Start did not have a random assignment design and could not be experimentally evaluated, the government did fund a quasi-experimental study, the National Evaluation of Sure Start (NESS). In the absence of experimental data, the NESS team compared outcomes for children in Sure Start areas with outcomes for children in similar areas that did not have Sure Start programs. The comparison was not perfect. Given the placement of programs in the poorest areas, it proved difficult to find areas that did not have Sure Start programs but were as poor as areas that did have programs. Also challenging was the fact that Sure Start programs did not use one consistent model but rather varied widely. Nevertheless, in spite of these challenges, the NESS analyses provide the best available evidence on the effects of Sure Start.

The NESS team has completed two major evaluation reports, along with a host of other studies of specific aspects of Sure Start operations and programming and with a third major evaluation report due to be released in spring 2010. The first evaluation report, released in November 2005, compared children in areas that were among the first to implement Sure Start to children in areas that did not yet have Sure Start programs but had applied to do so.[35] This early evaluation found few significant positive effects of the program on children and families in Sure Start areas. Moreover, for some disadvantaged groups outcomes seemed, if anything, to be worse in Sure Start areas than in the comparison areas. This latter finding suggested that Sure Start was not working hard enough to reach the most vulnerable families or that other mainstream service providers (such as health or social services staff) were cutting back their involvement in Sure Start areas, to the detriment of the most vulnerable families.

Defenders of Sure Start argued that the evaluation had been done prematurely, before programs had a chance to get their new services fully up and running. They also noted that the control group—consisting of areas that had already applied for Sure Start programs and were waiting for funding—might not accurately represent what would have happened in the absence of the Sure Start program. If a key element of Sure Start was the integration and coordination of local services, many of the control group areas would have already achieved this as part of putting together their applications for Sure Start funding.[36]

Nevertheless, the initial evaluation findings were worrisome; the government, to its credit, reacted by providing a firmer direction to the local programs—in particular, by emphasizing the importance of outreach and engagement with the most-disadvantaged families. At the same time, the government began looking into ways to engage high-risk families, and in 2007 it started piloting a more intensive home visiting program for disadvantaged families, drawing on the U.S. nurse-family partnership model.[37]

Three years after the initial evaluation, in 2008, the second major NESS study was released, and the results were quite different.[38] Comparing children in established Sure Start areas with children in areas that were as (or nearly as) poor but did not have Sure Start programs, the evaluators found that outcomes for children in Sure Start areas were significantly better than for those in the comparison areas on seven of the fourteen measures assessed. Children in Sure Start areas scored better than their peers in non–Sure Start areas on three measures of behavior, two measures of child health, and two measures of parenting. Moreover, there were no negative effects for disadvantaged subgroups (as there had been in the first evaluation).

As important as the seven outcomes where the 2008 evaluation found gains are the seven where it did not. In particular, it is noteworthy that Sure Start did *not* improve children's performance on a test of cognitive and language development. This finding makes sense given that most programs did not offer much formal early education beyond what was already being offered through the government's expansions of preschool (which would have reached children in both the treatment and control groups), but it is nevertheless disappointing. Sure Start also did *not* significantly alter fathers' involvement or mothers' smoking, weight, life satisfaction, or rating of their local areas. These latter results probably reflect the fact that the focus of the program was on parenting and child health and development rather than on parents' own well-being.

How could the second evaluation differ so much from the first? And which one should we believe? Most analysts—including the NESS team—would agree that to a large extent the differences are a matter of timing. The first evaluation probably provided an accurate picture of the effects of Sure Start at that time, whereas the second shows us the effects of Sure Start after several more years in operation. The Sure Start programs included in the second evaluation were longer-standing programs and thus had had more time to get their services up and running. They also were programs that had absorbed the lessons from the early evaluation about the importance of focusing on the most-disadvantaged families. Of course, with the passage of time, other background factors may have changed as well. For instance, there is some indication that the child health improvements found in the 2008 evaluation reflect overall health improvements in the country rather than specific effects of Sure Start per se. (This problem arises because outcomes in the control areas were sampled somewhat earlier in time than in the Sure Start areas.)

So were Sure Start programs worth the investment? To answer this question, we would have to total up the costs of the local programs and evaluate them against the benefits. This is hard to do because we do not yet know what the full benefits have been (or will be in the future). The 2008 evaluation suggests that there have been gains in terms of child behavior, child health, and parenting, but we do not yet know what the long-term benefits of those gains will be. And there may be other benefits that have not been formally measured. Qualitative interviews with families in low-income areas suggest that they value Sure Start not only as a provider of services for their children but also as a source of family support and social cohesion.[39] These kinds of benefits are important, even if they are hard to quantify. It is also likely that Sure Start has yielded some benefits in terms of lessons for other programs. Several of the government's current initiatives—the Children's Centers in particular, but also the intensive home visiting pilots—are probably more effective because they have been able to build on the Sure Start model and learn from its strengths as well as its limitations.

As mentioned earlier, we lack data with which to evaluate rigorously the impact of the other early childhood investments made during this decade. In particular, we would like to know whether children are starting school more ready to learn and whether the early childhood policies have been successful in closing gaps in school readiness between low-income children and their more-advantaged peers. However, there is remarkably little evidence available with which to answer these questions. One study of primary school children found that levels of school readiness among entering four-year-olds—as assessed by performance on a brief cognitive test—did not improve substantially over the period 2000 to 2006, nor did gaps narrow between lower-income and higher-income children.[40] However, this study did not use a large, nationally representative sample, did not have information as to which programs children had been exposed to, and did not include a sample of children who entered school before the reforms began (or a sample who entered school after all the reforms were in place). The study authors note that its results may also be affected by other factors that changed over that time period. For instance, the share of children in the sample whose first language was not English increased significantly over time, a factor that would have depressed overall performance and widened income-related gaps in school readiness. Thus, firmer conclusions must await analyses that use nationally representative data, from before and after the reforms, and that take into account which children participated in particular programs as well as the underlying characteristics of the children and families. It would also be desirable to have data on children's progress on a broader set of noncognitive as well as cognitive outcomes.

The government is moving in this direction with its new assessments of children's development at age five (at the end of the so-called Foundation Stage, which runs from birth to age five).[41] These assessments cover aspects of the children's physical, emotional, and social development as well as their intellectual development. These assessments did not begin until 2003, however, so they cannot be used to gauge the effects of the preschool expansions that occurred in the late 1990s.[42]

In the absence of firm evaluation data, there are still some accomplishments, and some shortcomings, that we can point to. On the accomplishment side, universal preschool has been rolled out to all three- and four-year-olds, and parents are now eligible for paid maternity and paternity leave, a period of unpaid parental leave, and the right to request part-time or flexible hours. Child care facilities have come under the inspection of Ofsted, the same agency that inspects schools, and the government is working to raise teacher qualifications in the child care sector.

The government's commitment of resources to the early years is certainly impressive. Government spending on early learning and child care quadrupled between 1997–1998 and 2007–2008, when it reached more than £5 billion per year. Investments in leave provisions also expanded. And all of this was on top of the measures to promote work and raise family incomes (discussed in chapters 2 and 3), many of which differentially benefited families with young children. Comparing the measures implemented by New Labour with what existed prior to 1997, the Cabinet Office was recently able to boast:

> This Government has doubled maternity leave and pay, introduced parental leave for fathers and given parents with young children the right to ask for flexible working. Free early learning and childcare places have been provided for all three- and four-year olds and over 3,500 Sure Start Children's Centres will be up and running by 2010. We have improved financial support for parents, created tax credits with extra support for families with infants, and introduced Child Trust Funds.[43]

Of course, there are also shortcomings. In particular, Britain still has a long way to go to address the challenge of providing child care that is available, affordable, and of good quality. A review that I conducted in 2008 with Alison Garnham, codirector of the Daycare Trust (for a child poverty project coordinated by the Joseph Rowntree Foundation) particularly highlighted the problems associated with cost and quality; of course, the two factors are linked, since raising quality raises costs to parents unless government subsidies increase.[44] We return to the subject of needed child care reforms in chapter 7.

But it is worth underscoring that the early childhood programs Britain put in place over the decade represent a truly remarkable set of accomplishments, reflecting major gains from where Britain started out, and providing a stark contrast to where the United States is today. Thus, while preschool in the year or two before school entry is now universal in Britain as it is in most European countries, in the United States universal prekindergarten programs reach fewer than one in five four-year-olds, while Head Start reaches only about half of poor three- and four-year-olds. And, while Britain and other European countries now provide an average of nine to twelve months of paid maternity leave, as well as some paid paternity leave, the United States still has no national policy guaranteeing a period of paid leave for all new mothers and fathers.

Chapter 5

Investing in School-Age Children

The third leg of the British reforms, investments in children, also included a set of reforms affecting school-age children. A major emphasis was placed on improving schools and closing gaps in achievement. In this respect, the British reforms were somewhat similar in spirit to the U.S. reforms under the 2001 No Child Left Behind Act, which also emphasized improving schools and closing achievement gaps. The British reforms differed, however, in being more directly led by the central government, which plays a much larger role in education than does the federal government in the United States.

EDUCATION, EDUCATION, AND EDUCATION

Campaigning for office, Tony Blair made clear the importance he placed on education in a speech before a Labour Party conference on October 1, 1996: "Ask me my three main priorities for government and I tell you: education, education, and education."[1] In staking his political fortunes on promoting education, Blair endorsed the views of economists, who have long emphasized the central role of education in the formation of what they call "human capital"—the stock of skills, knowledge, and experiences that workers bring to the labor market. And in the closing decades of the twentieth century, improving education had taken on a new urgency.

Much to their chagrin, the British found themselves well below the leading countries on international education rankings. Newly available international data on children's educational performance, published in "league tables," showed Britain performing below many of its peers among advanced countries. In an increasingly globalized economy, these poor results prompted concerns that Britain needed to raise its skill levels if it was to not lose its place as an advanced knowledge economy. As Blair warned in his 1996 education speech, "Britain was 35th in the world's education league table and that would eventually translate into Britain being 35th in the economic table, unless education was tackled."[2]

And there were also the trends in inequality. At the end of the twentieth century, most economists had concluded that the single most important factor driving the increase in income inequality in Britain (as in the United States) was the increased return to education in the labor market.[3] Britain had always had substantial gaps in educational attainment (like the United States), but with the increased demand for skill in the labor market, the penalties for having a low level of education—and the rewards for having a high level—had accelerated. If Britain was to rein in or even reverse some of the growth in income inequality, improving the educational attainment of those at the bottom of the skills and income distribution would be essential.

INVESTMENTS IN EDUCATION

When the Labour government came into office in 1997, 4.9 percent of gross domestic product was being spent on education.[4] Ten years later, that share had risen to 5.6 percent. This increase may appear to be a small gain, but it was sufficient to move Britain from the back of the pack internationally to a position where its spending equaled the 5.5 percent average share of GDP that its peers among industrialized countries devoted to education.[5] Moreover, given the growth in GDP over this period, the actual increase in expenditure was much larger than it appears when measured as a percentage of GDP. In fact, the government calculates that per capita spending on education *doubled* in real terms between 1997 and 2007.[6] By 2009 the government was spending £35 billion per year on education.[7]

How was the money spent? Initially, the main focus of the reforms was on primary schools, in keeping with the emphasis on investing early in the life cycle. One of the first commitments Blair made during the campaign in 1996 was to reduce class sizes in the primary schools to not more than thirty pupils per class. To meet this goal, as well as to provide more staff to offer individualized attention to children, an additional 35,000 teachers were put in place over the next ten years, alongside an additional 172,000 teacher aides.[8] Over the same time period, teacher salaries were raised (a total of 18 percent in real terms), as was pay for school principals (who saw increases of 27 percent in real terms).[9] Spending on renovations and capital improvements also increased.

Another early initiative was the literacy hour. Part of the National Literacy Strategy, the literacy hour required primary school teachers to spend an hour each day on literacy instruction and provided guidelines as to how that hour was to be spent: one-half was to be dedicated to whole-class instruction, and the other half to individual or small-group instruction.[10] The nationwide rollout of the literacy hour in September

1998 built on a prior initiative, the National Literacy Project, which had piloted the literacy hour in some four hundred primary schools in 1996–1997 and 1997–1998. The economists Stephen Machin and Sandra Mc-Nally, directors of the Center for the Economics of Education at the London School of Economics, evaluated the pilot program, comparing outcomes for children whose schools had the literacy hour with those for children from comparable schools that did not.[11] They found that children who were exposed to the literacy hour had small but significant gains (about two percentile points) in reading scores and that those gains persisted when the children were tested later, at age sixteen. Gains were larger for boys than girls, an important finding given that boys typically lagged girls in reading. And there was some evidence that the program also raised math achievement—which made sense given that improved reading skills would help in tackling math problems. Machin and Mc-Nally also found that the program was highly cost-effective. The literacy hour cost just £25 per pupil because the bulk of the costs involved one-time teacher training, and once teachers were trained they could teach many pupils. These costs paled in comparison to the benefits. The lifetime boost in earnings associated with a gain of two percentile points in reading skills was estimated to be somewhere between £2,000 and £5,500.

A similar initiative—the numeracy hour—required primary school teachers to spend an hour a day on math instruction. This too was found by Machin and McNally to be cost-effective in raising student achievement.[12] Over time both strategies have evolved and become less prescriptive, with teachers no longer required by the central government to spend an hour a day on particular tasks (especially since 2009, when the literacy hour was officially abandoned), but it appears that they were effective in accomplishing the change they set out to make—to ensure that all primary school children were receiving at least a minimal amount of focused literacy and math instruction each day.[13] Although some teachers chafed at the lack of freedom to organize their class time as they wanted, parents in low-income areas applauded the initiatives, saying they were happy to know what their children were learning each day.[14]

Improving secondary school achievement received less attention initially but grew in importance over time, especially during Labour's second and third terms in office.[15] A challenge in the British context was not just to increase the quality of secondary schooling but also to increase the share of young people staying on in school. Historically, Britain had low rates of young people remaining in school beyond the minimum school-leaving age, which had been age sixteen since 1972. In 1996, immediately prior to Labour coming into office, only 32 percent of British eighteen-year-olds were in full-time education, the lowest percentage in the European Union, except for Greece (see figure 5.1). Reflecting this shortfall in

Figure 5.1   Share of Eighteen-Year-Olds in Full-Time Education in European Union Countries, 1996

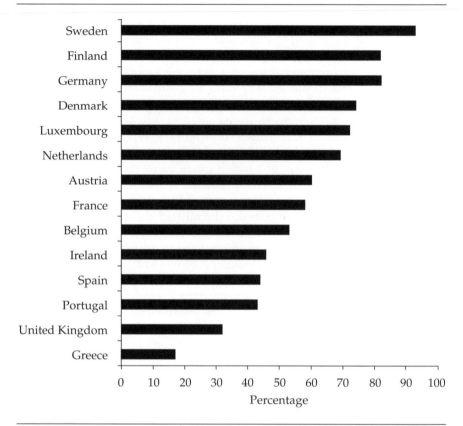

Source: Author's compilation based on OECD data, available from National Statistics (1996).

schooling, a 1999 task force on basic skills chaired by Sir Claus Moser found that 20 percent of adults had problems with literacy and 40 percent had problems with numeracy—rates that were much higher than those found in peer countries.[16]

Moreover, staying on in school was strongly linked to social class. In the period 1994 to 1996, immediately before the Labour Party came into office, 61 percent of seventeen- to eighteen-year-olds from the lowest-income families had received some education beyond age sixteen, compared to 84 percent of their peers from the highest-income families.[17]

To provide an incentive for low-income youth to complete more education, the government began a pilot program of educational maintenance allowances (EMAs) in the fall of 1999.[18] The EMA gave sixteen- to nineteen-year-olds from low-income families a payment of between £5 and £40 per week (depending on their family income) so long as they were enrolled in school; the program also provided some bonuses for those who satisfied particular attendance and achievement goals. Because the EMA initiative was piloted rather than rolled out nationwide, outcomes for low-income youth in treatment areas could be compared with outcomes for low-income youth in comparable areas that did not have the EMA. Taking advantage of this quasi-experiment, evaluators at the independent Institute for Fiscal Studies found that the EMA raised school enrollment after the school-leaving age by nearly six percentage points, with 71.3 percent of youth in EMA areas staying on versus 65.5 percent in control areas. About half of the youth who were induced to stay on would have otherwise entered work, while the other half would not have been in employment or education.[19] A later study, also at the Institute for Fiscal Studies, confirmed that not only were more youth staying on in school, but they were also completing more education.[20]

By 2005, 76 percent of all sixteen-year-olds were enrolled in full-time education, up from 70 percent in 1997, while the enrollment rate of seventeen-year-olds increased from 59 to 63 percent.[21] Nevertheless, staying-on rates for British youth still lagged behind those in peer countries. So, in 2005, the government released a white paper announcing a number of new initiatives to improve secondary schooling.[22] In 2008 it announced its intention to raise the school-leaving age to seventeen in 2013 and to eighteen in 2015, the first increases in the minimum school-leaving age since it was raised from fourteen to sixteen in 1973. This commitment was enacted in the 2008 Education and Skills Act. Also in 2008, the government introduced the "September guarantee": a promise of a place at a school or work-based training or education program for every sixteen-year-old leaving secondary school (later extended to cover seventeen-year-olds as well).[23] In spite of severe budget constraints, the 2009 budget restated this commitment and included funds for the initiative.

Another thrust of reform, particularly at the secondary level, has been a set of measures to increase choice and diversity of provision. These measures include the establishment of publicly funded but privately run academies (analogous to U.S. charter schools), starting in 2000. There has also been an expansion in religious schools, schools supported by charitable trusts, and specialist schools. As Ruth Lupton, an education analyst at the Centre for Analysis of Social Exclusion at the London School of Economics, and others have pointed out, these measures have been controversial because they create the risk that the secondary schools children attend could become even more unequal.[24]

However, efforts were also made to deliver more resources to the mostdisadvantaged areas and schools. As Ruth Lupton documents, these efforts began with Education Action Zones and later evolved into the Excellence in Cities initiative, which directed extra funding to all secondary schools (and later some primary schools) in the most-disadvantaged urban areas. Schools with a high proportion of students eligible for free school meals also received extra funding through programs such as Pupil Learning Credits.

The pace of educational reform was intense. The economist Howard Glennerster at the Centre for Analysis of Social Exclusion counted thirty-six major policy initiatives in the first five years alone.[25] And as we have seen, funding for education was increased dramatically, both during those first years and thereafter.[26]

THE RESULTS

Were these investments effective in meeting the twin goals of raising student achievement and narrowing gaps between less- and more-advantaged students? In his review of the period 1997 to 2001, Glennerster concludes that the answer to both questions is yes.[27] Drawing on both national education data (from the tests administered to all primary and secondary school students at regular intervals) and data from tests administered for international surveys, he provides evidence that overall achievement rose over this period and that gains were stronger at the bottom of the distribution, so that gaps in achievement between low-income students and their higher-income peers narrowed (as did gaps in average attainment between schools with high and low shares of children on free school meals). These gains are stronger for primary school students than for those in secondary school, which makes sense given the emphasis on primary schools in many of the initial reforms (such as class size reductions, the literacy hour, and the numeracy hour). And these gains are more apparent on national tests than on international ones, probably reflecting the tighter alignment of the curriculum with the former than the latter. Glennerster also cites data from surveys of parents in poor areas, half of whom reported that their local schools had improved.

Were the gains documented by Glennerster over those first five years maintained over the decade? The answer to this question has been hotly debated.[28]

So what does an objective reading of the data show? Let's start with results from tests administered to primary school students at age seven, known as Key Stage 1 (results shown in table 5.1). In 1997, 80 percent were performing at the expected level in reading, 80 percent were doing so in writing, and 84 percent in math. By 2001 these percentages had risen to 84, 86, and 91 percent, respectively, confirming the progress that Glennerster found in his analysis. But after 2001 no further progress was made, as

Table 5.1 Seven-Year-Olds at Expected Level (Level 2 or Above) at Key Stage 1, by Free School Meal (FSM) Status

	All	FSM	Non-FSM	Gap
Reading				
1997	80%			
1998	80			
1999	82			
2000	81			
2001	84			
2002	84	69%	88%	19%
2003	84	69	88	19
2004	85	70	88	18
2005	85	70	89	19
2006	84	69	88	19
2007	84	69	87	18
2008	84	69	87	18
Math				
1997	84			
1998	85			
1999	83			
2000	90			
2001	91			
2002	90	81	93	12
2003	90	80	93	13
2004	90	80	93	13
2005	91	81	93	12
2006	90	80	92	12
2007	90	80	92	12
2008	90	79	92	13
Writing				
1997	80			
1998	81			
1999	83			
2000	84			
2001	86			
2002	86	72	89	17
2003	81	64	85	21
2004	82	66	85	19
2005	82	66	86	20
2006	81	65	85	20
2007	80	63	84	19
2008	80	64	84	20

Source: Author's compilation. Data for 1997 to 2001 from Glennerster (2001); data for 2002 to 2008 from Department for Children, Schools, and Families (2004, 2005, 2006, 2007a, 2007b).
Note: Data by pupil characteristics are not available prior to 2002.

key government staffers such as Michael Barber, head of Blair's Delivery Unit, acknowledge.[29] As of 2008, the proportions of seven-year-olds at the expected level in reading and math were pretty much unchanged from 2001, and the share at the expected level in writing was back at the 1997 figure. The reading and math figures suggest that gains were made in that initial five-year period and maintained (but not increased) thereafter, while the writing results suggest some deterioration in the latter period.

Of course, we would like to know not just whether progress was made on average, but also whether gaps between low-income and other children narrowed. Unfortunately, data by pupil characteristics—such as free school meal (FSM) status, which is the best available indicator of low income—are not available until 2002. Thus, although the data clearly indicate that progress was made in overall achievement between 1997 and 2001, we cannot determine whether the gains were greater for low-income children. After 2001, when data by FSM status are available, progress stalled overall (as already discussed), and data by FSM status (table 5.1) show that no progress was made in closing gaps.

Turning to results for eleven-year-olds tested at the end of primary school—known as Key Stage 2 (shown in table 5.2)—the results are much more striking. First, not only are there large gains between 1997 and 2001 in the three subjects tested—English, math, and science—but there are continued improvements in English and math after 2001. These improvements were not sufficient, however, to meet the high targets the government had set for these subjects—namely, that by 2002, 80 percent of children would be at the expected level in reading and 75 percent at the expected level in math. The pattern for science is somewhat different: a large gain was made from 1997 to 2001, but no further progress was made thereafter.

The second striking finding for the eleven-year-olds is the evidence of the gap between low- and high-income students closing between 2002 and 2007 (the only years for which data by pupil characteristics are available for these test scores). Across each of the three subjects, children eligible for free school meals made more progress than their higher-income peers, and gaps in achievement narrowed (table 5.2). Although sizable gaps still remain, this is clearly evidence of progress in reducing them.

School-level data confirm that progress was made by the worst-performing primary schools. In 1997 only about half of primary schools had two-thirds or more of their eleven-year-olds scoring at expected levels in English and math, but by 2006 this proportion had risen to 87 percent for English and 81 percent for math, meaning that only a minority of schools were performing below this target.[30] Data comparing schools with a high versus low proportion of children eligible for free school meals tell a similar story.[31]

Table 5.2   Eleven-Year-Olds at Expected Level (Level 4 or Above) at Key Stage 2, by Free School Meal (FSM) Status

	All	FSM	Non-FSM	Gap
English				
1997	63%			
1998	65			
1999	71			
2000	75			
2001	75			
2002	74	53%	79%	26%
2003	75	54	79	25
2004	77	58	81	23
2005	79	60	82	22
2006	79	61	83	22
2007	80	62	83	21
Math				
1997	62			
1998	59			
1999	69			
2000	72			
2001	71			
2002	73	54	77	23
2003	72	53	76	23
2004	73	55	78	23
2005	75	56	78	22
2006	75	58	79	21
2007	77	60	80	20
Science				
1997	69			
1998	69			
1999	79			
2000	85			
2001	87			
2002	86	72	89	17
2003	86	72	89	17
2004	86	71	89	18
2005	86	72	89	17
2006	86	73	89	16
2007	87	75	90	15

Source: Author's compilation. Data for English and math from 1997 to 2001 from Department for Work and Pensions (2006b); data for science from 1997 to 2001 from Glennerster (2001); data for English, math, and science from 2002 to 2007 from Department for Children, Schools, and Families (2004, 2005, 2006, 2007a, 2007b).
Note: Data by pupil characteristics are not available prior to 2002 and were not yet available for 2008.

So the picture for primary school students provides a fair amount of evidence that the early reforms were successful in raising achievement for seven- and eleven-year-olds and that further gains—and progress in gap closing—were made for eleven-year-olds in the later years. As discussed earlier, we lack the data to determine whether gaps were closed among seven-year-olds in the early period, but given the pattern of reduced gaps among eleven-year-olds in the later period, it seems a safe bet that gaps were reduced among seven-year-olds in the early period, since this was the same cohort of children.

Of course, these data do not tell us whether the education reforms were responsible for the improvements or, if so, which reforms were most consequential. As discussed earlier, it is difficult to demonstrate the overall effects of the reforms and to tease out the effects of specific reforms, given that entire cohorts were treated. One recent study by the economists Helena Holmlund, Sandra McNally, and Martina Viarengo of the Centre for the Economics of Education takes advantage of the variation in funding across areas and over time to estimate the effect of increases in school expenditures on student achievement.[32] Examining the pupil-level data on eleven-year-old students' achievement at the end of primary school (Key Stage 2) over the period 2002 to 2007, they find robust evidence that increased spending was associated with significantly higher scores for students in English, math, and science and that spending increases boosted achievement more for low-income students (those eligible for free school meals) than for their higher-income peers.

However, the spending results do not tell us which specific expenditures were most consequential, or whether spending increases would have had as much impact in the absence of the comprehensive reforms. It is difficult to get inside the "black box" of school reform and understand which specific elements were consequential. Michael Barber, who played a key role in the education reforms as the director of the Standards and Effectiveness Unit at the Department of Education from 1997 to 2001 and later as director of Blair's Delivery Unit from 2001 to 2005, has written extensively about the reforms. He attributes the success in raising primary school achievement and in narrowing gaps in that achievement to several factors. During the 1997 to 2001 period, he and others focused intense attention on literacy and numeracy, setting ambitious targets and also rolling out national strategies for both. Barber also credits the strong and capable support for reform provided by Secretary of Education David Blunkett and Minister for Schools Estelle Morris, as well as the role played by Chris Woodhead, the tough and independent head of Ofsted inspections. But then there were the setbacks in 2001 and 2002. Barber describes this period:

The problem was that, by late 2002, the system which had worked so well between 1997 and 2000 had lost its edge at every level. Morris had been distracted, her top officials focused on other things, and after I had left there was no one at Education to have those restless, sleepless nights worrying about where the next percentage point was coming from. Moreover, after Chris Woodhead's resignation in the autumn of 2000, the impact of Ofsted inspection—a key lever in the strategy—had been weakened. In addition, with performance at a much higher level than just a few years earlier, it was of course increasingly difficult to make further gains.[33]

Additionally, there was a sense by 2001 that "we've done primary schools; now for the secondary schools."[34] Without sustained attention, however, progress in the primary schools stalled. According to Barber, the primary school reforms got back on track again after 2002 because he and others—in particular, Minister for Schools David Miliband—renewed the emphasis on literacy and numeracy and implemented initiatives to provide intensive support to struggling primary schools, to have leaders of successful schools mentor leaders of less successful ones, and to expand school choice and the establishment of new schools.

What about secondary school? Here the main data collection points are at age fourteen (known as Key Stage 3) and age sixteen, the minimum school-leaving age during this period and the age when students take national exams called General Certificates of Secondary Education (GCSEs). Data for fourteen-year-olds show progress throughout the ten-year period from 1997 to 2007 (table 5.3). The proportion of students scoring at the expected level rises from 57 percent to 74 percent in English, from 60 percent to 76 percent in math, and from 60 percent to 72 percent in science. Data by pupil characteristics for 2002 to 2007 show gaps closing between students eligible for free school meals and other students.

Data for sixteen-year-olds also show sustained progress (table 5.4). Aggregate data show that the share of sixteen-year-olds passing five or more GCSE exams rose from 45 percent to 65 percent from 1997 to 2008 (table 5.4, top panel, column 1). Data broken down by students' FSM status show that those gains were greater for students eligible for free school meals than for other students (table 5.4., top panel, columns 3 and 4); the result was a narrowing of the gap, although at the end of the decade a sizable gap remains. A tougher standard is passing five or more GCSEs, including English and math. On that standard, levels of attainment are lower and there is less overall progress and less progress in gap closing, though some progress is still evident (table 5.4, bottom panel).

School-level data confirm that the worst-performing secondary schools have improved. In 1997 some 360 schools (more than 10 percent of the

Table 5.3   Fourteen-Year-Olds at Expected Level (Level 5) at Key Stage 3, by Free School Meal (FSM) Status

	All	FSM	Non-FSM	Gap
English				
1997	57%			
1998	65			
1999	64			
2000	64			
2001	64			
2002	67	43%	72%	29%
2003	69	44	74	30
2004	71	46	76	30
2005	74	51	78	27
2006	73	50	77	27
2007	74	52	78	26
Math				
1997	60			
1998	59			
1999	63			
2000	65			
2001	66			
2002	67	43	72	29
2003	71	46	75	29
2004	73	50	77	27
2005	74	51	78	27
2006	77	56	81	25
2007	76	55	79	24
Science				
1997	60			
1998	62			
1999	55			
2000	69			
2001	66			
2002	67	40	72	32
2003	68	42	74	32
2004	66	39	71	32
2005	70	44	74	30
2006	72	48	77	29
2007	72	49	77	28

Source: Author's compilation. Data for 1997 to 2001 from Glennerster (2001); data for 2002 to 2007 from Department for Children, Schools and Families (2004, 2005, 2006, 2007a, 2007b).
Note: Data by pupil characteristics are not available prior to 2002 and were not yet available for 2008.

Table 5.4   GSCE Results for Sixteen-Year-Olds, by Free School Meal (FSM) Status

	All-1	All-2	FSM	Non-FSM	Gap
Percentage with five or more GCSEs (grades A to C)					
1997	45%				
1998	46				
1999	48				
2000	49				
2001	50				
2002	52	49%	23%	54%	31%
2003	53	51	24	55	31
2004	54	52	26	56	30
2005	57	55	30	59	29
2006	59	57	33	61	28
2007	61	59	36	63	27
2008	65	64	40	67	27
Percentage with five or more GCSEs, including English and math (grades A to C)					
1997	36				
1998	37				
1999	39				
2000	40				
2001	41				
2002	42				
2003	42				
2004	43				
2005	45	43	18	46	28
2006	46	44	20	48	28
2007	46	45	21	49	28
2008	48	48	24	51	27

Source: Author's compilation. Data for all students from 1997 to 2008 (All-1) from Department for Children, Schools, and Families (2008b); data for all children (All-2), FSM, and non-FSM for 2002 to 2008 from DCSF (2004, 2005, 2006, 2007a, 2007b; 2008b).
Note: Data by pupil characteristics are not available prior to 2002.

roughly 3,000 secondary schools nationwide) had fewer than 20 percent of students passing five or more GCSEs, and over 600 (more than 20 percent of all schools) had fewer than 25 percent passing; by 2006 these numbers had been reduced to 15 schools and 47 schools—representing 0.5 percent and 1.5 percent of all schools—respectively.[35]

School-level data also confirm that schools with larger proportions of low-income children have made more progress than schools serving more affluent children.[36] In 1999 only 19 percent of children passed five or more GCSEs in schools where half or more of the children were eligible for free school meals, but this proportion rose to 55 percent in 2008, a thirty-six-percentage point gain. Large gains (twenty-four and twenty-eight percentage points, respectively) were also seen in the passing rate for the next two groups of schools (serving 35 to 50 percent, or 21 to 35 percent, free-school-meal-eligible children). These gains contrast with the much smaller gains for schools serving more affluent children. As a result, gaps in GCSE attainment between the lowest- and highest-income schools narrowed dramatically, from forty-seven percentage points in 1999 to twenty-one percentage points in 2008. Patterns for a higher standard—the proportion of students passing five or more GCSEs, including English and math—are similar but display lower overall pass rates, less overall progress, and less narrowing.

So the data indicate that progress was made in raising achievement and in closing income-related gaps at the secondary school level as well. In some instances, the progress was greater in the latter part of the period, while in others there is evidence of steady progress throughout the period. This is not to say that all, or even most, of the gaps have been closed. Large attainment gaps persist at the end of secondary school, and these are reflected in continuing gaps in the share of children staying on in education past age sixteen, taking A-level exams (which they need to apply for university), and attending university.[37]

Nevertheless, the government largely succeeded in its aspiration of doing away with failing secondary schools. As at the primary level, the comprehensive approach to school reform was crucial. As Michael Barber points out, the reforms included three key elements: enhanced accountability, which included both inspection and testing; collaboration, as exemplified by mentorship programs for school leaders; and competition, through mechanisms such as school choice and new schools.[38] Also important were efforts to use marketing and pay raises to increase the popularity of teaching as a profession, thus improving the recruitment and retention of talented young graduates into teaching.[39]

THE VIEW FROM INTERNATIONAL ASSESSMENTS

Results on international assessments, on which British children had lagged in the mid-1990s, provide an independent source of information on their progress over the decade. It is important to note that the international data come from different sources, measure different constructs, and represent a varying sample of participating countries.[40] In some sources, data are available separately for England and Scotland, whereas in others, data are for the United Kingdom (England, Scotland, Wales, and Northern Ireland); this is relevant because the school reform initiatives, for the most part, applied only to England, and the national data just discussed (in tables 5.1 to 5.4) represent only England. The international data also are available only for selected years (with different years available for different tests). Thus, they are not an ideal or consistent measure of British progress in meeting the goals of the reforms over the decade. Nevertheless, when taken together, they do provide an external frame of reference and a useful supplement to the British data.

The most useful data set to track progress over the decade is the Trends in International Math and Science Study (TIMSS), administered in 1995, 1999, 2003, and 2007.[41] Figures 5.2 to 5.5 display the available data from TIMSS on changes in the test scores of British children and their international peers. Each figure includes all the countries that participated in the relevant years, which varied from year to year. Each figure is ordered to display on the left the countries that made the greatest gains in scores over time, and on the right the countries that made the smallest gains (or actually lost ground).

Figure 5.2, for fourth-graders (typically nine- to eleven-year-olds), shows that English children experienced the sharpest increase in math scores between 1995 and 2007 among the countries present in both years, with most of that progress coming between 1995 and 2003. Figure 5.3 shows more modest gains in science for English children over the same period: their performance put England roughly in the middle of the pack in terms of progress made. (Scotland, which appears separately, displays slightly declining science scores over the period.) Turning to eighth-graders (typically thirteen- to fourteen-year-olds), figure 5.4 shows that math scores for English children rose more over the 1995 to 2007 period than for children in most other countries, with most of that increase occurring from 1999 to 2007. Science scores also rose more for England than for most other countries (figure 5.5).[42]

Taken together, the international data provide some evidence of quite sizable gains for primary school students in Britain, particularly in math and particularly in the late 1990s. Gains at the secondary level, where present, tend to be smaller and occur later in the period. Although we must be cautious in drawing conclusions from the international data for the reasons discussed earlier, both these findings reinforce the overall patterns we saw in the national data.

One further piece of international evidence comes from public opinion surveys, which show the British public to be increasingly positive about the state of education in their country, relative to their European peers. Quality ratings from European Quality of Life Survey (EQLS) data show Britain moving up from ninth place to seventh place among the EU-15

Figure 5.2   Math Scores for Fourth-Graders in 1995, 2003, and 2007

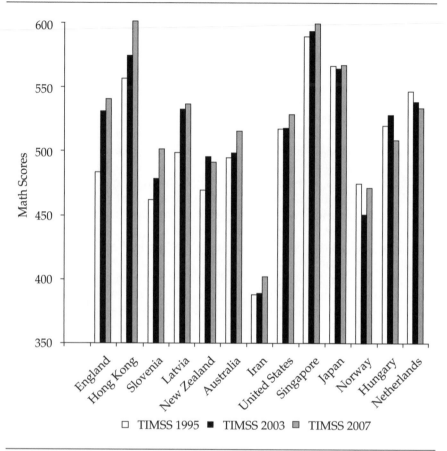

Source: Author's compilation based on data from the 1995, 2003, and 2007 Third International Math and Science Studies (TIMSS) (2009a, 2009c, 2007).

countries over the period 2003 to 2007 on the average rating that respondents provided when asked, "How would you rate the quality of the education system in this country?"[43]

PERSISTENT ACHIEVEMENT GAPS

In spite of the progress in Britain in closing the achievement gap between low- and higher-income children, it is still the case—ten years into the reforms—that sizable gaps remain.[44] In part, this is a reflection of the gap in the experiences they have before they start school (and in their out-of-

Figure 5.3   **Science Scores for Fourth-Graders in 1995, 2003, and 2007**

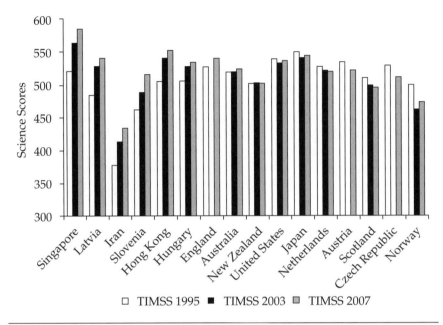

□ TIMSS 1995   ■ TIMSS 2003   ▨ TIMSS 2007

Source: Author's compilation based on data from the 1995, 2003, and 2007 TIMSS (TIMSS 2009a, 2009c, 2007).

school time). In this regard, it is important to note that many of the children currently in school will not have benefited from the early childhood reforms; for instance, children who were fifteen or sixteen years old in 2007 had already entered school by 1997 and thus did not benefit from the preschool expansions.

The persistent achievement gaps are also in part a function of the very different schools that low- and higher-income children attend; higher-income families do all they can to ensure that their children attend the best schools. Giving more low-income children access to the high-quality schools that their higher-income peers attend, through measures such as entrance lotteries, is an important goal, but so too is improving the schools that low-income children attend. In this regard, there is a good deal of discussion of ways to shift national and local funding formulas so that schools serving disadvantaged children get more resources, including resources to recruit and retain better-quality teachers.[45] The London Challenge—a successful initiative to improve schools throughout the city—has recently been extended nationwide, through the National Challenge.[46] There is also an increased emphasis on tracking the performance of spe-

Figure 5.4   Math Scores for Eighth-Graders in 1995, 1999, and 2007

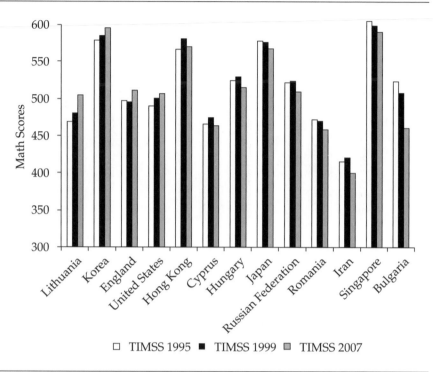

□ TIMSS 1995   ■ TIMSS 1999   ▦ TIMSS 2007

Source: Author's compilation based on data from the 1995, 1999, and 2007 TIMSS (TIMSS 2009a, 2009c, 2007).

cific subgroups such as children on free school meals (as a proxy for low income), setting specific targets for improving their achievement, and developing programs to make sure all children succeed in school.[47] Recent initiatives here include Every Child a Reader, Every Child a Writer, and Every Child Counts.

It is worth mentioning that, while the focus of the reforms has been on raising overall achievement and narrowing income-related gaps, some attention has been paid to other types of inequality. For instance, as discussed earlier, there has been concern about gender gaps associated with the poorer performance of boys, and some of the initiatives (such as the literacy hour) have been effective in helping to reduce these. There are also some ethnic groups—in particular, Pakistani and Bangladeshi children— whose average achievement has tended to lag behind that of white British children, although there is evidence that these children catch up quite a bit at age sixteen, when they face the high-stakes GSCE exams.[48] In many in-

Figure 5.5   Science Scores for Eighth-Graders in 1995, 2003, and 2007

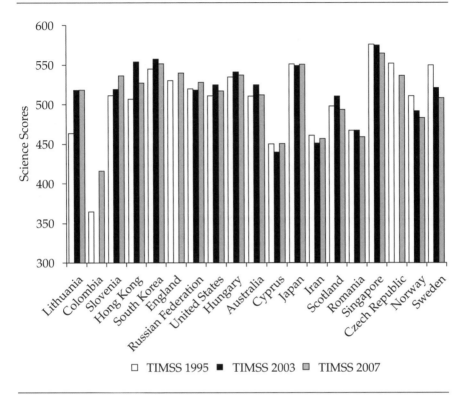

☐ TIMSS 1995   ■ TIMSS 2003   ▨ TIMSS 2007

Source: Author's compilation based on data from the 1995, 2003, and 2007 TIMSS (TIMSS 2009a, 2009c, 2007).

stances, as income-related gaps in achievement have narrowed, the ethnic gaps in achievement have narrowed as well. For instance, between 1998 and 2005, while the proportion of white British eleven-year-old children scoring at the expected level in English and math at the end of primary school rose by fourteen to sixteen percentage points, the proportion of Pakistani and Bangladeshi children scoring at the expected level rose by twenty-two to twenty-nine percentage points.[49] This makes sense since there is a good deal of overlap between low-income children and children from ethnic minority groups, and both populations would have benefited from efforts to raise the achievement of children at risk of low attainment.

In the long run, as achievement gaps are narrowed, children's eventual attainment should be less influenced by the attainment of their parents. Research by Paul Gregg and Lindsay Macmillan provides some evidence that this is starting to happen for the most recent cohorts: children born in 1990 are experiencing more social mobility than children born in 1970.[50] This trend will be important to follow as the 2000 cohort comes of age.

Nevertheless, gaps remain. A particular source of concern is the continuing gap in higher education enrollment. The progress in narrowing gaps in achievement in primary and secondary school has not yet been reflected in reduced gaps in higher education enrollment. It is still the case in Britain that parental education and social class are strong predictors of children's enrollment in university and other forms of higher education. What makes this of particular concern is that in Britain, as in the United States and other advanced economies, a higher education is increasingly necessary for workers who hope to be competitive in the labor market.

OTHER INVESTMENTS IN CHILDREN

The investments in early childhood and the improvements in the schools left one large gap unaddressed: the time that young people spent outside of school. Prior to 1997, schools differed widely in how much programming they offered to cover the hours before school, after school, or during school vacations. Although many schools had some form of after-school care available, the programs were of poor quality and tended to be used primarily by children of low-income working parents, who had little choice but to use the care, while middle-class children tended to participate in privately purchased activities outside of school (music lessons, sports, and so on). To improve the availability and quality of out-of-school programs and narrow gaps in access to such programs, the government in 2002 began taking steps toward instituting what it called "extended schools"—schools that would be open and provide a range of services before school, after school, and during school vacations. That year legislation was passed giving local authorities extra powers that would allow them to provide before- and after-school care, and twenty-five "pathfinder" local authorities were identified to pioneer extended schools.

In July 2005, the government announced its ambition to have all schools be extended schools by 2010 and to have half of schools attaining that target by 2008. A year after the 2005 announcement, progress was already evident. The share of primary schools offering before-school care had risen from 40 to 53 percent, while the share offering care during school vacations had risen from 26 to 43 percent. (The share of schools offering after-school care, already high in 2005, had risen from 87 to 91 percent).[51] An evaluation found that attainment gaps between low-income and higher-income students were lower in full-service extended schools than in other schools.[52]

A related initiative had to do with the provision of "positive activities" for youth. The Education and Inspections Act of 2006 placed an obligation on local authorities to ensure access to positive activities (such as sports and cultural events) for the young people in their area. Again, the idea was to improve the quality of out-of-school experiences for young people and to narrow gaps between low-income and more-advantaged youth.

Troubled youth or youth from struggling families received special attention. A series of reforms were introduced to strengthen the child protection and foster care systems, although these continued to be rocked by scandals, as they had so often been in the past.[53] More aggressive measures were also tested to address the issues associated with youth and families engaging in antisocial behavior. After an initial pilot that served some 2,600 families who were identified as engaging in antisocial behavior, Family Intervention Projects were slated to be rolled out to serve 20,000 such families by 2011.[54]

Health services for children were also expanded. In addition to Sure Start, which included an array of services focused on the health of young children and their parents, other health measures focusing on children included expansions in child and adolescent mental health services alongside improvements in health care services for children and young people, as well as maternity services. Overall, spending on the National Health Service doubled in real terms between 1997 and 2007, although much of this increased spending was aimed at improving services for middle-class consumers through measures such as reduced waiting times.[55] The various child health initiatives were brought together and expanded in a child health strategy issued in February 2009.[56]

Nutritional supports for children were also emphasized. As mentioned earlier, programs providing nutritional support to pregnant women and women with young children were expanded.[57] In addition, a major campaign was launched to improve the quality of nutrition in schools. In 2000 a pilot program was begun to provide every four- to six-year-old primary school child with a piece of fresh fruit every day, and this program subsequently was rolled out nationwide, with all schools participating by 2004.[58] Efforts were also made to improve the quality of school meals. The famed television chef Jamie Oliver partnered with schools to increase their use of fresh and nutritious foods. Although the reforms were primarily intended to improve child health, proponents argued that children eating healthier meals would also pay better attention and learn more in school. A 2009 analysis focused on schools in Greenwich provided some evidence in support of this claim, finding that children in schools that participated in Jamie Oliver's "Feed Me Better" initiative scored better in English and science and also had fewer absences from school than children in peer schools.[59]

Children's Centers were envisioned as hubs that would coordinate the delivery of a range of services to children and families. Other efforts along these lines included the establishment of Children's Trusts, which provided pooled funding that could be accessed across agencies in local areas, and Young People's Funds, which, again, provided pooled funding. The "Every Child Matters" initiative, announced in a green paper in September 2003, emphasized local coordination and information sharing, principles that were enshrined in law the following year in the Children Act of 2004. Within the central government, Britain's first minister for children was appointed in June 2003, followed by the first children's commissioner in March 2005.

When Gordon Brown took over as prime minister in the summer of 2007, he set up a new integrated Department of Children, Schools, and Families and, in a sign of the importance he placed on these areas, put one of his closest allies, Ed Balls, in charge. In December 2007, Balls published a Children's Plan that set out the new department's commitment to promote children's health and well-being by improving services and providing better support to families.[60]

CONCLUSION

This chapter and chapter 4 have chronicled a very extensive set of investments in children, fueled by large increases in spending for the early years and for school reforms. At the end of a decade of effort, to what extent had these investments—in tandem with the welfare-to-work policies and measures to raise family incomes—succeeded in reducing poverty and improving child well-being in Britain? What further steps would be needed to reach Britain's ambitious goals, and what lessons do these reforms offer for the United States and other countries? We turn to those questions in the final three chapters.

Chapter 6

Ten Years Later

How have the British antipoverty reforms affected child poverty and other measures of child well-being? And how do these results compare to those for the U.S. welfare-to-work reforms? The answers reveal some commonalities but also some notable differences. Child poverty has been reduced in both countries, but to a greater extent in Britain, reflecting the more generous measures enacted for low-income families in that country. Data on family expenditures also point to divergence across the two countries. In Britain, low-income families affected by the reforms are spending more money on items related to children, while in the United States low-income single-mother families affected by welfare reforms are primarily spending more money on items related to employment. This pattern of results is to be expected, given the emphasis in the British reforms on increasing benefits for children versus the emphasis in the United States on boosting single parents' employment.

Evidence on more direct measures of child well-being is more limited but suggests that the British reforms have probably been more successful in improving the health and development of children in low-income families, although substantial income-related disparities in child well-being remain.

We can also compare the British record over the decade with the record of other European countries. This is an important comparison because it provides a counterfactual as to what might have happened in Britain had the reforms not occurred. Here, too, Britain compares favorably, in both trends in poverty and inequality and trends in associated measures of deprivation and well-being.

THE BRITISH REFORMS

As we have seen in earlier chapters, the British government's agenda to reduce poverty and to improve the life chances of children in low-income families had the overall theme of "work for those who can, security for those who cannot," and included three main elements: policies to promote work and make work pay; increased benefits and tax credits for low-income families with children; and direct investments in children.[1] A key difference, as noted earlier, is that the British policies did not have a special focus on single-mother families.

The British policies to promote paid work and make work pay had much in common with the U.S. welfare reforms and included the introduction of Britain's first national minimum wage in 1999 as well as the Working Families Tax Credit (WFTC) (similar to the EITC). However, Britain's welfare-to-work program for lone parents, the New Deal, was primarily a voluntary program in which lone parents receiving means-tested Income Support had to attend job-focused meetings but were not required to take up training or work.

The other two elements of the British reforms were more distinctive. To further reduce child poverty (beyond what could be accomplished through the work-focused reforms), Britain's Labour government introduced a series of tax credit and benefit changes, including significant real increases in the value of Child Benefit, the universal child allowance, and substantial increases in the generosity of benefits for low-income families, whether or not the parents worked, with particularly large increases for families with children under age eleven. The British reforms also included a set of direct investments in children designed to reduce disadvantage and combat social exclusion. Early years programs that deliver child care or other services for preschool-age children were particularly emphasized, and part-time universal preschool provision is now in place for all three- and four-year-olds. Another important area of emphasis was improving schools; additional spending on education has reduced class sizes in the primary grades and provided support for other reforms in schools.

Although the new programs were not mandatory for lone parents, the British reforms did reduce the number of lone parents claiming means-tested cash assistance; with the number on Income Support falling from 1 million in 1997 to 783,000 in 2006, a much smaller fall than in the United States.[2] Over the same period, lone-mother employment rates rose from 45 percent to 57 percent, a remarkable rise given that, as noted, the reforms did not include a work requirement for this group.[3] As in the United States, it is hard to disentangle the effects of the reforms from the effects of the strong economy, but econometric estimates suggest that half of the increase in lone-mother employment that occurred between 1998 and 2002 was due to the policy reforms, with expansions in tax credits playing a particularly important role.[4] Comparable estimates for the period after 2002 are not available, but given that the economy was slowing, it seems likely that the reforms played an even larger role (relative to the role of the economy) in those years. Thus, over the entire reform decade, it is fair to conclude that the reforms accounted for at least half of the gain in lone-mother employment, and probably more.

THE U.S. WELFARE REFORMS

Before comparing the outcomes of the reforms in Britain with those in the United States, it is helpful to first review the overall contours of the U.S. reforms.[5] One important difference to make clear at the start is that the U.S. welfare reforms, unlike the British reforms, were focused on single-mother families receiving means-tested welfare rather than on low-income families more generally. In some instances, the welfare reforms and associated reforms did affect other families, but their main target was single mothers. So most of the U.S. evidence applies to low-income single-mother families rather than to low-income families more generally. This is an important limitation. As discussed later, while single-parent families in the United States experienced both losses (due to cuts in welfare benefits) and gains (due to increases in work-related benefits) under welfare reform, low-income two-parent families saw only gains, since few of them had been eligible for welfare in the first place, and many gained from the expansions in the EITC, child care, and child health insurance coverage. So if we focus only on how single-parent families fared under welfare reform, we miss an important part of the U.S. story—the part related to low-income two-parent families. This is an aspect of the U.S. welfare reforms that has not received much attention but is important to recall.

Welfare reform in the United States began in the early 1990s as states used the waiver process to apply for permission from the federal government to make changes in the way they administered the major federal cash welfare program, Aid to Families with Dependent Children (AFDC). These state waiver reforms were quite varied, but what they had in common was a dual focus on reducing welfare use and increasing parental employment. The federal Personal Responsibility and Work Opportunity Reconciliation Act (PRWORA), passed in 1996 and implemented in all states by 1998, cemented these elements of welfare reform by replacing the long-standing cash assistance program, AFDC, with a new time-limited and work-focused program, Temporary Assistance to Needy Families (TANF).

A key element of the U.S. welfare reform package was the expansion of provisions to promote work and make work pay. These provisions were mainly aimed at single mothers on welfare, but they also increased work incentives for parents in low-income two-parent families. Particularly important in this regard were expansions in the Earned Income Tax Credit for low-income workers, at both the federal and state levels.[6] In addition, the value of the minimum wage was increased. And there were substantial expansions in child care subsidies and child health insurance programs, with two-parent families in many states becoming eligible for these benefits for the first time. These reforms were implemented in the context of a very strong economy in the United States in the 1990s; the unemployment rate from the latter half of 1997 through most of 2001 was under 5 percent, which was lower than it had been since the early 1970s.

The fact that many reforms occurred together, and in a strong economy, has made it difficult to sort out the precise role that specific reforms have played. It is clear, however, that the welfare reforms (including the EITC and other measures to make work pay), in combination with the strong economy, resulted in very steep declines in welfare caseloads and dramatic increases in single-mother employment. The expansions in the EITC are thought to have played a particularly important role.[7]

The magnitude of the impact of welfare reform in the United States is truly striking. Welfare caseloads fell from a high of nearly 5 million families in 1993 to about 2 million in 2000.[8] Over the same time period, the share of single mothers who were employed grew from 67 percent to over 80 percent.[9]

Data on EITC and welfare expenditures and caseloads illustrate the dramatic shift that occurred.[10] Prior to 1996, when PRWORA was enacted, the federal government spent more on cash welfare benefits through AFDC than it did on the EITC. After 1996, that pattern was reversed, with spending on the EITC vastly outstripping spending on TANF. While cash welfare spending under AFDC/TANF was cut from $40.9 billion in 1995 to $22 billion in 2005 (in constant 2007 dollars), EITC spending rose from $35 billion to $45 billion. Over the same time period, the number of AFDC/TANF recipients fell from 13.4 million to 4.5 million, while the number receiving EITC rose from 19.3 million to 22.7 million.

Both single-parent and two-parent families are eligible for the EITC, although about 75 percent of the funds spent on the EITC goes to single parents.[11] The EITC has played an increasingly important role in boosting family incomes in both types of families. Rebecca Blank of the Brookings Institution has shown that from 1979 through 1990 there was little difference in the pre- and post-tax income of a family with a minimum-wage earner, but that from 1990 onward, post-tax income was notably higher, owing to expansions in the EITC.[12] By the mid-1990s, post-tax annual income for a single-parent family with a minimum-wage earner was about $4,000 higher than its pre-tax income ($15,000 versus $11,000), a pattern that continued through 2007 (the most recent year of data analyzed). Figures for two-parent families with minimum-wage earners tell a similar story.

THE EFFECTS OF THE REFORMS ON
CHILD POVERTY

Reducing child poverty was the explicit goal of the British reforms, and an implicit goal of the U.S. ones. How have the two countries' efforts fared?

As we have seen, Britain measures poverty in both relative and absolute terms. When Prime Minister Tony Blair declared war on child poverty in 1999, 3.4 million children—one in four—lived in poverty, whether defined in relative or absolute terms. But how much poverty changed over the ensuing decade depends very much on whether a relative or absolute definition is used.

Using the government's preferred relative measure of child poverty— the percentage of children in families with income below 60 percent of median income—the child poverty rate fell from 26.7 percent in 1998–1999 to 22.5 percent in 2007–2008, a 16 percent reduction from the 1998–1999 base.[13] While a sizable decrease—from 3.4 million children to 2.9 million—this reduction was not fast enough to place the government on track to cut poverty in half in ten years, or to end it in twenty, according to a relative definition. This was particularly disappointing to the government given the progress it made in the first five years of the initiative. As of late 2003, the government was widely viewed as being on track to reach its first child poverty target of a 25 percent reduction in relative poverty in five years.[14] And in fact, it came very close to meeting that target in 2004.[15] Progress in reducing child poverty stalled after 2004, however, and indeed the number of children in relative poverty and the relative child poverty rate were higher in 2007–2008 than they had been in 2003–2004 (see detailed data in table 6.1). As we shall see, this stalling was the result of a slowing economy—unemployment rates were still at record low levels through 2004 and 2005, but began to rise thereafter—but it was also due to a slowdown in government investments in the antipoverty initiatives.

Using a relative measure imposes a very tough standard, because if median income is rising, more low-income children will be counted as poor even if their incomes have not fallen in real terms.[16] This was in fact the case in Britain, where over the decade from 1996–1997 to 2006–2007, median income rose 20 percent, with average annual increases of 1.9 percent, although these slowed in the latter part of the decade.[17] This was a faster rate of growth than had occurred under the previous eighteen years of Conservative government, when average annual growth was 1.6 percent.[18] Table 6.2 shows that real income growth was more evenly distributed across the income distribution than it was under the former Conservative government—when incomes had risen the most for those at the top of the income distribution and the least for those at the bottom—but rising

Table 6.1   Trends in Child Poverty Using the British Government's Three Official Measures, 1997 to 2008

	Relative Poverty		Absolute Poverty		Material Deprivation	
	Percentage	Number (Millions)	Percentage	Number (Millions)	Percentage	Number (Millions)
1996–1997	26.7%	3.4				
1997–1998	26.9	3.4				
1998–1999	26.1	3.4	26.1%	3.4	20.8%	2.6
1999–2000	25.7	3.4				
2000–2001	23.4	3.1				
2001–2002	23.2	3.0				
2002–2003	22.6	2.9	14.1	1.8		
2003–2004	22.1	2.9	13.7	1.8		
2004–2005	21.3	2.7	12.9	1.7	17.1	2.2
2005–2006	22.0	2.8	12.7	1.6	16.3	2.1
2006–2007	22.3	2.9	13.1	1.7	15.6	2.0
2007–2008	22.5	2.9	13.4	1.7	17.1	2.2

Source: Author's compilation based on Brewer et al. (2008, tables 4.2, 4.5, and 5.2).
Note: Income is measured before housing costs.

real median incomes still made it challenging to reduce poverty defined in relative terms.

Before leaving table 6.2, it is worth noting that the Family Resources Survey data on which the income statistics are based show a fall in real income for the bottom income quintile and a zero percent gain for the second to bottom quintile from 2004–2005 to 2006–2007. Although this was a period of slower income growth throughout the income distribution as the economy slowed, it nevertheless is striking that income growth is negative or nonexistent for the bottom 40 percent of families. Detailed comparisons of the Family Resources Survey data and administrative data, carried out by analysts at the Institute for Fiscal Studies, point to a discrepancy in the figures on benefit receipts, with low-income families reporting less income from benefits than official government records show was expended on them. If low-income families are underreporting their incomes, income growth may have been more positive at the bottom than it appears, and poverty reduction may not have stalled as much as the survey data suggest. Nevertheless, it is unlikely that underreporting accounts for all the stagnation of incomes at the bottom; some of this must have been due to the slowing economy.

If we look at Britain's progress using its second official measure, an absolute poverty line—measured as the share of children below 60 percent of the median income in 1998–1999, with the poverty line indexed only for

Table 6.2   Real Income Growth Under Conservatives and New Labour, by Income Quintile

	1 (Lowest)	2	3	4	5 (Highest)
Conservatives: 1979 to 1996–1997	0.8%	1.1%	1.6%	1.9%	2.5%
New Labour: 1996–1997 to 2006–2007	1.8	2.1	1.9	1.7	1.9
Blair 1: 1996–1997 to 2000–2001	2.4	2.7	2.4	2.5	2.7
Blair 2: 2000–2001 to 2004–2005	2.6	2.5	2.0	1.6	1.4
Blair 3: 2004–2005 to 2006–2007	–1.1	0.1	0.7	0.6	1.2

Source: Author's compilation based on data from Brewer et al. (2008, table 3.1).

inflation, as it is in the United States—we see a very substantial reduction in child poverty, from a rate of 26 percent of children in 1998–1999 to a rate of 13 percent in 2007–2008, a remarkable reduction of 50 percent from the 1998–1999 rate and a fall from 3.4 million poor children to 1.7 million (table 6.1). Moreover, although progress on this measure also stalled after 2004, absolute poverty did not rise significantly between 2004–2005 and 2007–2008, unlike the trend seen for relative poverty.

How can we reconcile the two sets of results? Britain's dramatic progress in halving child poverty as measured in absolute terms confirms that incomes have been rising for families at the bottom. But the slower progress on reducing relative poverty suggests that incomes at the bottom did not rise enough to counteract the fact that incomes have also been rising for middle- and higher-income families. This is not surprising since the British policies were focused on raising the incomes of those at the bottom; they were not focused on raising taxes on the rich or constraining the labor market, which continues to favor more-educated and higher-income workers. So, in a period when overall income inequality was continuing to rise, the improvement in poverty in relative terms was less than the improvement in absolute terms.

Because the United States uses an absolute poverty line, it is straightforward to compare the progress of the United States and Britain in reducing child poverty in absolute terms. Tim Smeeding, director of the Institute for Research on Poverty at the University of Wisconsin, and I do so using comparable data from the U.S. Census Bureau and Britain's Department for Work and Pensions.[19] For each country, we plot the share of children below the country's official absolute poverty line (the government's absolute poverty line for Britain and the official U.S. poverty line for the United States). This is a tough comparison for Britain to do well on, since its absolute poverty line is set higher up in the income distribution than the U.S. poverty line is. For example, in 2000 Britain's absolute poverty line was just below 60 percent of median income, whereas the U.S. poverty line was at about 35 percent of median income. The results (displayed in figure 6.1) show that the reduction in child poverty in Britain has been larger and more sustained than in the United States. This divergence was already apparent five years into the New Labour administration and was visible in both relative and absolute poverty statistics.[20]

Whether considering relative or absolute poverty trends, we would like to know not just whether children were moved above the poverty line, but also whether living standards for children in low-income families have improved. Analysts studying welfare reform in the United States have raised concern that incomes and living conditions may have deteriorated for the lowest-income families. Several studies have found that incomes fell for the bottom quintile of the income distribution because some families affected by welfare reform were not able to replace their lost benefits with increased earnings from work.[21]

Rebecca Blank estimates that the number of single mothers who are not connected to welfare or work doubled between the mid-1990s and the mid-2000s and that this disconnected group now makes up 20 to 25 percent of all single mothers.[22] We have more to learn about how these women are supporting themselves and their families. Blank points out that many of these women do not live with other adults and that on average they are very poor, with median household incomes under $13,000 per year. She also notes that there is probably a good deal of overlap between these disconnected women and women who have been sanctioned for noncompliance with welfare work requirements or who have reached welfare time limits; many of the women in this situation suffer from poor mental health or other barriers to work.[23]

Of course, counteracting this fall in living standards for some single-parent families has been the rise in living standards for low-income two-parent families who benefited from the expansions in the Earned Income Tax Credit (EITC), the Child Health Insurance Program (CHIP), and food stamps, as well as the increased minimum wage. In contrast to single-parent families, low-income two-parent families would not have lost benefits under welfare reform. So, in the case of two-parent families, the gain in income for low-income working poor families through expansions in the work-based safety net was not offset by a loss in welfare income for low-income couple families who did not manage to move into work or increase their work effort.

Figure 6.1   Trends in Child Poverty in Britain and the United States

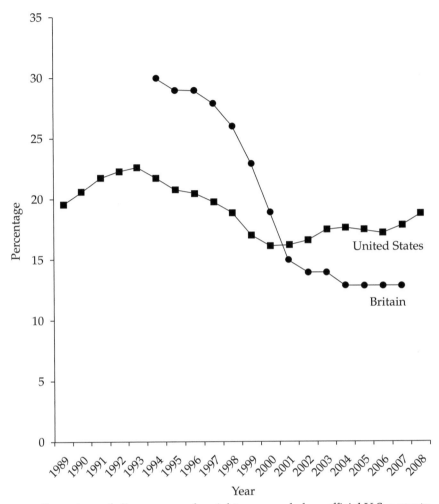

Percentage of all persons under eighteen years below official U.S. poverty line, (about 35 percent of median in 2000)

Percentage of U.K. children below the absolute poverty threshold (about 60 percent of median in 1998–1999)

Source: U.S. Bureau of the Census (2009a); Department for Work and Pensions (2009a, 73).

Although concerns about living standards at the bottom of the income distribution have been raised in Britain as well, the picture there appears to be brighter.[24] In Britain, in contrast to the United States, real income grew over the 1996–1997 to 2006–2007 period for all income quintiles, although with some apparent stalling of growth at the bottom in the most recent data (as discussed earlier). The only place in the British income distribution where real incomes may have fallen over the reform period are the bottom few percentiles, where the measurement of income is notoriously noisy and particularly likely to be affected by how income is measured: British surveys typically ask about income over the past two weeks rather than over the past year, as is customary in the United States.[25] And, unlike in the United States, there are virtually no single mothers who are disconnected from both work and welfare, because of the universal availability in Britain of cash income support to all families with children.

Overall, then, the evidence indicates that both countries have seen improvements in child poverty, but with Britain having achieved larger reductions than the United States.[26] As with the employment and caseload changes, it is difficult to partition the poverty changes into a portion driven by the policy reforms as distinct from a portion caused by the strong economy. In both countries, both the policy changes and the strong economy played an important role, and there are also likely to have been interactions between the two, since pro-employment policies are more effective at reducing poverty when the labor market is stronger.

It is also important to note that the role of a strong economy differs depending on whether one is using an absolute or relative poverty measure. Clearly, a strong economy was an important factor in raising incomes at the bottom (as well as elsewhere in the distribution) and reducing absolute poverty. At the same time, because the strong economy raised median incomes, it would have had the effect of increasing relative poverty unless income gains at the bottom kept up with gains for the median. Indeed, estimates by Mike Brewer from the independent Institute for Fiscal Studies suggest that the strong economy would have led to relative child poverty *rising* in Britain over the past decade if the government had not implemented its antipoverty strategy.[27] The government estimates that had it merely adjusted the 1997 tax and benefit system in line with prices, something like 2 million more children would now be in poverty.[28]

THE EFFECTS OF THE REFORMS ON MATERIAL DEPRIVATION

When Britain reassessed how it defined poverty in 2003, it established a third official measure of child poverty.[29] Less often used than the two measures of income poverty, this measure is designed to capture information about children who are materially deprived owing to their family's lack of financial resources, taking into account that not all children in income poverty are materially deprived. The material deprivation measure therefore tracks the share of children whose families are materially deprived as defined by not being able to afford a set of specific items *and* having income below 70 percent of median income (70 percent being used because some children just above the 60 percent relative poverty line may nevertheless be deprived).

Deprivation for children is defined as not being able to afford the following items: a holiday away from home at least one week a year; swimming at least once a month; having friends over for tea or a snack every two weeks; enough bedrooms for every child over age ten to have his or her own bedroom or to share only with a child of the same sex; leisure equipment, such as a bicycle; celebrations on special occasions, such as birthdays or Christmas; some form of preschool at least once a week (for preschool-age children); going on a school trip at least once a term (for school-age children); and having safe outdoor space or facilities nearby. The government selected these items by reviewing all available deprivation data for Britain and selecting those items that best distinguished between poor and nonpoor families, recognizing that the specific items included in the index would need to be updated periodically as living standards changed.[30] The government also uses several measures of adult deprivation, such as not being able to keep the home warm or in good repair.

Data are gathered on both child and adult deprivation through the annual national Family Resources Survey. Families' responses are weighted to take into account the frequency of deprivation on a particular item—an item receives more weight in the deprivation score if most people have it—and then adjusted so that scores range from 0 (lowest possible deprivation) to 100 (highest possible). The government uses a score of 25 or higher, in conjunction with income below 70 percent of contemporary median, to indicate material deprivation according to the official government definition.[31]

As shown in table 6.1, Britain has made considerable progress in reducing material deprivation. In the baseline year—1998–1999—20.8 percent of British children were materially deprived on this measure, and this rate had fallen to 15.6 percent by 2006–2007 before rising again to 17.1 percent in 2007–2008 (the latest year for which data are available). It is noteworthy that the rate of material deprivation continued falling after 2004–2005, a period during which progress on relative and absolute child poverty measures diverged. This suggests that what is driving the better record on material deprivation is an improvement in living standards among the low-income, in line with the progress on absolute poverty, which is why most American researchers tend to favor an absolute poverty line. Some of this improvement also may reflect the effect of government initiatives that affected the well-being of families with children without directly raising their incomes. For instance, increased subsidies to local leisure centers would reduce the cost of swimming, making that more affordable for low-income families. So too would increased subsidies for preschool child care and school trips.

One criticism of this kind of measure of material deprivation is that, in tracking the ownership of a select set of items (and using an arbitrary income cutoff), it is essentially arbitrary. It is also an incomplete measure, to the extent that it captures only a portion of families' budgets and expenditures. For this reason, some analysts prefer measures of family expenditures, which we consider in the next section.[32]

A further limitation of a material deprivation measure is that it may not capture the kind of material hardship that is most stressful for families and most harmful for children. In this regard, results from a second survey, the Families and Children Study (FACS), are very informative. Results from this survey indicate that low-income families not only made gains in terms of the types of items measured in the material deprivation survey but also reduced their levels of reported financial distress (as measured by items such as worrying about money all the time, running out of money, and so on).[33] Results for lone parents (shown in table 6.3) are particularly striking: reductions in the share experiencing financial stress as well as the share unable to afford particular items were dramatic, in particular between 1999 and 2002, when many of the income-related elements of the reform were rolled out.

How do trends for the United States compare? Data on trends for food insecurity in single-mother families are consistent with what we saw earlier in trends for child poverty in the United States: children's living conditions improved in the mid- to late-1990s, when welfare reform was first implemented, but then plateaued or slightly deteriorated thereafter. As shown in table 6.4, between 1995 and 1997 the share of single-mother households in the United States that were food-insecure fell from 32 to 28 percent, while the share that were food-insecure and experiencing hunger fell from 12 to 9 percent.[34] Looking at the data after 1998, we see that the pattern is one of flat or slightly increasing food insecurity, and by 2007 the shares of those who were insecure or insecure and experiencing hunger had risen slightly, to 30 and 10 percent, respectively.[35] Table 6.4 also shows trends in food insecurity for married-couple families. As expected, they have much lower levels of food insecurity throughout the period, but they also show some declines in the years when single-parent food insecurity declined, suggesting that both groups were affected by common trends in

Table 6.3   Changes in Financial Stress and Material Deprivation
Among British Lone Parents

	1999	2002	2005	2006
Lone parents with financial stress				
Almost always worries about money	45%	30%	27%	29%
Always runs out of money before end of week	27	19	19	18
Problems with debt almost all the time	15	12	14	n.a.
Lone parent who cannot afford:				
Going away for one-week holiday	74	58	53	53
Having company over for a meal	34	20	18	16
Celebrating special occasions	27	14	11	10
Toys and sports gear for children	24	12	7	7
Best outfit for children	20	13	10	n.a.
Fresh fruit on most days	17	8	6	n.a.

Source: Author's compilation based on data from Stewart (2009a, table 3.2), using data from Families and Children Survey.

the economy or by increases in the benefits available to both types of families—in particular, food stamps and the EITC.

Data on other types of deprivation, available for selected years from the Survey of Income and Program Participation (SIPP), show some declines in deprivation for the lowest-income families between 1995 and 2003.[36] Among families in the bottom fifth of the income distribution, 20 percent were behind on their utility bills and 14 percent were behind on their rent or mortgage payments in 1995. By 1998 these rates had improved to 15 and 10 percent, respectively. They remained at roughly this level (16 and 10 percent, respectively) in 2003. So, again, the picture is of improvements in living standards in the immediate aftermath of welfare reform, but with less evidence of improvement thereafter. However, data for single parents for 1998 to 2003 suggest that there was continued improvement for this group: 21 percent were behind on their utility bills and 12.5 per-

Table 6.4   Food Insecurity Among Families with Children, 1995 to 2007

	Married-Couple Families		Single-Mother Families	
	All Insecure	Insecure with Hunger	All Insecure	Insecure with Hunger
1995	9.9%	2.6%	32.2%	11.9%
1996	7.0	2.9	31.3	11.4
1997	7.5	1.8	27.9	9.2
1998	9.6	2.0	31.9	10.4
1999	9.6	1.6	29.7	8.1
2000	10.9	1.9	31.0	9.0
2001	10.7	2.1	31.9	8.7
2002	10.4	1.9	32.0	8.7
2003	10.8	1.9	31.7	8.7
2004	11.6	2.3	33.0	9.2
2005	9.9	2.3	30.8	8.7
2006	10.1	2.1	30.4	10.3
2007	10.5	2.7	30.2	10.3

Source: Author's compilation based on data from *Household Food Security in the United States* (Bickel, Carlson, and Nord 1999; Cohen, Parry, and Yang 2000; Nord et al. 2001, 2002, 2003, 2004, 2005, 2006, 2007).

cent were behind on their rent or mortgage bills in 2003, compared to 26 percent and 15 percent, respectively, in 1998.

THE EFFECTS OF THE REFORMS ON FAMILY EXPENDITURES

Another way to assess the material well-being of children in low-income families is to examine the level and pattern of their families' expenditures and, in particular, their spending on items for children.[37] Income and poverty measures capture the resources potentially available to children but do not measure the resources actually spent on them. Low-income families may be able to borrow or share resources with other families, in which case measures of income and poverty may understate the resources available to children. At the same time, low-income families typically spend more of their income paying for essential items such as housing and food costs, as well as back bills and debt, in which case measures of current income may overstate the resources available for other items for children.[38]

A further limitation of income data is that they do not tell us how resources within the family are allocated. One concern that is sometimes raised is that low-income parents might just squander additional benefits by spending them on items for themselves or on harmful goods such as alcohol and tobacco. The counterargument is that low-income parents, like other parents, try to do the best they can for their children and will spend benefits responsibly, particularly if those benefits are labeled as being for the children. Examination of detailed expenditure data, reported later in the chapter, can directly address this question.

In particular, such analyses can shed light on whether families are purchasing items for children (such as children's clothing) as well as whether they are purchasing items thought to be related to child health and development (such as fresh fruits and vegetables, books and toys, or computers), although, of course, one cannot determine with certainty which of these items are actually consumed or used by children.[39] At the same time, analyses of family expenditure data are more comprehensive than analyses of material deprivation, which, as discussed earlier, are based on a select set of items rather than families' full set of purchases. Accordingly, there has been a good deal of interest in studying the effects of the policy reforms on family expenditures, both as a measure of effects on children's material well-being and as a source of information as to possible effects on child health and development.

The economists Bruce Meyer and James Sullivan have carried out several studies examining the effects of welfare reforms on the expenditures of single-mother families in the United States.[40] They find that average total expenditures rose, at least slightly, for most single-mother families following the welfare reforms. However, they also find that these expenditure increases were largely focused on transportation and housing (with some additional spending going to food away from home and child care costs) and came at the cost of a decline in single mothers' nonmarket time (time available for leisure and household production).

Does this pattern of results extend to more detailed categories of expenditures, and how do results for Britain compare? With colleagues from Britain and the United States, I carried out a series of studies looking at detailed patterns of expenditures of both U.S. and British families following the welfare and antipoverty reforms. These studies shed light on changes in how families are allocating their spending and, specifically, on the question of whether they are shifting their spending toward items related to employment or items related to child health and development.[41]

The first of these studies, which I carried out with Paul Gregg and Elizabeth Washbrook in 2005, provided preliminary evidence on how family expenditures changed following the reforms in Britain by comparing low-income families' expenditures in 1996–1997 (pre-reform) to their expenditures in 2000–2001 (after the wave of reforms implemented between 1998 and 2000).[42] Using data from Britain's Family Expenditure Survey (FES), a large-scale survey of household expenditures and income that has been in existence since 1957, we found evidence across a number of expenditure categories and durable items that low-income families' spending was converging to that of higher-income families.[43] This study spurred two further studies, one in Britain and one in the United States.

The British study, carried out by Gregg, Washbrook, and myself in 2006, again used data from the FES and applied a difference-in-difference-in-difference (DDD) methodology.[44] This methodology begins with the estimation of the change in expenditures of the treatment group—the group most affected by the reform; in this case, low-income families with children under age eleven—between the pre-reform period and the post-reform period. This is the first difference. This difference is compared to the change in expenditures over the same time period for a group that is similar but less affected by the reforms—in the British case, this is low-income families with children ages eleven to fifteen who benefited from the reforms, but not as much as those with younger children. This is the second difference. Finally, the difference in changes in expenditures between these two groups is compared to the difference in changes in expenditures for two control groups—higher-income families with children under age eleven and higher-income families with children ages eleven to fifteen—resulting in the third difference (the DDD).[45]

The 2006 British study examined the impact of the antipoverty reforms that occurred between October 1998 and April 2000, pooling data from April 1995 to March 1998 to capture expenditure patterns prior to the reforms and data from April 2000 to March 2003 to capture patterns after reform.[46] The study found strong expenditure gains for low-income families with children ages zero to ten, relative to other groups, with significantly positive DDD increases for five of the nine major categories of expenditure: housing (spending was up thirteen percentage points), food (up nine percentage points), clothing and footwear (up twenty-eight percentage points), leisure goods and services (up thirty-four percentage points), and motoring and travel (up forty-four percentage points, but from a very low base). However, the same families significantly *reduced* their spending on alcohol and tobacco, again relative to other groups (in DDD estimates). This study thus provided striking evidence that the extra spending by low-income families eligible for more direct financial support from the British government was being allocated to housing, food, clothing and footwear, leisure, and motoring, clearly switching away from alcohol and tobacco.[47] Also striking was the finding, in the analyses of more detailed expenditure categories, that low-income families with a youngest child age zero to ten were significantly increasing their spending on children's clothing and footwear, fruits and vegetables, books, newspapers, magazines, and holidays—all items with potential benefits for child health and development.

As families' incomes rise, they may also be more likely to own durable goods such as a car or van, telephone, or computer. The 2006 British study considered a broad set of goods: a car or van, a telephone, a washing machine, a freezer, a microwave, a tumble dryer, a computer, a videocassette recorder, and a CD player. Some of these goods may make a direct contribution to a child's health and development, while others may make an indirect contribution by helping the family connect with employment or leisure activities or by reducing parental stress and isolation. Before reform, there were large gaps in ownership of items from this broad set of durable goods in Britain. Low-income families with children ages zero to ten were substantially less likely to own a car or computer than were higher-income families with children in the same age range; gaps also existed in the ownership of goods such as telephones, microwaves, or CD players. Analyses of the post-reform period show that there were sharp increases in ownership of all these goods among low-income families with young children. However, the DDD results show that the increase outpaced that of other groups for only two of the items—car ownership and having a telephone. Low-income families, if anything, lost ground in computer ownership, because although low-income families increased their ownership, their gains were dwarfed by even larger gains by higher-income families (although the DDD estimate was not significant).

How do the effects of welfare reform on families' expenditures in the United States compare? With my colleagues Neeraj Kaushal and Gao Qin, I carried out a similar DDD analysis for the United States using data from the Consumer Expenditure Survey (CEX), a large-scale survey of U.S. families' expenditures.[48] In this case, the treatment group was low-educated single-mother families. This group was chosen because low-income single-mother families were the main target of welfare reforms in the United States, and low education is an excellent marker for low income. The analyses compared the change in the focal group's expenditures over the reform period (the first difference) with the change in those of more highly educated single mothers (the second difference). The study then contrasted that with the differential between low-educated and more highly educated married mothers to estimate the third difference.

Before turning to those results, it is worth recalling two major points of difference between the reforms in the two countries. First, the benefit increases for low-income families in Britain were not contingent on employment, while in the United States the only low-income single-mother families who saw benefit or tax credit increases were those who moved from welfare to work (or who increased their work effort). Second, the British reforms were explicitly child-focused, while in the United States the focus of welfare reform was mainly on the employment behavior of adults. If either or both of these factors contributed to producing the child-oriented shifts in expenditures among British families affected by the antipoverty reforms, we might not see comparable effects in the United States. Rather, we might expect to see more employment-oriented shifts in expenditures, in addition to or instead of the child-oriented ones.

The results for the United States are indeed different. The analyses indicated that the welfare reforms of the mid- to late-1990s were not associated with any statistically significant change in total expenditures in households headed by low-educated single mothers. However, patterns of expenditure did change: the welfare reforms were associated with an increase in spending on transportation, food away from home, and adult clothing and footwear. In contrast, there were no statistically significant changes in expenditures on learning and enrichment activities or child care. This pattern of results suggests that the welfare reforms in the United States have shifted expenditures in single-parent families toward items that facilitate work outside the home but, at least so far, have not allowed low-income families to catch up with more-advantaged families in terms of their expenditures on child-focused or learning and enrichment items.[49]

Many of the changes in expenditures observed in the U.S. data, while statistically significant, are small in magnitude (and many others are not statistically significant). Thus, the conclusions we can draw about the changes in low-income single-mother families' expenditures in the United States remain somewhat tentative. Also, as noted earlier, the treatment group analyzed for the United States—low-educated, single-mother families—is different from the treatment group analyzed for Britain (all low-income families). Nevertheless, the overall pattern of results is consistent in suggesting that to the extent that patterns of expenditures did change for the families most affected by welfare reform in the United States, the direction of that change was mainly to increase expenditures on work-related items rather than on child-related or learning and enrichment items, as was the case in Britain. These results make sense given the work-oriented nature of welfare reform in the United States, but they leave open the question of the extent to which children affected by the reforms in the United States are better off than they were previously.

THE EFFECTS OF THE REFORMS ON
CHILD WELL-BEING

Ideally, we would like to know how low-income children are faring not just in terms of income poverty, material deprivation, and family expenditures but also in terms of broader measures of well-being. After all, one of the main reasons that societies care about child poverty is that it is associated with poorer child health and development. The idea that raising family incomes leads to improved child well-being was a key underlying assumption of the reforms, as we saw in chapter 3.

Before turning to the evidence on the effects of the reforms on child health and development, it is important to note that the evidence is somewhat limited and that what evidence we do have mainly relates to short-run effects. If we think that the effects of reduced poverty will be larger in the long run, then the short-run evidence will understate these. It is also worth noting, however, that if policies have little or no effect in the short run, they are unlikely to have large effects in the long run. Seen from that perspective, the short-run evidence is quite useful.

THE EFFECTS ON CHILD HEALTH AND DEVELOPMENT

How have the British antipoverty reforms and the U.S. welfare reforms affected the health and development of children in low-income families? To the extent that the reforms have reduced poverty and associated hardship, they should also be accompanied by improvements in child well-being. Although parents try hard to protect their children from the effects of low income and hardship, even young children are aware of their parents' financial situation and the constraints that it places on their families.[50] As incomes rise and those constraints are eased, if parents are less stressed or depressed or are able to purchase more beneficial items for their children, we would expect to see improvements in child health and development.[51] However, there may also be countervailing effects of parents' spending more time in employment, particularly if parents are working low-wage jobs that provide little scope for flexibility and autonomy, entail long commutes, or require work at nonstandard or variable hours.[52] Thus, it is not clear a priori how the British antipoverty reforms and the U.S. welfare reforms should be expected to have affected child health and development, and assessing those effects is not straightforward. For the most part, we lack experimental evidence that would allow us to determine with confidence the impact of the reforms. Moreover, as discussed earlier, in both countries the policy change was not a unitary phenomenon but rather a set of initiatives that encompassed many different types of reforms, enacted in quite varied settings. A further obstacle is that measuring child health and development is expensive and time-consuming, and therefore data on these outcomes tend not to be as readily available as are data on welfare caseloads, parental employment, or family incomes and expenditures. In addition, it is possible and even likely that the effects of the reforms on children vary by factors such as the age, temperament, or gender of the child; if so, estimating average effects across children may not provide a full or accurate picture of how specific types of children are affected.

With these limitations in mind, what can we conclude about the effects of the British and U.S. reforms on child health and development? In the United States, a great deal of weight tends to be placed on evidence from a series of welfare-to-work experiments evaluated by researchers at MDRC.[53] These experiments, which preceded the passage of the federal welfare reform legislation (PRWORA) in 1996, tested reforms undertaken by states that had obtained permission through the waiver process to try alternative approaches to welfare policies and programs. (MDRC also evaluated a few experiments carried out in Canadian provinces.) They are therefore a good source of information about how families may be affected by welfare-to-work reforms, although they did not include the full array of reforms that affected low-income families over that decade.

The MDRC studies suggest that the effects of the reforms depend on the child's age.[54] For preschoolers (children who were age two to five when their mothers were exposed to the reforms), there were few significant effects on behavior or health, although health outcomes did tend to be better when the reforms raised incomes.[55] With regard to cognitive development, seven of ten programs had no significant effects. Positive effects were found in the remaining three programs, the largest being in the two programs that provided earnings supplements: the Canadian program, Self-Sufficiency Project (SSP); and the Wisconsin program, New Hope.[56]

Turning to children who were school age (ages six to ten) at the time their parents were exposed to the welfare reforms, the findings for child health parallel those for the younger children. However, the effects on cognitive outcomes differed. The same types of welfare-to-work programs that had positive effects on school achievement for children who were preschoolers when their mothers were encouraged to work had *no* such effects for children ages six to nine, and *negative* effects for children ages ten to eleven.[57] Analyses focusing specifically on adolescents found significantly poorer school outcomes for youth whose mothers were exposed to welfare-to-work reforms and also some possible adverse effects on behavior.[58]

As emphasized earlier, the MDRC studies preceded the passage of PRWORA and thus cannot directly address the question of how that sweeping set of reforms affected child health and development in the United States. Observational studies that are following children and families in the years since welfare reform face the familiar challenge of not being able to identify conclusively the counterfactual—that is, what children's health and development would have been in the absence of the reform. Nevertheless, these studies shed some light on how children are faring since welfare reform. Particularly notable is the Three-City Study of Welfare Reform, which has followed large samples of children in Atlanta, Boston, and Chicago. Overall, the researchers have found few significant effects on children as their mothers moved from welfare to work; if anything, there has been some evidence of improvements in mental health for adolescents when their mothers moved from welfare to work.[59]

Econometric studies that take advantage of variation in welfare policies over time and across states to estimate the effects of welfare reforms on child health or development are few.[60] One topic that has been examined is the effect of changes in work exemption policies on mothers with infants.[61] Given the evidence on the adverse effects of maternal employment in the first year of life and the beneficial effects of maternity leave, we might expect these shortened work exemption policies to have some adverse effects on child health and development.[62] Two studies to date have examined the effects of these policies. One found that the tougher work requirements are hastening low-income mothers' entry into work following childbirth, while the other found that the tougher work requirements are significantly reducing breast-feeding.[63]

If it is challenging to evaluate the effect of the reforms on child health and development in the United States, it is even more so in Britain, which did not have a series of welfare reform experiments like those evaluated by MDRC in the United States. Instead, many of Britain's antipoverty reforms were implemented nationwide, meaning that there was no control group of families who were not treated. A further challenge is that the reform package included many distinct elements—changes in benefits and tax credits, expansions in parental leave and early childhood care and education, and improvements in the schools, to name just a few—most of which were delivered, often at the same time, to the same cohorts of children, making it difficult to tease out the impact of any one element on child health or developmental outcomes.

In addition, many of the British reforms are still under way or still relatively new. Welfare reform in the United States began in 1992 (with the state waiver reforms) and was extended nationally in 1996 (with the passage of PRWORA, which all states implemented by 1997 or 1998), whereas the British Labour government did not come to power until 1997; its antipoverty reforms did not begin until 1999, and they have continued to evolve since then. Thus, it is still too early to assess the impact of many of the British reforms. Although government indicators point to progress by low-income children on an array of outcomes, as shown in table 6.5, it is difficult to determine whether the reforms were responsible for particular gains, and if so, which ones.[64] Thus, determining how the sweeping reforms in Britain have affected child health and development—and the extent to which they have narrowed the gaps in health and development

Table 6.5   Changes in Child Health and Development Between 1997 and 2007 on the "Opportunity for All" Indicators

	Improvement?
Children in workless households	n.a.
Low income	
Relative	✓
Absolute	✓
Persistent	✓
Teen pregnancy	
Teen conceptions	✓
Teen parents in education, employment, or training	✓
Children in disadvantaged areas with "good" development	n.a.
School achievement of eleven-year-olds	✓
School achievement	
Sixteen-year-olds	✓
Schools below floor target	✓
Nineteen-year-olds with at least Level 2 qualification	n.a.
School attendance	—
Outcomes for looked-after children	
Education gap	X
Not in education, employment, or training	—
Stability	✓
Sixteen- to eighteen-year-olds in learning	—
Infant mortality	X
Serious unintentional injury	✓
Smoking prevalence for	
Pregnant women	✓
Children ages eleven to fifteen	✓
Obesity for children ages two to ten	X
Re-registrations on Child Protection Register	✓
Housing that falls below standard of decency	✓
Families in temporary accommodation	X

Source: Author's compilation based on data from Department for Work and Pensions (2007c, Indicator Summary Table, 5–7).
Note: The table compares the status of children on each indicator as it was in 1997 and 2007 (or the closest year for which data are available). "✓" indicates improvement over the period, "X" indicates worsening, "—" indicates no change, and "n.a." indicates data were not available in or around 2007.

outcomes between low-income and more-advantaged children—remains challenging.

As in the United States, few studies have directly examined child health and development outcomes for cohorts of children affected by the British reforms. Exceptional in this regard is a 2009 study by the economists Paul Gregg, Susan Harkness, and Sarah Smith, who analyzed outcomes for adolescents in lone-mother families affected by the Working Families Tax Credit (WFTC) and related reforms over the 1999 to 2003 period.[65] They find robust evidence that these youth have improved mental health, school attendance, and school aspirations compared to other youth whose families were not affected by the reforms. This set of results is particularly striking given the negative findings for similar outcomes for adolescents in the MDRC studies in the United States. The difference probably reflects the different focus of the British and U.S. reforms—requiring parental employment in the United States versus raising incomes (without regard to parental employment) in Britain.

Other evidence on the impact of the British reforms on child health and development comes from several analyses of specific initiatives that take advantage of the fact that some were piloted or phased in on a staggered basis. As discussed in chapter 4, probably the single largest evaluation of a component of the antipoverty strategy is the National Evaluation of Sure Start (NESS): the conclusive implementation study, released in 2008, compared children in Sure Start and non–Sure Start areas and found that Sure Start led to significant improvements in seven of the fourteen outcomes assessed.[66] There is also some positive evidence from evaluations of the education initiatives, as we saw in chapter 5.[67]

HOW DOES BRITAIN'S RECORD COMPARE TO THAT OF THE REST OF EUROPE?

Britain began its antipoverty campaign with an ambitious goal—ending child poverty by 2020. Ten years on, although the government has made excellent progress against absolute poverty and substantial progress against relative poverty, it looks very unlikely that this goal will be met, particularly if poverty is measured in relative terms, against a backdrop of an economy characterized by growing overall inequality.

But of course, there are limits to what any antipoverty policy can achieve. Is it realistic to imagine a society where no child is in poverty ever? Just as economists identify a natural rate of unemployment—below which no society could aspire to go—there is probably also a natural rate of poverty. No matter how strong a country's labor market is, and how generous its safety net, there will always be some individuals who fall on hard times, at least temporarily, and who will therefore be counted as poor. There will also always be some individuals who have serious difficulties engaging with the labor market and other aspects of society. And in our increasingly global societies, there will be immigrant groups who may have different values, norms, and skill sets and who may, at least in the short term, have lower incomes.

In recognition of these realities, the British government in 2003 introduced the idea that a realistic goal for ending child poverty in Britain would be to have a record that was "among the best in Europe."[68] Thus, if the best-performing countries in the European Union were only able to reduce their child poverty rate to a single digit, that would be a more reasonable target for Britain to aspire to than a goal of reducing child poverty rates to zero.

In this regard, then, it is useful to compare child poverty rates in Britain with the rest of the European Union. When we do so (using data on relative poverty rates, as is customary in Europe), we see that Britain has made considerable progress, although it still has a long way to go to be among the best in Europe.[69]

As we saw in chapter 1, one of the factors motivating Britain to undertake its child poverty initiative was its poor showing relative to its European neighbors, as well as other advanced industrialized countries. In 1999, when Blair declared war on child poverty, Britain's relative child poverty rate, at 29 percent, was ten percentage points higher than the average of 19 percent for the EU-15—the fifteen countries that made up the European Union at that time. (After seven mostly eastern European countries joined the EU when it was expanded in 2004, it became known as the EU-22.) Over the ensuing years, Britain's position improved (see figure 6.2), so that by 2007, although Britain still had a high child poverty rate relative to its EU-15 peers, its rate, at 24 percent, was only six percentage points higher than the EU-15 average of 18 percent. (The United States does not appear on this chart, but if it were included, its child poverty rate, at roughly 30 percent defined in relative terms, would be higher than that of any country in the EU-15).[70]

The dramatic improvement in Britain's position reflects the fact that while Britain's child poverty rate was falling during its antipoverty initiative, poverty on a comparable relative measure was rising or holding constant for most of its EU-15 peers.[71] For example, Denmark, which had the lowest child poverty rate in the group in 1995—at 6 percent—saw its rate rise to 10 percent by 2006. Its Nordic neighbors Finland and Sweden saw similar increases. In southern Europe, in contrast, countries began the period with relatively high rates and saw those rates primarily maintained (or saw them fall in the case of Portugal). The northern European countries provide a particularly interesting point of comparison, since they include Britain's nearest neighbors. Comparing child poverty in 2006 to its

Figure 6.2   Child Poverty Rates in Britain and the EU-15, 1995 to 2006

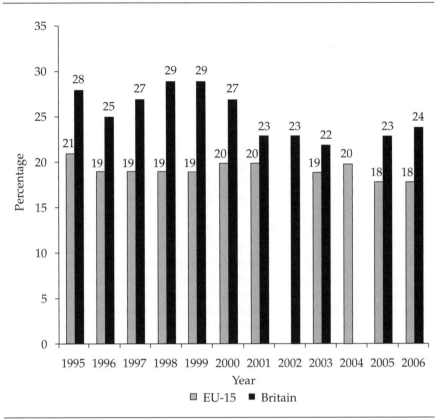

Source: Author's calculations using data from Eurostat (2008b; see chapter 6, note 24); data from 1995 to 2001 from the European Community Household Panel. Data from 2002 and 2005 are provided by national sources, with some countries providing data from a new survey, European Union Statistics on Income and Living Conditions (EU-SILC), in 2003 and 2004. From 2005 onward, all country data are from EU-SILC.
Note: The poverty rate is defined as the percentage of children with an equivalized disposable income below a poverty threshold set at 60 percent of the national median equivalized disposable income (after transfers).

level in 1999, no country in that group experienced a fall in child poverty comparable to that seen in Britain. Indeed, with the exception of Germany, where poverty fell one percentage point, poverty rates in this group either held steady or increased during the period when child poverty was falling five percentage points in Britain.[72]

The European data indicate that Britain's relative position in terms of child poverty improved dramatically over the decade. Thus, although in

2006 Britain still ranked among the worst in Europe in terms of its child poverty rate, it had closed the gap with its peers in the EU-15, and at a time when underlying trends were acting to make poverty reduction more difficult. This was remarkable progress, even though not sufficient to place Britain among the best in Europe. Moreover, the European data support the conclusion that in the absence of the reforms, relative poverty in Britain would probably have increased or at best held constant over the decade.

Data on measures of material deprivation also shed some light on how trends in Britain compare to those for its European neighbors. The European Quality of Life Survey tracks changes in several aspects of material deprivation between 2003 and 2007 (comparable data from earlier years are not available), including: cannot afford to keep home adequately warm; cannot afford a week's holiday; cannot afford to replace worn-out furniture; cannot afford to have friends or family for a drink or meal once a month; cannot afford new rather than secondhand clothes; and cannot afford a meal with meat, chicken, or fish every second day. Britain saw improvements on all six of these measures between 2003 and 2007, in contrast to the trend for the EU-15 as a whole (as illustrated in figure 6.3 using data on home heating). Only Portugal, which had a large decline in poverty, reported consistently greater improvements in living standards than did Britain (although the data also indicate some improvements in other low-income southern European countries, such as Greece and Spain, as well as sizable improvements in Ireland, which had its own antipoverty initiative). Unfortunately, comparable data for the United States on these items is not available.

Some comparative data on broader measures of well-being are also available.[73] How does the well-being of Britain's children compare to the well-being of children in other European countries? On Valentine's Day 2007, the British public awoke to the news that their country was "failing children."[74] A report by UNICEF comparing the well-being of children in twenty-one industrialized countries found that British children ranked last on many of the outcomes.[75] The news for the United States was hardly better. As a headline in *USA Today* announced: "UNICEF ranks well-being of British, U.S. children last in industrialized world."[76] Britain had the poorest record on the items related to family and peer relationships as well as those related to behavior and risks. The U.S. record was not much better in those categories and was even worse on the items related to health and safety.

The Conservative Party's shadow chancellor, George Osborne, was quick to use the UNICEF report to accuse Chancellor Gordon Brown of having "failed this generation of children. . . . After 10 years of his welfare and education policies, our children today have the lowest well-being in

Figure 6.3 **Percentage of Poplulation that Cannot Afford to Keep Home Adequately Warm**

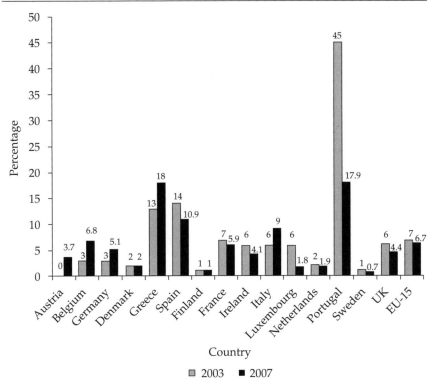

Country

☐ 2003 ■ 2007

Source: European Foundation for the Improvement of Living and Working Conditions (2003, 2007).

the developed world."[77] However, it soon emerged that the UNICEF report did not refer to the cohort of children who had experienced ten years of Labour policies. Indeed, nearly half of the indicators used in the report came from data collected in 2000 and 2001 on children who were born between 1985 and 1990—years before Labour came into office in 1997.

Kitty Stewart, a researcher at the Centre for Analysis of Social Exclusion, updated the UNICEF analysis in 2009, taking advantage of the fact that the same information was collected again in 2005 and 2006, on a cohort of children born between 1990 and 1995. In contrast to the earlier cohort, this later cohort would have spent a majority of their childhood years under the Labour government. Her analysis of this later cohort tells a very different story about the well-being of children in Britain under Blair and Brown. As she notes, the results "are little short of astonish-

Table 6.6   Change in the Well-Being of Young People in Britain Relative to Young People in Other OECD Countries, 2000–2001 and 2005–2006

	2000–2001 Score and Rank		2005–2006 Score and Rank		Change in Rank
Eat fruit every day	27%	18/21	43%	3/21	(15)
Like school a lot	20	16/21	37	4/21	(12)
Agree that peers are kind and helpful	47	20/21	72	10/21	(10)
Used condom last intercourse[a]	70	11/14	82	5/14	(6)
Ever used cannabis[b]	40	19/20	25	15/20	(4)
Overweight according to BMI[c]	15	17/22	13	14/22	(3)
Smoke cigarettes once a week	13	16/21	8	13/21	(3)
In at least three fights in last year	14	16/21	14	13/21	(3)
Above middle in life satisfaction	84	16/21	85	13/21	(3)
Health fair or poor	23	20/20	19	18/20	(2)
Eat breakfast every day	56	16/21	64	15/21	(1)
Have had sexual intercourse[b]	37	16/16	29	15/16	(1)
Bullied at least twice in past few months	10	12/21	10	12/21	(0)
Drunk at least twice	30	21/21	24	21/21	(0)

Source: Author's compilation based on data from Stewart (2009b, table 13.5).
Notes: Score indicates the percentage of British eleven-, thirteen-, and fifteen-year-olds who replied "yes" to a given item (unless otherwise indicated); ranking is Britain's place among twenty-one OECD countries (unless otherwise indicated), with a ranking of 1 indicating the best-performing country and 21 the worst.
a. Indicates question was asked only of fifteen-year-olds who had had sexual intercourse.
b. Indicates question was asked only of fifteen-year-olds.
c. Indicates question was asked only of thirteen- and fifteen-year-olds.

ing."[78] Of the fourteen measures for which comparable data are available at the two time points, Britain's ranking improved on twelve of them, and in some cases very substantially (for details, see table 6.6). For instance, the share of young people eating fruit every day increased from 27 percent to 43 percent, moving Britain's ranking from eighteenth place (out of twenty-one OECD countries) to third place. Very large improvements were also evident in the share of young people who like school a lot and who agree that peers are kind and helpful. On the question of how satisfied British young people are with their lives (a question that aims to measure happiness), Britain's ranking improved from sixteenth place (among twenty-one countries) to thirteenth.[79] Averaging across the fourteen indicators in the table, Britain's ranking moved up from seventeenth place in 2000–2001 to twelfth place in 2005–2006.

As Stewart points out, Britain's progress on these indicators of well-being is consistent with the progress it has shown in other survey data. For instance, data on young people from the 2006 Health Survey for England confirm the decline in the share who smoke or drink alcohol, the decline in obesity, and the increase in fruit consumption.[80]

Not all the indicators tracked in the UNICEF report have improved. In particular, it is noteworthy that there was no improvement between 2000–2001 and 2005–2006 in the share of young people who had been bullied or in the share who had been in fights (although Britain's relative ranking improved on the latter item as the share rose in some other countries). In addition, although the percentage of young people who had been drunk fell, British youth still ranked at the bottom of the league table on this indicator.[81] Drinking and violence may involve only a minority of youth, but they appear to be deep-seated problems associated with British youth culture. Government policy has recently begun to tackle them in a more serious way, but we do not yet know how effective those efforts will be.[82]

Parallel analyses for the United States tell a different story (see table 6.7). In contrast to Britain, where children made gains on twelve of fourteen items, children in the United States made gains on only seven of the twelve items for which data are available (the United States did not ask questions about sexual intercourse or condom use), as their well-being relative to youth in peer countries stagnated on two items and worsened on three others. While Britain's average ranking rose five positions, from seventeenth to twelfth, the average ranking of the United States rose only two positions, from fifteenth to thirteenth.[83]

CONCLUSIONS

Comparing the effects of the British antipoverty reforms and the U.S. welfare and related reforms, we find some commonalities but also some notable differences. Common to both countries is a reduction in child poverty. In Britain, explicit targets were set, and although the relative poverty targets have not been met and overall income inequality has not been reduced, the child poverty reductions are nevertheless very impressive— child poverty has been cut in half in U.S. terms—and they have been accompanied by reductions in measures of material deprivation and hardship. In the United States, the reductions in child poverty have been smaller, and some families appear to have been left behind by the reforms and are possibly worse off or no better off than before.

These differences make sense given the differential treatment across the two countries of those who are not working. The work-focused U.S.

Table 6.7   **Change in the Well-Being of Young People in the United States Relative to Young People in Other OECD Countries, 2000–2001 and 2005–2006**

	2000–2001 Score and Rank		2005–2006 Score and Rank		Change in Rank
Eat fruit every day	28%	18/21	40%	8/21	(10)
In at least three fights in last year	12	12/21	10	6/21	(6)
Drunk at least twice	12	6/21	9	4/21	(2)
Above middle in life satisfaction	83	18/21	84	16/21	(2)
Ever used cannabis[a]	36	17/20	31	16/20	(1)
Eat breakfast every day	47	20/21	49	19/21	(1)
Bullied at least twice in past few months	12	14/21	12	13/21	(1)
Overweight according to BMI[b]	25	21/21	30	21/21	(0)
Health fair or poor	20	19/20	23	19/20	(0)
Agree that peers are kind and helpful	53	19/21	48	20/21	(–1)
Like school a lot	23	8/21	27	9/21	(–1)
Smoke cigarettes once a week	7	5/21	5	9/21	(–4)

Source: Author's compilation based on data from World Health Organization (2004b, 2008).
Notes: Score indicates the percentage of United States eleven-, thirteen-, and fifteen-year-olds who replied "yes" to a given item (unless otherwise indicated); ranking is the place of the United States among twenty-one OECD countries (unless otherwise indicated), with a ranking of 1 indicating the best-performing country and 21 the worst.
a. Indicates question was asked only of fifteen-year-olds.
b. Indicates question was asked only of thirteen- and fifteen-year-olds; data on sexual intercourse and condom usage were not available for the United States.

reforms provide little or no support to those who do not work, and this is reflected in the trends for those at the very bottom of the income distribution. In Britain, in contrast, benefits for those who do not work have been raised (along with benefits for those who do work), and this increase has provided a more generous floor for those at the bottom. These differing approaches reflect cultural differences across the two countries. The strong work requirements in the United States, which are applied even to mothers of infants, would not be acceptable in Britain, where mothers spend more hours on child care than in any other European Union country.[84] It is telling that Britain was extending its period of paid maternity leave at the same time that the United States was shortening the time that low-income mothers could stay home with a newborn.

Analyses of expenditure data, which shed further light on which families have seen gains and in particular on how those gains are being spent, point to more divergence across the two countries. In Britain, low-income families affected by the reforms are spending more money on items related to children and are more likely to own a car and a phone, goods that are essential if families are to be connected to friends, family, and work. In the United States, the story is different: the single-parent families who were the main target of the welfare reforms primarily spend more money on items related to employment, not on items for children. The U.S. results make sense given that parents had to go to work or increase their work effort if they were to increase their incomes subsequent to welfare reform, but these results are troubling if the intent of those reforms was to benefit children through increased expenditures on them.

When it comes to more direct evidence on the well-being of children, and specifically how the reforms have affected child health and development, a common challenge across both countries is the lack of large-scale, long-term studies of child health and development that could shed light on how the reforms have affected important domains of child well-being. At the end of a decade of reforms (longer in the United States), we still know relatively little about how children's health and development have been affected by these sweeping changes.

One clear conclusion that can be drawn from the British and U.S. experiences is how much outcomes for children are likely to vary depending on the type of reform selected. There is a logic to the results for these two countries—to a large extent, the results are what we would expect given the design of the reforms. Britain made an exceptional effort to improve the position of children in low-income families, and this is reflected in its success in reducing child poverty and material deprivation as well as in raising the expenditures of low-income families on child-focused and learning and enrichment items. The United States, in contrast, made an exceptional effort to increase employment among single mothers, even at the risk of leaving some who could not work without a source of safety net income, and it has been remarkably successful at attaining that goal: more single mothers are working, incomes are rising, and poverty rates are falling, but families are spending much of those income gains on work-related—rather than child-focused—investments, and some families have been left behind. We know less about actual health and developmental outcomes for children, but given these patterns of results, it seems fair to conjecture that low-income children and adolescents in Britain may have gained more in terms of health and development than did their low-income peers in the United States.

These conclusions are borne out by the data from Europe. While indicators of child well-being improved for young people in Britain relative to their peers in Europe, the same is not true for youth in the United States.

Moreover, the European data provide a useful lens through which to view the British poverty results. The European data help establish what is likely to be feasible in terms of poverty reduction, particularly if one uses a relative measure, which is affected by trends in inequality. These data also provide further proof of the success of the British reforms. Not only did Britain outperform the United States in reducing poverty on a U.S.-style absolute poverty measure, but it also appears to have outperformed its European peers in reducing poverty on a European-style relative measure.

Chapter 7

The Next Steps for Britain

A decade after Prime Minister Tony Blair declared war on child poverty in March 1999, ending child poverty continues to be an aspiration of the British government. What is the status of the antipoverty campaign? Who are the remaining poor children, and looking ahead, what further reforms might help move them out of poverty?

THE STATUS OF THE BRITISH ANTIPOVERTY CAMPAIGN

The British record of achievement in reducing child poverty over the past decade is both exhilarating and sobering. On the one hand, the British government's success in halving child poverty in absolute terms is truly an accomplishment to celebrate—and one for other countries to emulate. But on the other hand, Britain has failed to reach its target of halving child poverty in relative terms, although it has reduced relative poverty in a period when, judging from the evidence from peer European countries, it would otherwise have risen. Indeed, it is remarkable for the British to have made any progress in reducing relative poverty given that the economy continues to generate inequality—which, all else being equal, would increase relative poverty unless something offsets it.

Nevertheless, British reformers are keenly aware that, on both the absolute and relative measures, many British children continue to be poor. If Britain is to come close to its target of ending child poverty by 2020, a crucial question for British reformers—and those seeking to learn from their experience—is whether building on the past decade's efforts will be sufficient to end child poverty, or whether new strategies are needed.

It is important that, in thinking about this question, we take the political context into account. A national election must be held no later than May 2010, and as of late 2009 the Conservative Party was favored to win. Thus, in assessing the status of the British antipoverty campaign, it is important to take into account the views of both the Labour Party and the Conservative Party (as well as the third major party, the Liberal Democrats).

It is also important to take into account the fiscal challenges that will face whichever party is in office. Britain, like the United States, has been severely affected by the worldwide financial crisis and recession, and whoever is elected in 2010 will face hard choices when it comes to public spending, as well the challenges associated with increases in unemployment and underemployment. The coming decade will be a difficult one in which to combat child poverty, whether the goal is ending it or very substantially reducing it.

Yet both the Labour and Conservative Parties (and the smaller Liberal Democrat Party) say that they are committed to this goal. The Labour government has filed legislation enshrining this commitment in law, and Conservative (and Liberal Democrat) members of Parliament have spoken in favor of the goal, even though they have objected to some of the specifics of the legislation.

What types of policies are the two main parties proposing for the next decade? Although neither party has spelled out all the details of their proposals, some general principles have emerged.

The consensus within the Labour government is that, to make further progress on child poverty, new approaches are needed. In the words of a 2008 interdepartmental review: "To reach 2020 . . . means exploring innovative policy approaches for the next decade that address the fundamental causes of poverty and will have a long-term and sustainable impact."[1]

In part, this interest in new approaches is a reflection of changed public attitudes toward welfare and the poor.[2] When the Labour Party came into office in 1997, after nearly two decades of Conservative government, there was widespread public support for expanding the welfare state and providing more generous benefits for the poor. Over the next decade, as the Labour government expanded programs and made benefits more generous, these attitudes changed. From the vantage point of 2006 (the latest year for which public opinion data are available), there was less reason than there had been in 1997 to assert that the welfare state needed further expansion or that benefits were inadequate. At the same time, the increase in in-work supports and the strong labor market of the late 1990s and early 2000s made emphasizing employment a more viable option. Thus, it is perhaps not surprising that from 1997 to 2006 the share of the population endorsing the idea that government should increase taxes to spend more on health, education, and social benefits declined from 62 to 48 percent, while the share of the public saying that most of the unemployed could find a job if they really wanted one rose from 39 to 67 percent.[3] And while in the decade prior to 1997 a majority of respondents had consistently said that benefits for the unemployed were too low and caused hardship, and a minority said they were too high and discouraged work, these positions reversed after 1997.[4]

With regard to lone parents, the share of the public agreeing that benefits for this group should be raised remained relatively flat (at roughly one-third), but the share endorsing the conditionality of benefits increased.[5] Although data are not available for the full decade of reform, data from 2000 to 2003 show that the share of the public supporting sanctions if a lone mother did not attend her work-focused interview rose from 30 percent in 2000 to 41 percent in 2003.

Reflecting these changed attitudes, as well as a continuing belief that work is the best route out of poverty, Labour policymakers have moved to implement tougher work requirements for lone parents, a step that would have been unthinkable ten years earlier. Another indication of the sea change in the Labour government's stance on welfare, and public opinion toward welfare, was the statement in March 2007 by the minister for welfare reform that the government would "never" pay benefits high enough to lift people out of poverty. As Nicholas Timmins noted in the *Financial Times*, "A decade ago, such remarks from a Labour MP would have caused a riot. Today they are a measure of how far public attitudes to welfare have hardened."[6]

Even if attitudes had not changed, however, there would still be a case for updating the child poverty strategy. The measures that were successful in moving some families with children out of poverty in the first decade of the antipoverty campaign might not be as successful with the families who remain poor today. It might also be the case that some measures that were tried need to be altered or that there are promising new approaches that are worth trying.

Accordingly, since 2007 the government has been pursuing "child poverty pilots" that experiment with new approaches to fighting poverty. For instance, drawing on the example of the conditional cash transfer programs that have been implemented throughout Latin America (and are now being piloted in New York City), low-income families with children under age five are being offered a new child development grant (a one-time payment of £200), conditional on their visiting their local Children's Center and taking advantage of services such as child care. And, through child care pilots, some low-income parents are being offered free or low-cost child care before they begin work, in response to criticism by myself and others that requiring copayments from such parents is a barrier to work. Although cynics have suggested that the pilots are being offered because they are less costly than full-blown national initiatives, it is also true that they allow the government to try some new approaches and gather evidence about what works and for which populations.

The government has also been rethinking existing strategies. In 2008 it launched comprehensive reviews of all the major elements of its child poverty strategy—including tax credits and child care. It also initiated a review of definitions of poverty and, in particular, what it would mean to end child poverty. These steps all suggest a recognition that the strategy engaged in during the first ten years of the antipoverty initiative would not be adequate for the second and indicate an openness to exploring new approaches (such as the child poverty pilots).

Another new direction for the government is placing more emphasis on local area initiatives. Recognizing that much of the child poverty problem is in London—and indeed, in specific neighborhoods in London—the government has supported local areas in setting up their own local antipoverty strategies. Tower Hamlets, a traditional immigrant-receiving area in the East End of London, which is now predominantly Pakistani and Bangladeshi, has the highest child poverty rate in London and is one of the most deprived local areas in the country on a host of measures. Its child poverty strategy has four key principles—partnership, family and community engagement, localization, and tackling inequalities—and contains a host of specific steps designed to tackle child poverty in that community.[7] For example, to address the challenge of families not enrolling their children in child care, members of the partnership are exploring with families ways to support and strengthen family child care. They are also working to better connect families with the benefits, tax credits, and services to which they are entitled.

Whatever approaches are undertaken, they will require a commitment of government resources. As we have seen, the Labour government made a substantial investment in the antipoverty initiative in the first five years after Blair's pledge (from 1999 to 2004)—leading up to the first target in 2004—but then took its foot off the gas after that. Tax credit and benefit increases were maintained but not accelerated, which is what would have been required to make further progress on child poverty. More recently, measures announced in the 2007 and 2008 budgets commit new resources (£125 million over the next three years) to the antipoverty initiative.[8] These resources are projected to move an additional 500,000 to 600,000 children out of poverty (defined in relative terms).[9] If those projections are met, analysts from the independent Institute for Fiscal Studies predict that the child poverty rate (defined in relative terms) would fall from its level of 22.3 percent in 2006–2007 to 18.1 percent in 2010–2011.[10]

As mentioned earlier, it is possible that the direction of the next decade of antipoverty efforts will not be in the hands of the Labour Party. An election must be held no later than May 2010, and polls in late 2009 favored the Conservatives. In 2009, anticipating a possible change in government, the Labour government was filing legislation to enshrine some of their most important initiatives into law. For example they filed legislation to make Sure Start Children's Centers a legally recognized part of the infrastructure of children's services in local areas.

In another example, on June 11, 2009, the Labour government filed legislation committing future governments to the goal of ending child poverty. The Child Poverty Bill defines four measures of child poverty—relative poverty, absolute poverty, material deprivation, and persistent poverty—and sets targets for each. It also requires the government to announce and report on its child poverty strategy each year and to establish a child poverty commission to work with it on this. As Yvette Cooper, secretary of state for Work and Pensions, said at the bill's second reading on July 20, 2009: "We know that no law alone can end child poverty, but the Bill will help to hold the Government's feet to the flames in pursuit of a fairer Britain."[11]

However, if the Conservatives are elected in 2010, they will have a good deal of latitude to change other elements of the antipoverty program. Based on what Conservative Party spokespeople were saying in 2009, what can we expect?

Conservatives say that they too are committed to reducing child poverty. As Conservative member of Parliament Theresa May declared in the House of Commons debate about the Child Poverty Bill:

> Eradicating child poverty is an ambitious but important aspiration for any Government of this country. Not only is it an economic imperative, as no advanced economy can afford to waste the potential of so many of its citizens, more importantly it is a moral imperative, as no decent society should allow children to grow up in poverty. . . . Some 10 years ago, the Government made a commitment to eradicate child poverty by 2020. We can disagree about the approach that has been taken and the lack of progress that has been made, but we should all recognize the importance of setting out that ambition.[12]

Another Conservative member of Parliament, David Gauke, elaborated on May's remarks and made the connection between child poverty and social exclusion:

> We strongly share the aspiration to eradicate child poverty by 2020. . . . It is not good for any of us if a section of society is excluded from the benefits of what we hope will be a growing economy in the years ahead, stuck in a culture of low aspiration and dependency and attaining poor educational qualifications. All that results in a cycle of deprivation, and it becomes increasingly hard for any child born into poverty to escape it. This is bad for those in poverty and for society as a whole. For those reasons, we support the aspirations behind the Bill.[13]

Whether the Conservatives would put real resources into meeting this aspiration if in office is, of course, unknown. The Conservatives' statements of support in Parliament were greeted by skepticism not just by Labour Party members but also by Liberal Democrats. Liberal Democrat member of Parliament Steve Webb, who prior to entering Parliament had analyzed poverty data at the Institute for Fiscal Studies, did not mince words:

> Monitoring poverty under the previous Conservative Government during the 1980s and early 1990s was, over many years, a profoundly politicizing piece of work. We would update the figures each year . . . and find that year after year the level of child poverty would remorselessly grow. Some people did very well in the late 1980s but children in poverty did not. . . . This is a bill that could never have been brought forward by a Conservative Government because they stood by and watched as child poverty reached record levels. To hear Conservative[s] suggest that they even care about this subject, and that it would be some sort of priority, is frankly unbelievable.[14]

However, the Conservatives who lead the party today are not those who were in power in the Thatcher years. And today's more moderate Conservatives have certainly expressed their aspiration to end child poverty. Party leader David Cameron emphasized child poverty in his speech at the Conservative Party conference in October 2009.[15] He also affirmed his party's commitment to the approach that Blair and Brown had articulated a decade earlier—security for those who can not work, and work for those who can.

If the Conservatives do uphold their pledge to tackle child poverty, what measures might they pursue? Like their counterparts in the United States, British Conservatives stress measures to support marriage and the family as a way to strengthen families and build social capital. They have also indicated that they would like to see local organizations and charities play a larger role in the provision of services. And they have stressed increased school choice as a mechanism to improve the quality of schools and reduce inequality in education. As the Conservatives explained in their landmark *Breakthrough Britain* report in 2007, and as Cameron reiterated in his October 2009 Conservative Party conference speech, these measures are grounded in the belief that "people must take responsibility for their own choices but that government has a responsibility to help people make the right choices."[16] Cameron and other Conservatives also emphasize that poverty will not be solved by money alone and that policy must tackle what Conservatives see as social breakdown.[17]

With regard to the specific reforms introduced by Labour over the past decade, the Conservatives have been critical of the tax credits, which they argue undermine work incentives, since the amount of the credit is reduced sharply as earnings increase). As we saw in Chapter 3, the design of the system creates strong incentives for single mothers to move from welfare into work of at least 16 hours per week, but little incentive to increase work hours beyond those 16 hours. Cameron hammered this point home during his October 2009 Conservative Party conference speech:

> In Gordon Brown's Britain if you're a single mother with two kids earning £150 per week the withdrawal of benefits and the additional taxes mean that for every extra pound you earn, you keep just 4 p. What kind of incentive is that? Thirty years ago this party won an election fighting against 98 percent tax rates on the richest. Today I want us to show even more anger about 96 percent tax rates on the poorest.[18]

The Conservatives have also been critical of the overall complexity of the system. They propose to replace the more than fifty distinct benefit programs with just two basic programs—one for those out of work or on low wages, and the other for all low-income families.[19] They have been supportive, however, of other components of the reform package—in particular the child care subsidies, which in fact had built on programs begun under the previous Conservative government. They have also pledged to maintain or expand Sure Start and home visiting by health visitors, as well as to introduce some new approaches to support families in the all-important early years.[20] This was another point stressed by Cameron at the Conservative Party conference:

> But it's not just about money. It's also about emotional support, particularly in those fraught early years before children go to school. Labour understood this and we should acknowledge that. That's why Sure Start will stay, and we'll improve it. We will keep flexible working, and extend it. And we will not just keep but transform something that was there long before Sure Start began – health visitors.[21]

In addition, although the Conservatives have historically not been very enthusiastic about the minimum wage, voting against it in 1998 and filing legislation to allow employees to opt out of its coverage in 2009, Cameron cited it in his October 2009 speech as one of Labour's positive accomplishments and one that he intends to keep.[22]

Fundamental to any effort to further reduce child poverty (whether under a Labour or Conservative government) is the need to understand which children are poor and which specific factors place children at an elevated risk of poverty. In the next section, I present data on the current demographics of poverty; I then discuss the policies that I think Britain should adopt to address the challenges suggested by those demographics.

THE DEMOGRAPHICS OF POVERTY

Using the government's preferred relative definition of poverty—children in families with incomes below 60 percent of median income, before housing costs—what types of families do poor children live in?[23]

The surprising answer—given the strong links between parent worklessness and child poverty—is that half of poor children live in families where at least one parent is already working in the labor market (see table 7.1). Most of these—43 percent of all poor children—live in two-parent families where at least one parent is working (often full-time; see table 7.1), while a further 8 percent live in one-parent families where the parent is working (typically part-time). The large share of poor families with working parents reflects the fact that workless families, while at much higher risk of poverty, make up only a small share of all families with children. But it also reflects the fact that parental work, while it substantially reduces the risk of family poverty, is not always sufficient to move families with children above the poverty line. Thus, one implication of the demographics of child poverty is the need to do more to raise incomes in working families.

The next largest share of poor children—30 percent—live in one-parent families where the parent is not working. The presence of this large group is a key motivating factor in the government's decision to impose new work requirements on lone parents, as well as to offer more generous in-work benefits and child care support to provide incentives for them to work. Clearly, if child poverty is to be reduced, either more lone parents will have to be moved into work or incomes will have to be raised for nonworking one-parent families.

The remainder of poor children—19 percent—live in two-parent families where no parent is working. Poverty in these families is likely to be very challenging to address, since it is probably related to several cross-cutting factors, including parental disability and large family size.

How have the demographics of child poverty changed since 1997?[24] One striking change is in the distribution of poor children across working versus workless households. As shown in table 7.1, the proportion of poor children who live with working parents has risen (from 42 percent to 51 percent), while the share living with nonworking parents has fallen (from 58 percent to 49 percent). This change primarily reflects the fact that fewer children overall are living with nonworking parents as the strong economy and measures to promote work and make work pay have moved more parents into work. In 1996–1997, 21 percent of all British children lived in workless households, but this share had dropped to 16 percent by 2007–2008.

The reduction in worklessness is all the more impressive given the rise

Table 7.1   Distribution of Poor Children by Family Type, 1996–1997 and 2007–2008

	1996–1997	2007–2008
Living with working parents	42%	51%
Two parents, at least one working	37	43
At least one full-time	19	20
At least one part-time	8	11
Self-employed	10	12
One parent, working	5	8
Full-time	1	2
Part-time	4	6
Living with workless parents	58	49
Two parents, neither working	24	19
One parent, not working	34	30

Source: Author's compilation based on Department for Work and Pensions (2009a, table 4.3, 4.5).
Note: Poverty is defined in relative terms as income below 60 percent of contemporary median income, before housing costs.

in the number of children living with lone parents, who have the highest risk of worklessness. In 1996–1997, 21 percent of British children lived with lone parents, and this share had increased to 25 percent by 2006–2007. If the employment rate of lone parents had not increased over this period, the increasing share of children living with lone parents would have led to a rise in the share of children living in workless households and an increase in child poverty (see table 7.2).[25]

The declining share of poor children living in workless households also reflects the fact that the risk of poverty for children with nonworking par-

Table 7.2   The Effect of Changing Family Structure and Poverty Risk on Change in Poverty, 1996–1997 to 2006–2007

Child poverty rate in 1996–1997	27%	
Child poverty rate in 2006–2007	22	18.5% reduction
Child poverty rate in 2006–2007 if:		
Only family structure had changed	28	3.7% increase
Only poverty risk for lone parents had changed	24	11.1% reduction
Only poverty risk for couples had changed	25	7.4% reduction

Source: Author's calculations using data from Department for Work and Pensions (2008a).
Note: Poverty is defined in relative terms as income below 60 percent of contemporary median income, before housing costs.

ents has fallen. This is particularly the case for children living with non-working lone parents. Although these children still have the highest risk of poverty, that risk was lower in 2007–2008 than it had been a decade earlier (75 percent versus 86 percent).

To understand the composition of poor families with children and the measures that might be needed to further reduce child poverty, we also need to take into account several crosscutting factors that are associated with an elevated risk of poverty and are present across family types. The first of these crosscutting factors is parental disability. The poverty rate is considerably higher for children who have a parent with a disability (33 percent) compared to those who have no family member with a disability (20 percent).[26] Parental disability is a particularly important factor in non-working couple families, more than half of whom have one or more adults with a disability.[27] So the factors associated with parental disability need special attention if further progress toward ending child poverty is to be made. At a minimum, it would be useful to know what share of these disabled parents might be able to enter work or increase their earnings with additional treatment or support and what share are not able to increase their income from employment and may need further income supports if their children are not to be in poverty.[28]

A second factor that must be taken into account is family size. The risk of poverty is 33 percent for children in large families—families with three or more children—in contrast to only 18 percent for children in smaller families. This excess risk is lower than it was in 1996–1997, when children in large families faced a 42 percent risk of poverty (while children in smaller families faced a risk of 18 percent), but it is nevertheless still substantial. There are several reasons why large family size is linked with poverty—in particular, higher child care expenses and other costs—but there are also other factors that co-occur with large family size (for example, parental disability or immigrant status) and that themselves are associated with higher poverty risk. Understanding these co-occurring factors is important because simply providing additional benefits to families with more children, which is what some analysts have recommended, may not address the root causes of their poverty and might create incentives for families to have more children.

Measures to address child poverty must also take into account differences by race and ethnicity. Child poverty rates in Britain vary sharply by race and ethnic group. At highest risk of poverty—with a poverty rate of 58 percent—are children from Pakistani or Bangladeshi families. Black non-Caribbean and Chinese families also have elevated child poverty rates, at 34 percent and 31 percent, respectively, as do children in Indian, black Caribbean, or families of mixed race-ethnicity—with child poverty rates of 28, 25, and 25 percent, respectively—compared to the average of

20 percent for white British families.[29] These poverty rates are all lower than they were pre-reform, with the largest reductions in poverty for those groups with the highest rates of poverty.[30] Nevertheless, it is still true that there is a disproportionate risk of poverty for groups other than white British families.[31] The presence of such stark differences by race and ethnic group—in particular, the very high poverty rate among Pakistani and Bangladeshi families—suggests the need to take race and ethnicity into account in assessing the success of existing antipoverty policies and designing further policies.

Why are Pakistani and Bangladeshi children at such high risk of poverty? One reason is that very few of their mothers work in the labor market. Only 20 percent of Pakistani and Bangladeshi women are employed, compared to about 70 percent of white British women; this difference probably reflects different cultural norms and values about the appropriate role of women in the family and the labor market as well as the fact that some Pakistani and Bangladeshi mothers are relatively new immigrants and may not be confident of their English or their ability to work in the British labor market.[32] Efforts to reduce child poverty among Pakistani and Bangladeshi families will have to come to terms with these issues. If families are forgoing higher income in order to have mothers stay home with the children, or if these mothers are not in the labor market because their families do not think it appropriate for women to go out to work, then government efforts to move those mothers into employment may not be very successful. Conversely, if the issue is limited English-language or other skills, education and training programs could be very helpful.

A second factor is low earnings. Even among working families, Pakistanis and Bangladeshis are more likely to be poor because they are disproportionately likely to have low earnings, reflecting both lower hours of work and lower pay.[33] More than half of Pakistani and Bangladeshi families in poverty are headed by a couple but lack a full-time worker.[34] We know too little about whether workers in these families are working shorter hours because of ill health or disabilities or because of difficulties finding full-time work. Another one-third of Pakistani and Bangladeshi families in poverty have at least one full-time worker, but that worker's earnings are too low to raise the family out of poverty.[35] It is also not clear to what extent this low pay is due to low skills, concentration in low-paid occupations and industries, or discrimination in the labor market.

A third factor is large family size. As we saw earlier, large families have much higher rates of poverty than smaller families, and Pakistani and Bangladeshi families tend to be larger than the average white British family. In part, this greater size is due to higher numbers of children: more than 60 percent of Pakistani and Bangladeshi children live in families of three or more children, compared to only about 30 percent of white British children who live in families this large.[36] But in part it also reflects how frequently these families live in multigenerational households: one-third of Pakistani and Bangladeshi children live in households with three or more adults, in contrast to only 10 percent of white British children.[37]

A fourth, and related, factor is disability and ill health. Families with a disabled adult are at higher risk of poverty, as we saw earlier, and Pakistani and Bangladeshi families are more likely than low-income white British families to have a disabled family member or a family member in ill health (typically one of the parents or an elderly relative). Roughly 35 percent of Pakistani and Bangladeshi children have a household member who has a disability or is in ill health, compared to 18 percent of white British children.[38] This factor, combined with the other factors just discussed, means that on average a Bangladeshi or Pakistani family with children has about 0.5 workers per dependent in the home, in contrast to the average white British family with children, which has about 1.0 workers per dependent.[39]

An additional, and related, factor that is relevant for understanding poverty trends and the current composition of the child poverty population is immigration. Although the impact of immigration on poverty trends in Britain has received little attention and is not well understood, what is clear from the available statistics is that the number of children of immigrants increased very sharply over the ten-year period from 1996 to 2006 (a period that overlaps with the first decade of the antipoverty reforms). In 2006, 22 percent of all births in Britain were to a foreign-born mother, a 70 percent increase from the rate of 13 percent in 1996.[40] Over the same period, there was a 50 percent increase in the number of immigrant children between the ages of zero and fourteen entering the country, alongside a 100 percent increase in the number of immigrants in their childbearing years (in the age groups fifteen to twenty-four and twenty-five to forty-four).[41]

How the increased numbers of immigrant children affect poverty rates depends, of course, on which groups they come from. In the decade between 1996 and 2006, the largest increases in immigrant numbers were from the European Union (in particular, Poland), with a particularly sharp increase following the accession of Poland and other eastern European countries into the European Union in 2004.[42] The relative living conditions of these recent migrants from Poland and other parts of the European Union, and in particular the question of whether they have higher poverty rates than native families, have not been studied, although we do know that their wages are significantly lower than those of British-born workers.[43] Immigrant numbers also increased from India, Bangladesh and Sri Lanka, and Pakistan, groups that have higher-than-average poverty rates.

So the increase in numbers from these groups would have led, all else being equal, to increased poverty over the decade.

NEXT STEPS FOR BRITAIN

The British record over the past decade and the current demographics of child poverty point to five key challenges that must be addressed if Britain is to be successful in further reducing child poverty.[44] Here I recommend the measures I believe would be most effective in meeting those challenges.

Challenge 1: Doing More to Raise the Incomes of Working Families

With fully half of all poor children living in families in which at least one parent already works, doing more to raise the incomes of working families is essential if Britain is to reduce child poverty any further. What kinds of measures might be useful here?

One way to raise incomes is to increase the hours that parents work. Many of the families in this group are poor because, although there are two adults in the family, only one is working; in other cases, the family is poor because the adult or adults, although working, are working only part-time (see table 7.1). As we have seen, the policies put in place over the past decade, in common with earlier policies in Britain, have mainly focused on rewarding single mothers who work at least 16 hours per week, or couples where at least one parent works at least 30 hours per week. But the rewards to additional hours worked, for both family types, are negligible. As discussed earlier, this is a point that the Conservatives have stressed, and they have pledged, if elected, to reduce the high marginal tax rates facing low-income workers.

For both types of families, another key area of focus should be raising mothers' employment and hours through expansions in child care and other in-work supports. Mothers with young children do get some free child care but for the most part, the free places are only for 3 and 4 year olds, and these slots are provided only part-time and part-year. Support for other child care is in the form of child care subsidies. Although these child care subsidies were made more generous under New Labour, the policies still require a substantial copayment on the part of even the lowest-income mothers. (As of 2009, the subsidies covered no more than 80 percent of the costs of care.) Although the government has understandably been concerned about keeping some incentive for parents to shop around for the best value in child care, that incentive could be maintained with lower copayments. And there may be some groups for whom the

157

interest in promoting work is so strong that it is worth providing care with little or no copayment from the parent, at least on a transitional basis to move parents into work or into more hours of work. This strategy is what the government is trying in its child care pilot, but I think it should be rolled out much more broadly for the lowest-income families.

A second way to raise the incomes of working families is to increase hourly earnings. In the short run, the most direct way for the government to do that is to maintain and indeed raise the value of the minimum wage. The minimum wage sets an income floor at the bottom of the labor market and is particularly important in raising women's earnings at the bottom. Raising the minimum wage is popular with the public: 81 percent of respondents in a recent survey said that they think the minimum wage is too low.[45] It also saves on public expenditures, as the amount spent on tax credits and other benefits would be reduced.

In the longer run, measures to improve the skills and qualifications of low-skilled workers are needed if their hourly earnings are to improve. The Labour government has recognized this need; as Gordon Brown said in 2008:

> In future, the best welfare will no longer be the benefits you have today but the skills you gain for tomorrow. . . . We will combine tough sanctions for those who refuse to work or train with better or more targeted support for those most in need to give them the skills and advice they need to get back on the jobs ladder.[46]

But whoever is elected in 2010 will have to do more in this area, in spite of constrained public finances. It is important that the government not let up on its focus on narrowing achievement gaps and raising skills for those at the bottom of the distribution, from early childhood through the school years through adulthood. Training and education programs for adults, which have received less emphasis than other education programs to date, may be a particularly fruitful area for expansion. Well-designed programs not only can raise earnings for the adult trainees but also have benefits for their children in terms of improved success in school.

In addition to these measures to increase parents' labor market earnings, it is of course also possible to increase in-work subsidies (or reduce in-work taxes) to increase parents' net incomes. The reforms of the past decade have gone a long way toward increasing the rewards to work provided through the tax and benefit system, and at a minimum those supports should be maintained in the coming decade, although fiscal limitations may make it difficult to invest substantial new funds in increased tax credits or benefits. In allocating those funds, policymakers will face the familiar tension between narrowly targeting the benefits on those with the lowest incomes—which risks eroding work incentives if benefits are withdrawn too sharply (as discussed earlier) as well as reducing public support for the policies among those a bit higher up in the distribution—and spreading the limited amount available for benefits more evenly, which often generates more public support but at the risk of losing some of the antipoverty impact. This is a hard one to get right, but if reducing poverty is the focus, there is a case to be made for more narrowly targeting these benefits to the lowest-income workers. As Steve Webb pointed out in the House of Commons debate on the Child Poverty Bill: "We should be prioritizing within existing budgets: for example, rather than paying tax credits right up the income scale, we could reallocate some of the money to lower-income families. That would assist in meeting the child poverty goal."[47] This is a point on which there seems to be fairly widespread agreement in principle, although with some difference of opinion as to exactly which specific programs to target and how narrowly to do so. For instance, at the 2009 Conservative Party conference, Cameron announced that if elected, he would stop funding Child Trust Funds for middle- and higher-income families and instead target the funds to low-income families.[48] Analysts at the independent think tank IPPR, while endorsing the concept of greater targeting within universalism, specifically argued against stopping Child Trust Fund payments for middle-income families, although they did call for more targeting of that program as well as the universal child benefit.[49]

Challenge 2: Moving More Lone Parents into Work

Despite the quite substantial increases in lone-parent employment over the past decade, it is still the case that living with a nonworking lone parent is a major risk factor for poverty. Nearly one-third of poor children live with a lone parent who is not working; clearly measures to generate further increases in lone-parent employment are essential. As discussed earlier, the government has recognized this need, and the coming years will see a vastly changed set of rules for lone parents in the benefit system. These changes should move substantial numbers of lone parents into employment.

Expansions in child care and other in-work supports will be important here. Nonworking lone parents are one group for whom the state's interest in getting the children into child care and the mother into employment may be so compelling that providing child care free of charge to the parent—at least on a transitional basis—could well be warranted. At the very least, copayments for such parents should be reduced below their current levels. And the offer of a child care subsidy should not be contingent on the parent first being in work. Rather, the family should be supported in its efforts to find and use child care, with the expectation that the parent will then seek and enter employment (or training or education, if appropriate).

There may also be a need to rethink how the benefit system views short-hours jobs. The British work-related income supports are set up to kick in when adults work at least sixteen hours per week. But it may not be realistic to expect women who have little or no work experience to make an initial leap from nonwork to working sixteen or more hours per week. The British labor market does offer some shorter-hours jobs, but currently the welfare system does little to reward women for moving into them. A question for policymakers is whether it would make sense to experiment with programs to try to shift mothers who are not currently working into short-hours jobs, on at least a transitional basis.[50] This could be accomplished, for instance, by making families eligible for the Working Tax Credit even if mothers are working fewer than sixteen hours per week, or by allowing families on Income Support to keep more of their earnings as an incentive to increase their hours. Such changes might risk eroding incentives for mothers to work at sixteen or more hours per week, so the full effects would need to be carefully considered. But it is likely that, if properly implemented, policies that promote short-hours employment on a temporary basis could help women who are not working get a foothold in the labor market and start them on the road to longer-hours jobs in future.

Once lone parents are working, measures to boost their skills and incomes continue to be important if they are not to backslide onto welfare again or find themselves working but poor. With public finances tight, the minimum wage is likely to play a particularly important role here. As mentioned earlier, further education for low-skilled adults is an area that has received too little attention to date and could be fruitfully expanded.

Finally, an important issue for lone-parent families, and one that did not receive much attention in the past decade, is the role of child support payments from absent parents in supplementing family incomes. Child support is a potential "win-win" policy because it raises family incomes for vulnerable lone-parent families while also discouraging their formation.[51] While it is true that there are limits to how much support low-income fathers can pay, even a modestly increased amount of child support could go a long way toward improving the living standards of lone-mother families. It would also help in achieving the child poverty targets. The typical lone mother in poverty has income not very far below the relative poverty line, often a matter of £10 pounds per week or less. Thus, even a small amount of child support could play a crucial role in moving lone mothers out of relative poverty. Whoever takes office in May 2010 should conduct a review of child support policy to see what improvements might be possible. Such a review can draw on the wealth of evidence from the United States on child support reform, and in particular, on the experience of pioneering states such as Wisconsin.[52]

Challenge 3: Addressing Poverty in Workless Two-Parent Families

We know from the demographics of poverty that nearly one in five poor children lives in a married- or cohabiting-couple family in which neither adult works. We also know that roughly half of these nonworking families have at least one adult with a disability, while the remainder presumably face other types of barriers to work. To move adults in these families into employment will require new types of programs that engage directly with the adults. For those receiving benefits, the starting point should be a personal adviser who works with the client to identify the factors that are preventing work and to develop and deliver a plan for addressing them. This is precisely what Paul Gregg proposed in his 2008 report, and the government is moving in this direction. But there is a lot of work to be done to develop effective programs for the varied groups making up this sector of poor families.

It is worth emphasizing that child care is also important here. British policymakers tend to assume that when there are two adults in the home, one adult can provide child care while the other works. But if in half (or more) of these families one of the adults has a disability (or some other limiting condition, such as a substance abuse or mental health problem), it may not be realistic to expect one adult to work while the other cares for the children. Policies should assume instead that any family with children may need child care if parents are to work. And a low-income family should not be barred from receiving a child care subsidy solely because there is a nonworking parent in the home, particularly if one parent in the home is working.

Challenge 4: Addressing the Disproportionate Risk of Poverty in Particular Population Groups

Policy to date has not really come to terms with the racial and ethnic differences within the British population. The demographic data clearly shows that some groups are at much higher risk of poverty than others and that their higher poverty risk is probably related to differences in cultural values and norms. This is particularly true for Pakistani and Bangladeshi families, whose children have a risk of poverty of 58 percent—nearly three times the risk for white British children. As noted earlier, a major factor in the elevated risk of poverty for these children is the fact that the majority of their mothers do not work in the labor market. It is not clear that more of the same measures—more generous tax credits, child care subsidies, and so on—would induce these mothers to enter work. Rather, it is likely that their not working reflects cultural preferences and values, as well as possible barriers related to limited English and low skills.

If the government is serious about reducing poverty in Pakistani and Bangladeshi families, the starting point would be ethnographic research with these families to understand their views of work and family life and also their views about poverty and inequality. It may be that these families do not view themselves as poor, or that they see themselves as poor but consider that a price worth paying to be able to have the mother stay home, or that views on this question differ across families. It is also likely that views differ within families, so it would be important to interview mothers, fathers, and children.

As noted earlier, it is also the case that Pakistani and Bangladeshi adults who work have work hours and hourly wages that are lower than those of white British adults. This may be a reflection of low skills, in which case there would be a role for programs to raise skills and qualifications, or it may be due to poor health or disability, in which case there would be a role for efforts to better connect such families to health and other services for those with disabilities. The low levels of pay may also reflect segregation or discrimination in the labor market. This is an area where further research is needed. There is also a useful role for local pilot antipoverty programs, such as the one in the Tower Hamlets section of London.

Challenge 5: Reducing Child Poverty Given Underlying Trends in Income Inequality

An important challenge inherent in meeting the British goal of ending child poverty defined in relative terms is the difficulty of altering underlying trends in income inequality. In Britain, as in the United States, income inequality has been rising since the late 1970s owing to a complex set of factors, including technological change and trade, which are difficult for government policy to alter. Inequality rose more slowly under Blair and Brown than it did under Thatcher, but it did rise.[53] In the long run, the investments that Britain has made in children may reduce or at least rein in the growth in inequality to the extent that they are successful in raising the skills of those at the bottom and therefore closing skills gaps. But to date, as Nicholas Timmins of the *Financial Times* commented, "the net result of all Labour's hard running has been to achieve barely a standstill on inequality, even if poverty has been reduced."[54] This does not negate the British record on reducing absolute poverty and material deprivation, but it does raise sobering questions about what any government can do to counteract the trends toward greater underlying inequality and to reduce relative poverty.

It is to the credit of the British government that it engaged in 2008 in a review of measures to promote social mobility, by which is meant both the movement of the next generation into more and better jobs and the narrowing of gaps in opportunities between individuals of different family backgrounds to get those jobs.[55] This review resulted in a white paper, released in January 2009, that pledged a set of coordinated activities to improve skills in early childhood, the school years, the transition to higher education, and adulthood.[56] This is the kind of long-run vision that is needed if the government is to succeed in changing underlying trends in inequality.

Another way to counter trends in overall inequality is to intervene to hold down earnings or income at the top of the labor market. This is something the New Labour government was reluctant to do, but toward the end of the Brown administration in 2009, the government was beginning to talk about raising tax rates at the top of the income distribution (a step the Obama administration was also proposing in the United States). With the financial crisis, there was also talk in both countries about restraining top executive pay and bonuses. If implemented, such measures would go some way toward slowing the growth in underlying inequality by holding back the growth of incomes at the top.

But the trends in inequality, and the links between those trends and relative poverty, also raise questions about how the government should measure poverty and what targets it should hold itself accountable for. In Britain it is generally assumed that poverty should be measured mainly in relative terms, as it is in Europe. Although official British poverty statistics throughout the past decade have included a relative, absolute, and material deprivation measure, the relative measure is seen as the primary one. As Yvette Cooper, secretary of state for the Department for Work and Pensions, has explained:

> Our main child poverty target has always been a relative poverty target and it must stay so. It means that as society becomes more prosperous, all our children must share in that prosperity. As the incomes of better-off families grow, the poorest families must not get left further behind, because if they do their children will fall further behind—and not just today, but potentially for decades to come.[57]

Indeed, when the government sought input on improving poverty measurement in 2009, it floated the idea of dropping the absolute measure in favor of adding other relative measures—in particular, a measure of persistent poverty—because the absolute measure was becoming outdated. As I pointed out in my reply to that consultation, eliminating the absolute measure would be a serious mistake. The measure of absolute poverty may need to be updated to reflect rising incomes and living standards, but this is a separate issue from whether an absolute measure should be abandoned altogether. If the purpose of a poverty measure is to help assess whether public policies are improving the living standards of the lowest-income families, then an absolute measure is incredibly useful, as is a measure of material deprivation. The relative poverty measure, in contrast, measures how much *inequality* between those at the bottom and those at the median has changed, something that is harder for a government to control. So I think it makes sense to keep all three measures (or four, if one includes a measure of persistent poverty).

The view that an absolute measure is a centrally important one is, I must point out, at odds with British government thinking and is also at odds with the position of most British academics and analysts working on poverty issues, who tend to see the relative measure as primary. However, it may not be so far from the view of the British public. The British Social Attitudes Survey asked a nationally representative sample of respondents about their definition of poverty.[58] The results are telling. When asked, "Would you say someone was or was not in poverty if they had enough to buy the things they really needed, but not enough to buy the things that most people take for granted?" only 22 percent said that this person is in poverty. When the scenario was changed to "if they had enough to eat and live, but not enough to buy other things they needed," the share agreeing that this is poverty rose to 50 percent. When a third scenario is presented— "if they had not got enough to eat and live without getting into debt"— then nearly all respondents (89 percent) said that this is poverty. Thus, the working definition of poverty for most of the British public seems to be linked to the idea of absolute need.

This conclusion is reinforced by the findings from some recent qualitative interviews carried out by the National Center for Social Research as part of a project to better understand how respondents think about these types of poverty questions. Although the sample interviewed was small (twenty respondents), the results suggested that when asked about child poverty, what respondents have in mind is something closer to absolute poverty than to relative poverty: "The phrase 'to end child poverty' was understood in a consistent way by respondents to mean that children would have their needs met in terms of clothing, housing, food, education, and health."[59]

The qualitative interviews also revealed problems in using a relative definition of poverty. When the concept of relative poverty was introduced, respondents differed in how they interpreted this term. In particular, respondents differed as to which reference group they had in mind:

some thought about poor children relative to children in other countries, while others thought of children in the past, and yet others thought of other children in Britain today.

So, whatever poverty measures the government uses, work may be needed to communicate those definitions to the public and make sure that government and public definitions of poverty are more closely aligned than they are currently.

CONCLUSION

Ten years into Britain's war on child poverty, with solid progress made but more to be done, both major political parties are considering some new approaches to child poverty. I argue here that such new approaches should be grounded in an understanding of the current demographics of British child poverty. Those demographics suggest that whichever government comes into office in 2010, Labour or Conservative, should focus on three types of policies: policies to do more to raise incomes in working families; policies to move more lone parents into work; and policies to address poverty in workless two-parent families. In addition, whichever party carries the antipoverty policy forward will have to adapt its policies to address the disproportionate risk of poverty in particular population groups.

Finally, a key challenge for government will be to make further progress on child poverty given underlying trends in income inequality. I have argued that this issue has implications not just for antipoverty strategy but also for how poverty is defined and measured. The British government's three measures reflect different underlying constructs, all of which should be tracked, but they are distinct and should have distinct targets. Reducing relative poverty is a key aspiration, but in setting a target for this measure, it is important to take into account that relative poverty is affected by trends in inequality, over which government may have little control. Measures of absolute poverty and material deprivation, in contrast, provide a better gauge of the success of government efforts in raising living standards for the lowest-income families, and their targets should reflect this.

Chapter 8

Lessons for the United States and Other Countries

Britain's war on child poverty is relevant not only for Britain but also for other countries that, in spite of their overall wealth, still face child poverty. This is particularly true of the United States, where, in spite of progress in the 1990s, child poverty rates remain stubbornly high and indeed reached a ten-year high in 2009. Reflecting this stalled progress in reducing child poverty is a wave of attention to poverty in the United States in the past few years that is unlike anything seen since the War on Poverty of the 1960s.[1] As discussed in this chapter, the new U.S. antipoverty campaigns include local efforts led by mayors such as Michael Bloomberg in New York City, as well as national campaigns by groups such as the Center for American Progress. Reflecting this new wave of attention and echoing the British pledge, the U.S. House of Representatives passed a resolution in 2008 calling on the United States to cut poverty in half in ten years, a goal that Barack Obama endorsed during his presidential campaign.[2]

With the United States taking these kinds of steps toward what might be a new commitment to ending child poverty, this is an opportune moment to identify lessons from the British experience. Such lessons may also be relevant to reformers in other countries. Child poverty is on the agenda in Canada, Australia, and New Zealand, all of which have cited the antipoverty campaign in Britain as an example.[3] Members of the European Union—which, as we saw in chapter 6, experienced increases in poverty at the start of the twenty-first century—have also been renewing their focus on child poverty.[4] These countries too can learn from the British experience.

Of course, there are many differences between countries, and we cannot simply extrapolate from the experience of one country to another. In drawing out lessons from the British experience, we must be mindful of the specific context in that country and how it differs from other countries. However, just as lessons have been learned in the United States from welfare reforms in specific states (or indeed, in Canada), lessons can be drawn from the British reforms. We also have to be mindful of the current economic context: the world is still in the grips of a major economic down-turn. At the same time, however, the economic pressures make the need to identify and implement effective antipoverty policies all the more urgent.

THE START OF A NEW WAR ON POVERTY IN THE UNITED STATES AND OTHER COUNTRIES?

The closing years of the twentieth century and the start of the twenty-first century saw a resurgence of interest in tackling child poverty in the United States as well as in other advanced industrialized countries that, in spite of their wealth, still have substantial numbers of children living in poverty. Although none have gone as far as Britain in establishing a goal for reducing child poverty and committing resources to meet that goal, there are signs in the United States and other countries of heightened attention to the issue of child poverty.

In the United States, President Barack Obama was elected on a platform that stressed increasing supports for working families and middle-class families (which in the United States is a broad category that often includes the working poor), as well as increased investments in children. Like Tony Blair when he came into office in 1997, Obama leads a party that has been out of office for some time and that has a number of poverty-related initiatives it is eager to enact. Just prior to the election in 2008, Speaker of the House Nancy Pelosi convened a Children's Summit, which, like the reviews convened by the Treasury in Britain, was a forum for focusing the attention of legislators and policymakers on children and on programs that might address child poverty.

Obama took office in January 2009 in the midst of the worst economic downturn since the Great Depression. Several of the measures that he and Congress implemented to address that economic crisis have involved expanding programs (such as unemployment insurance and food stamps) that particularly benefit low-income families with children. Indeed, the stimulus package contained many of the anti-poverty policies that Maria Cancian and Sheldon Danziger called for in their 2009 volume, *Changing Poverty, Changing Policies*.[5] It increased the value of food stamp grants for non-working single mothers (and all other food stamp recipients) by nearly 15 percent, extended unemployment benefits and also raised unemployment benefit levels by $25 per week, and added $3 billion in funding for more generous EITC benefits for families with three or more children.[6] Arloc Sherman of the Center for Budget and Policy Priorities in Washington estimated that the stimulus funding would keep 6 million people, including 2.4 million children, out of poverty.[7] The Obama stimulus packages also included expanded funding for programs that serve low-income or at-risk children (such as Early Head Start and Head Start), as well as substantial increases in funding for education.

Nevertheless, even with the expanded spending on programs for children, the government has not been able to fully protect children from the impact of the economic downturn. Statistics released in August 2009 showed that child poverty in the United States had risen to a ten-year high, at 19 percent.[8] And new statistics on food insecurity, released in November 2009, showed that child hunger had risen to record levels as well.[9] This reversal of what had been a downward trend in child poverty (and associated hardships) in the 1990s is likely to provide a further impetus for attention to child poverty in the United States. At the same time, public spending constraints will put pressure on the government to identify and implement programs that use scarce government dollars effectively. With the downturn affecting the economies of other countries worldwide, attention to child poverty, and the need for effective programs to tackle child poverty, will be greater in other countries as well.

LESSONS FROM THE BRITISH EXPERIENCE

What lessons can the United States and other nations draw from the British experience over the past decade? The most important lesson is that *it is possible to make a sizable reduction in child poverty*. Britain may not succeed in ending child poverty in a generation, but it has made a very substantial reduction in child poverty, in particular if measured on a U.S.-style absolute poverty line (which, as I have argued, is the most appropriate way to assess the effect of government antipoverty policies).

Britain's efforts over the past decade provide a very clear message: where there is a serious public intention and effort to tackle child poverty, substantial reductions can in fact be achieved. If we think that there is nothing government can do to reduce child poverty, the British example clearly provides strong evidence to the contrary. Child poverty is not an intractable problem, nor are high child poverty rates an inevitable feature of our advanced industrialized economies.

A related lesson is that *it is not necessary to work out all the details of the policy in advance*. Stating a goal and setting a target—as Blair and Brown did in 1999—can mobilize government and drive the development of specific strategies. Targets, of course, are not a cure-all, and they do carry risks. They can be set so low that their achievement is meaningless, or so high that no one aspires to meet them. And once the deadline for a target passes, it can lose the attention of policymakers, who may be focused on other targets. So targets need to be chosen judiciously, and it is best to not have too many at the same time. But if chosen well and prioritized, targets can be a very effective way of mobilizing government. Just as President John Kennedy declared his intention to put a man on the moon (well before NASA knew how it was going to do that) and President Lyndon Johnson declared war on poverty (and then hired Sargent Shriver and a host of other advisers to figure out how to do this), a U.S. mayor, governor, or president could unleash a wealth of innovation by making a commitment to reduce or end child poverty.[10]

Mayor Bloomberg's antipoverty initiative in New York City provides a striking example of what an antipoverty campaign might look like in the U.S. context. His Commission on Economic Opportunity, led by Geoffrey Canada (the founder of the Harlem Children's Zone) and Richard Parsons (then-chairman of Time Warner), brought together individuals from various sectors to brainstorm on how the city could meet the mayor's goal of making a substantial reduction in poverty.[11] The work of the commission led to a plethora of innovative antipoverty reforms that are being implemented by a new agency, the New York City Center for Economic Opportunity.[12] For instance, to help low-income working families, New York City instituted a local child care tax credit and also implemented an innovative program to help eligible families claim the Earned Income Tax Credit without having to go through for-profit tax preparers. New York City also became the first city in the United States to conduct a trial of a conditional cash transfer program, similar to what has been implemented in many Latin American countries; the program, Opportunity NYC, provides cash rewards to children and families who meet program expectations in the areas of health, work, and education.[13] Not all the programs being tried in New York City will be successful, but some will be, and all are being evaluated, so there will be opportunities for other cities and jurisdictions to learn from the city's efforts.

At the national level, the work of the Center for American Progress Task Force on Poverty provides another example of what an antipoverty campaign in the U.S. context might look like.[14] Led by Angela Blackwell (the founder of PolicyLink) and Peter Edelman (professor of law at Georgetown University) and directed by Mark Greenberg (then at the Center for American Progress), this task force called for a national goal of cutting poverty in the United States in half in the next ten years as a step toward ending poverty in a generation, and it identified a set of twelve specific policies to achieve that goal. Since the report was issued in 2007, the goal of cutting poverty in half has been picked up and endorsed by several other groups. A national campaign called "Half in Ten" has been formed to advocate for cutting poverty in half in ten years, and a resolution endorsing this goal has been introduced — and passed — in Congress.

Recent efforts in Ontario, Canada, provide an example of what a

British-style antipoverty campaign might look like in that country. Drawing inspiration from the British reforms, as well as from reforms in other Canadian provinces and in New York City, the Ontario minister for children and youth services Deb Matthews released an ambitious antipoverty strategy in December 2008, setting a goal of reducing child poverty by 25 percent in the next five years and setting out the steps it would take to achieve that goal.[15] In 2009 the Ontario legislature passed the Poverty Reduction Act, enshrining that goal in law and committing the government to update its target every five years, to implement initiatives designed to improve the living conditions of the poor, and to collect data to monitor progress toward that target.[16] In common with the British strategy, the Ontario strategy stresses investments in programs for preschool-age children and school-age children, as well as measures to raise family incomes and help connect parents to employment.

Australia too has seen renewed interest in tackling child poverty. After Prime Minister Bob Hawke promised in 1987 that no child would be poor in Australia in 1990 and then failed to meet that target, Australian politicians have been wary of setting antipoverty targets.[17] In 2004, however, a Senate report reviewed the evidence on poverty and inequality in Australia and called on the federal government to develop a national poverty strategy.[18] It also called on the government to set up a poverty unit to coordinate the strategy, develop poverty reduction targets, and report back to the legislature on its progress. Testifying before the Senate committee, advocates cited the example of Britain's antipoverty campaign, as well as Ireland's national poverty strategy.

In New Zealand too there are indications of heightened attention to child poverty. A 2008 report produced by the Children's Commissioner, in collaboration with the Barnardo's charity, called on the government to establish a comprehensive plan to address child poverty in New Zealand.[19] Echoing the concerns that prompted the British war on child poverty, the New Zealand report noted that child poverty and inequality had risen steeply in the late 1980s and 1990s and called on the government to set an overall target of eliminating child poverty. And it called for a multipronged antipoverty strategy, including expanding investments in children in early childhood, providing more support for parents to work, and ensuring an adequate income for all families with children.

If the United States and other countries are to launch antipoverty campaigns, what other lessons can they draw from the British initiative? I would highlight three types of lessons. The first set has to do with the package of reforms that Britain enacted, the second involves the process of reform, and the third concerns the politics. In discussing each of these types of lessons, I pay particular attention to drawing out the implications for the United States where the most direct comparisons can be drawn.

The Package of Reforms

The specific package of reforms that Britain enacted offers several lessons. Like the United States under welfare reform, Britain emphasized reforms to promote work and make work pay—but in contrast to the United States, Britain also emphasized two other components: reforms to raise family incomes and investments in children. Although it is difficult to determine which specific elements of the reform package were the most consequential in reducing child poverty, it is likely that all three components played a role and that there were important synergies between them. As a recent review of European Union efforts to reduce child poverty concluded: "The more successful Member States seem to recognize that neither employment nor income support measures on their own are sufficient. The two need to go hand in hand."[20] A 2008 OECD report reached a similar conclusion, emphasizing that both employment and income support measures are needed.[21]

Given that the United States has gone about as far as it can go in terms of work-oriented welfare reform, and given that Britain drew on the U.S. reforms in designing its reforms to promote employment and make work pay, there are not many specific lessons for the United States to draw from this first leg of the reforms. However, I would suggest two.

First, it is worth noting that Britain, in implementing its national minimum wage, set it at a higher level than in the United States, and Britain has updated the minimum wage much more regularly ever since, through a process that ensures annual review and updating. The United States, which has allowed its minimum wage to decline to a lower level and has had a much patchier record of updating it, could usefully emulate this aspect of the British reforms. Sheldon Danziger, director of the National Poverty Center at the University of Michigan, has called for the minimum wage to be set at 45 percent of the median wage and indexed so that it moves with the median wage.[22] A more ambitious goal, drawing on the British example, would be to set the minimum wage at 50 percent of the median, again indexing it annually. So my specific recommendation: *The United States should set an appropriate level for the minimum wage—at 45 to 50 percent of the median wage—and ensure that it is updated annually*. Ideally, this should be done at the federal level, but since many states set their own minimum wages (at levels higher than the federal minimum), this could also be done at the state level.

Second, although Britain's Working Tax Credit is quite similar to the U.S. Earned Income Tax Credit, there is one key difference. The British tax credit is paid regularly to the family, unlike the U.S. credit, which is mainly received as a once-a-year, lump-sum payment. U.S. workers may choose an advance payment option, but few do so. It may be that receiving the payment as a lump sum acts as a form of enforced savings and allows families to make better use of the additional income. But it might be that families would be better off if they had the income available on a regular basis, as they do in Britain. A further consideration in the U.S. context is that many low-income families use the services of tax preparers to claim the EITC because it is linked to tax refunds, and they often pay fairly substantial fees to do so. Such fees would not apply if workers received the EITC through their employers. My recommendation: *The United States should experiment with programs to increase the take-up of the advanced payment option for the EITC, as well as additional programs to help families claim the credit without paying exorbitant fees to tax preparers.* Again, although ideally this should be done at the federal level, it could certainly be piloted at the state or even local level (as New York City's recent efforts to boost take-up of the EITC demonstrate).

There are further lessons the United States could learn from the other two legs of the British reforms. With regard to the measures to raise family incomes whether or not the parents are working, I would highlight the expansions of the universal or near-universal child benefits through the Child Benefit and Child Tax Credit programs. Although the United States has historically been reluctant to implement a universal child benefit, it has been willing in recent years to expand the reach and generosity of its child tax credit. However, an estimated 10 million poor children still receive only a partial credit or no credit because their families have no earnings, or earnings that are too low to qualify.[23] My recommendation: *The United States should make the federal child tax credit fully refundable so that it reaches all poor children.*

Another aspect of the British measures to raise family incomes worth highlighting is the targeting of extra benefits to families with the youngest children. As mentioned in chapter 1, one of the motivating factors for this targeting is that families with young children are at much higher risk of poverty than families with older children. There is also evidence from research—most of it carried out in the United States—that preschool-age children are more adversely affected by poverty than older children. Benefit increases in Britain were specifically targeted to families with the youngest children, and this strategy was successful in reducing poverty gaps between families with younger and older children.[24] Although not conclusive, the best available evidence suggests that raising incomes for families with young children would lead to more investments in items that are beneficial for children and could help to close gaps in school readiness between low-income children and their more affluent peers.[25] My recommendation: *The United States should give some consideration to targeting additional benefits to families with the youngest children.* Again, this is a reform that should be enacted at the federal level, but could be begun with initiatives at the state or local level.

With regard to the third leg, the investments in children, I would particularly highlight the expansions in early childhood programs and supports, including greater supports for families with newborns, more flexible work arrangements for families with young children, and the provision of universal preschool in the two years prior to school entry.

At the start of its reforms, Britain had one of the least generous maternity leave policies in Europe, and one of its first steps was to make that program more generous and to extend its duration. Britain also introduced paid paternity leave and the right for parents of young children to request part-time or flexible hours. Although these British programs have not yet been evaluated, a wealth of evidence from prior research supports the conclusion that such programs will yield benefits in child health and development.[26] The United States has a long way to go to catch up to Britain and other countries in terms of the support it provides to families with young children. My recommendation: *The United States should implement a period of paid parental leave to allow parents to stay home with their newborn. And the United States should enact a right for parents of young children to request part-time or flexible hours so that working parents with young children will be better able to balance their work and family responsibilities.* Ideally, these supports for families with young children would be enacted at the federal level, but the best prospects for passage may be in state legislatures. Several states have parental leave laws that are more generous than the federal Family and Medical Leave Act (FMLA), and three have recently enacted paid maternity leave.[27]

The British reforms also included the introduction of universal preschool for three- and four-year-olds. This is another area where Britain had lagged pre-reform, relative to peer countries, most of which already offered free and publicly funded universal preschool for children in the year or two prior to school entry. The British reforms have accomplished a sea change in attitudes towards preschool, as Naomi Eisenstadt, the original director of Sure Start has pointed out:

> We may argue about what works and what doesn't work in early years services but we don't argue about whether there should be an early years service. We don't have those arguments about whether the state should pay for universal provision for three- and four-year olds. That's no longer contested.[28]

The U.S. can certainly learn from this aspect of the reforms. A large body of evidence documents that high-quality preschool programs increase children's school readiness, with particularly large effects for the most-disadvantaged children.[29] Hence, expanding quality preschool programs can raise overall school readiness as well as close gaps between low-income children and their more-affluent peers. However, not all preschool programs are alike; the evidence suggests that higher-quality programs yield larger gains. Research in Britain, for example, strongly suggests that children learn more in preschool when they are in school- or center-based settings (as opposed to less formal types of child care settings) and when those programs are led by staff who have a university degree.[30] Yet, as I highlighted in my discussion of the reforms, some of the programs that British three- and four-year-olds attend are not formal school- or center-based programs, and relatively few are led by university-educated staff. In this regard, the British experience offers a cautionary note for the United States, which, like Britain, has a heavily privatized child care system and one in which the type and quality of provision is highly variable. If the United States follows the British example and provides subsidies that parents can take to a wide range of child care programs, the quality of that provision will vary widely, and the gains that have been seen from the best-quality preschool programs will not be realized. Fortunately, there are many other models to draw on, including the universal pre-kindergarten programs in the United States itself, which are now operating in several states, with programs located in the public schools or in approved preschool settings that meet standards set by the public schools. These universal pre-kindergarten programs have a strong track record of promoting children's school readiness and have been well received by parents, who view them as part of the public education system.[31] Thus my recommendation: *The United States should draw inspiration from how quickly and decisively Britain moved to universal preschool provision, but should draw on the best evidence on U.S. preschool and pre-kindergarten programs in deciding what type of provision to support.*

A similar caveat applies to drawing lessons from Britain's ambitious Sure Start program. Britain's decision to invest substantially increased resources in low-income families with infants and toddlers is certainly to be applauded. At a time when scientists were underscoring the importance of investments in the early years, British policymakers made the important observation that they were underinvesting in the early years, relative to the amounts they were investing in school-age children and adolescents. The Sure Start program was part of the British government's effort to redress this balance (another important part being the increases in benefits and tax credits for families with the youngest children). However, the British government's decision effectively to let areas design their own programs, within reasonably flexible, centrally specified program parameters (a minimal number of home visits shortly after birth and the offer of a preschool place at age three), is more open to question. Sure Start did lead to significant improvements for low-income children on about half of the outcomes measured. But in hindsight, the Sure Start programs might have had even more impact if they had included more intensive early home visiting as well as a stronger push to enroll children in formal child care, and perhaps at an earlier age; indeed, policy in Britain has since moved in these directions with pilots of the nurse family partnership home visiting programs for pregnant women and newborns, pilots of preschool for disadvantaged two-year-olds, and universal preschool for three- and four-year-olds. The United States has approached these goals from the opposite direction: there are many state and local early intervention programs for disadvantaged families with young children, but few operate on a large scale, and they have had little support or direction from the federal government until quite recently. My recommendation: *The United States should emulate Britain and direct more investments to the youngest disadvantaged children, but in doing so it should consider carefully the strongest empirical evidence as to which programs would most effectively improve child health and development for low-income children.*

For school-age children, there is potentially a good deal for the United States to learn from Britain's centrally led education reforms. Britain's education system differs from that of the United States in many respects—in particular, in having national standards and tests as well as a strong set of external inspectors. Although these components of the British education system cannot simply be imported and installed in the U.S. context, there may nevertheless be something for the United States to learn from the British example. I agree with Richard Rothstein of the Economic Policy Institute that the United States could usefully learn from the British inspection system.[32] The United States might also experiment with initiatives like the literacy and numeracy hours, which proved to be very cost-effective in the British setting. My recommendation: *The United States should consider whether some of the British reforms (in particular, curriculum initiatives such as the literacy hour and numeracy hour and accountability initiatives such as the inspection system) might work in the U.S. context.* Such initiatives could be tried at the state or local level, or they could be supported through programs created at the national level.

The Process of Reform

A second set of lessons has to do with the process of reform. Here I would highlight the role of evidence-based policymaking in Britain; the tension between implementing large-scale and comprehensive initiatives, on the one hand, and piloting and experimenting, on the other; and the importance of including work on how poverty is defined.

One of the most striking features of the British reforms was the extent to which they were grounded in evidence. The United States could learn from this aspect of the reforms. The British reform policies were for the most part carefully thought through and designed and based on the best available evidence. During my many meetings with civil servants and policymakers over the past decade, I was stunned at their detailed knowledge of—and keen interest in—the research on child poverty and antipoverty policies. Some of this attention to evidence reflects the heavy representation in the Treasury and in key departments of economists and other staff with research training, but some of it is also the result of the culture of public policymaking in Britain. Before a major policy decision can be taken, it is expected that the government will review the evidence and seek advice from experts and stakeholders, and it is also expected that in announcing a new policy, the government will cite the evidence and advice that informed that decision. The United States has been moving in the direction of giving more attention to evidence in policymaking, but it should take further steps in this direction. My specific recommendation: *The United States should emulate the British practice of writing or commissioning background papers to review the evidence before enacting major new social policies.* It is encouraging that the Obama administration is doing just this in deciding how to allocate funds under its new home-visiting initiative.[33]

When it came to implementing the reforms, policymakers in Britain faced the familiar tension between the desire to implement large-scale initiatives and the need for pilots and experiments to provide information about what works. In hindsight, some reforms were rolled out nationwide prematurely, depriving the government and researchers of the opportunity to learn from pilots or phased-in reforms and make adjustments as they went along. More piloting and experimentation would have yielded important insights that subsequently could have informed more sweeping policies. Ten years into its efforts, the government began a series of child poverty pilots to test out innovative new approaches to end child poverty. Such pilots might have been even more informative had they been undertaken at the start of the antipoverty effort.

A related point has to do with how many initiatives can be implemented at the same time. Although Britain is to be lauded for the scope of its efforts, it is also true that because its initiatives were so numerous and so wide-ranging, it was difficult for the government and the public to focus on any given one. One view is that the antipoverty strategy might have been more effective had the government focused on a few key priorities or initiatives rather than undertaking such sweeping reforms. Of course, identifying those key priorities is easier said than done—arguably, the reforms were a package, and all the pieces needed to be in place for any one element to succeed. And the sweeping reforms must be seen in context. When the Labour Party was elected in 1997, poverty and inequality had soared to record highs in Britain, and there was a strong sense among the public that government should do something to reduce them. It is hard to fault the government for launching a comprehensive assault on child poverty rather than testing out a series of small-scale reforms or targeting a few key policy areas. This is clearly a challenge that faces President Barack Obama as well. After eight years of a Republican presidency, many Democrats are impatient and display little tolerance for small-scale or incremental reforms, as has been evident in the debate that occurred in 2009 over extending health insurance coverage.

Another view is that the British government's reforms were not ambitious enough. The child poverty lobby has strongly criticized the government for not doing more to reduce child poverty. This view is shared by Steve Webb, Liberal Democrat member of Parliament:

> One of my greatest concerns is that an opportunity has been missed in the last 12 years. . . . If we could not achieve the goal when we had the political will and the money in the bank, when the public finances looked relatively good and the economy was growing . . . is it credible that we will accelerate progress . . . when the public finances are crippled?[34]

While I appreciate the points made by Webb (and the child poverty advocates), I think their assessment is too harsh. Britain may have missed its ten-year target of reducing relative child poverty, but it did meet its goal for reducing absolute poverty, which, as I argued earlier, is a more accurate measure of the success of government policies. The absolute child poverty measure is also the one most relevant to the United States, which uses an absolute measure. Moreover, during the periods when Britain did invest real resources (in particular, during the first five years of the reforms), it made substantial reductions in child poverty, whether measured in absolute or relative terms. And as we have seen, the reforms were in fact very large in scope and very wide-ranging. It is hard to fault the British for having done too little.

So what can we conclude about how these types of reforms should be implemented? The lesson I would draw from Britain's experience over the past decade is the following: *In tackling child poverty, it would be prudent to use a dual-track strategy, mounting comprehensive initiatives in key priority areas where the mandate for change and evidence about what works is strong, while at the same time piloting and experimenting in other areas where the support for change or the evidence base is weaker.*

A third crucial aspect of the process of the British reforms was its attention to how poverty is defined. The government realized early on that if it was to make a commitment to reduce and eventually end child poverty, it had to be very clear about how child poverty was defined and it also had to ensure that the definition was meaningful to relevant stakeholders. The review that the government conducted at the start of the reforms resulted in the establishment of three official definitions of poverty—including a new measure of material deprivation—as well as the development of a new national data set to measure poverty on an ongoing basis.[35] Definitions of poverty were reviewed again at the end of the decade of reform, and that review resulted in the establishment of a fourth official definition (persistent poverty) and the recommendation that a Child Poverty Commission be established to continue to work with the government on updating and refining the definitions on an ongoing basis.

The question of how to define poverty is, of course, very relevant to the United States. The United States has a poverty line that dates from the 1960s and has fallen considerably in value over time (its value today is roughly 35 percent of median income, in contrast to European poverty lines, which are set at 60 percent of median income). The U.S. poverty measure has been widely criticized. Several major flaws are often cited: it does not adequately take into account necessary family expenses, such as work-related expenses and medical out-of-pocket expenses; it does not reflect families' receipt of major government transfer programs, such as food stamps; and it does not adjust for differences in the cost of living across areas. A National Academy of Sciences panel reviewed the issues with the current measure and recommended an extensive set of changes in a report released in 1995, but as of 2009 these had yet to be implemented.[36]

If the United States is to move forward on an antipoverty agenda, revising the official poverty measure is essential. And the lesson from Britain is that such revision and updating may need to be ongoing. My recommendation: *The United States should revise its official poverty measure along the lines of what was recommended by the National Academy of Sciences, and it should set up a mechanism to renew and update that measure on an ongoing basis.*

The experience of New York City's antipoverty initiative is instructive here. Early on, the New York City reformers realized that if they were to undertake a serious antipoverty campaign, they would have to revise the poverty measure. Not only did the official measure not provide accurate information about how many, and which, individuals and families were poor, but it also was not able to capture the impact of many of the initiatives they intended to try out. For instance, since the official measure did not take child care costs or subsidies into account and did not include the EITC in calculating income, statistics based on it would not reflect the city's new child care tax credit or efforts to expand EITC receipt. Under the leadership of Mark Levitan, its director of poverty research, the New

York City Center for Economic Opportunity undertook the ambitious project of developing its own alternative poverty measure, along the lines of what had been recommended by the National Academy of Sciences panel.[37] The result has been informative not only for New York City, as it tracks the impact of its reforms, but also for other cities and states that are interested in developing similar measures.[38] And Levitan's work is now informing efforts at the national level to improve the official U.S. measure: legislation was filed in Congress in 2008 and 2009 to implement an alternative measure along the lines of what the National Academy of Sciences panel recommended—and New York City has developed.

The Politics of Reform

The politics of the British antipoverty campaign also offer some lessons for reformers in the United States and other countries. After the initial fanfare of the Blair announcement, the British government for the most part waged its war on poverty by stealth. Fearful of being viewed as Old Labour–style tax-and-spenders, New Labour kept fairly quiet about its antipoverty campaign, although it did publicize its welfare-to-work reforms as well as its campaigns against benefit fraud.

The welfare state analyst Tom Sefton, who has extensively studied public attitude data, argues that, as a result of this approach, a large share of the British public was not aware of the war on child poverty or of its successes.[39] Sefton also argues that the way the war on child poverty was presented led the public to develop tougher attitudes toward the poor.[40] He points out, for example, that the share of the public saying that most of the unemployed could find a job if they really wanted one rose from 39 percent in 1996 to 67 percent a decade later, while over the same period, support for increasing spending on social welfare programs fell.

However, some of this change in attitudes is likely to have been a consequence of the reforms. For example, given that benefits were made more generous, it makes sense that fewer of the public would now say that benefits are inadequate. And it is hard to know what to make of the data on public attitudes about poverty. Trend data show that the share of the public saying that there was a quite a lot of poverty in Britain declined from 71 percent in 1994 to 52 percent in 2006 (see table 8.1). This may reflect a hardening of attitudes, but it may also accurately reflect the fact that poverty rates did fall over the period.

The most recent evidence suggests that British attitudes toward welfare policy continue to be nuanced, as they were a decade ago. According to a survey of two large, nationally representative samples conducted by the Fabian Society for the Joseph Rowntree Foundation in late 2008 and early 2009, there continues to be strong public support for providing benefits

Table 8.1   Perceptions of Poverty in Britain, 1986 to 2006

	1986	1989	1994	2000	2003	2006
Respondents agreeing that there is:						
Quite a lot of poverty	55%	63%	71%	62%	55%	52%
Very little poverty	41	34	28	35	41	45
Don't know or refused	4	3	1	3	4	3

Source: Data from Taylor-Gooby and Martin (2008, table 11.3).
Note: Respondents were replying to the question: "Some people say there is very little real poverty in Britain today. Others say there is quite a lot. Which comes closest to your view? That there is very little real poverty in Britain, or that there is quite a lot?"

and other supports to those who are seen as fulfilling their obligation to society (by working or by caring for dependents); thus, there is strong support for raising the minimum wage and for increasing benefits for carers.[41] There is also strong support for expanding measures to reduce inequality in the early years (such as home visitors) as well as measures to reduce gaps in school achievement (such as higher pay for teachers in disadvantaged areas). This latter finding suggests support for an agenda framed around social mobility; the government is now focusing on such an agenda, and observers such as Lee Elliot Major of the Sutton Trust have argued that it should now be the "No. 1 social policy issue."[42]

Public support is less strong when it comes to providing benefits to those who are neither working nor caring for dependents. Because the public tends to overestimate the share of benefit recipients who are out of work or not caring for dependents, support for the welfare system is not as strong as it might be. As Labour member of Parliament Karen Buck noted during the debate on the Child Poverty Bill:

> [People] do not understand that half of all households in poverty contain at least one person who is in work. As long as we have a public assumption that poverty is associated with out of work benefit dependency, we will have our work cut out in winning public support for what needs to be done.[43]

If Labour had made a stronger case for its war on child poverty and more aggressively publicized its initiatives and successes, would it now be in a stronger position in the polls? It is hard to tell. It may be that after a decade of Labour government, voters would have tired of Labour in any case. And it is likely that other factors were more consequential in leading to the decline in the party's popularity. Britain's involvement in the war in Iraq was deeply unpopular and played a key role in the fall in public support for Tony Blair. In addition, a series of events in the fall of 2007—in particular, the government's waffling about whether to call an election, followed by the fall of a British bank, Northern Rock, and mishaps involving the loss of personal data by government agencies—seriously undermined the standing of Gordon Brown. Although Brown recovered a good deal of ground through his astute handling of the financial crisis in 2008 and his continuing global leadership on economic issues, his standing was harmed again by the scandal that erupted in the spring of 2009 over expenses claimed by members of Parliament. (Although the scandal involved members of both major political parties, public anger was directed more strongly at the Labour Party, since it had the majority at the time.) As of late 2009, Brown still lagged behind the Conservatives in the polls.

But even if the way the war on child poverty was promoted (or not promoted) did not play a major role in undermining support for the Labour Party, it does seem to have played a role in shaping attitudes toward poverty and antipoverty efforts. At the end of a decade of antipoverty efforts, the Labour government had to admit that "none of us has done a terribly good job at convincing the public of the need to tackle child poverty."[44] The lesson for reformers in the United States and other countries is clear: *Reformers must carefully nurture public support, making the case for tackling child poverty, framing the issue in a way that elicits rather than undermines public support, publicizing the actions they are taking, and also making sure the public knows when they have been successful.*

This aspect of the British experience may have implications for President Obama, who thus far has emphasized his efforts on behalf of working families and middle-class families while saying less about child poverty. Although much of what Obama is proposing (and has done already as of late 2009, particularly through the economic stimulus packages) will in fact benefit poor children, by not speaking out more forcefully on child poverty, is he losing an opportunity to build public support for efforts on behalf of poor children? The lesson from the British experience suggests that the answer is yes, in that the public may not support child poverty efforts unless the government actively makes a case for such efforts. But of course, other aspects of the U.S. context may be different. In particular, the United States has historically had much less public support for welfare and antipoverty programs than Britain and other peer countries, in part because of its tendency to view welfare and poverty issues in racialized terms.[45] So perhaps Obama is right to emphasize support for "working families" and "middle-class families," terms that evoke stronger public support than "poor families" or even "poor children." In addition, it is also important to acknowledge that, one year into his administration, President Obama has a full agenda of pressing domestic issues, such as the economy and health care reform, that are directly related to child poverty.

THE FIFTEEN LESSONS

So what lessons have we learned? I have discussed fifteen lessons in this chapter. First, there were two big-picture lessons that would be relevant to any advanced industrialized country trying to tackle child poverty:

1. It is possible to make a sizable reduction in child poverty.

2. It is not necessary to work out all the details of the strategy in advance.

Next, there were nine specific recommendations, based on aspects of the British reform package. These recommendations are made with the United States in mind, since the details of specific policies will clearly vary by country:

3. The United States should set an appropriate level for the minimum wage and ensure that it is updated annually.

4. The United States should experiment with programs to increase the take-up of the advanced payment option for the EITC, as well as additional programs to help families claim the credit without paying exorbitant fees to tax preparers.

5. The United States should make the child tax credit fully refundable so that it reaches all poor children.

6. The United States should explore ways to target additional benefits to families with the youngest children.

7. The United States should enact paid parental leave to allow parents to stay home with their newborn.

8. The United States should enact a right for parents of young children to request part-time or flexible hours to help working parents with young children better balance their work and family responsibilities.

9. The United States should emulate the British in moving quickly and decisively to universal preschool provision for three- and four-year-olds, but should draw on the best available evidence in deciding what type of provision to support.

10. The United States should emulate the British in directing more investments to the youngest disadvantaged children, but should consider carefully the strongest empirical evidence as to which programs would most effectively improve child health and development for low-income children.

11. The United States should consider what aspects of the British education reforms might be applicable in the U.S. context—in particular Britain's curriculum initiatives (such as the literacy and numeracy strategies) and accountability reforms (such as the reforms to the inspection system).

Next, there are three key lessons to be gleaned from the process of reform in Britain. These are developed specifically for the United States, but to a large extent they would apply to other countries undertaking antipoverty reforms as well:

12. To support evidence-based policymaking, it would be useful to emulate the British practice of writing or commissioning background papers to review the evidence before enacting major new social policies.

13. To address the tension between the need for large-scale initiatives and the useful role of smaller pilots, it would be prudent to use a dual-track strategy, mounting comprehensive initiatives in key priority areas where the mandate for change and evidence about what works is strong, while at the same time experimenting in areas where the support for change or the evidence base is weaker.

14. Having an appropriate and up-to-date measure of poverty is critical; to this end, the United States should revise its official poverty measure along the lines of what was recommended in 1995 by the National Academy of Sciences, and should set up a mechanism to review and update that measure on an ongoing basis.

Finally, the British case offers a cautionary tale with regard to the politics of reform, suggesting that:

15. Reformers must carefully nurture public support, making the case for tackling child poverty, framing the issue in a way that elicits rather than undermines support for the issue, publicizing the actions they are taking to do so, and also making sure the public knows when they have been successful.

CONCLUDING THOUGHTS

From the vantage point of the United States and other advanced industrialized countries that still face child poverty, there is much food for thought in the British case. Over the past decade, Britain has implemented not just ambitious reforms to promote work and make work pay—as the United States did under its welfare reforms—but also reforms to strengthen the non-work-based safety net for families with children while also boosting investments in programs and services for children. Although raising parental employment and earnings must be central to any antipoverty approach, the United States and other countries can learn a great deal from the other two legs of the British reforms.

As we have seen, Britain's reforms included a number of measures to raise family incomes whether or not the parents were working. Thus, when the worldwide recession hit and employment slowed in 2008 and 2009, Britain had a safety net in place that did not rely as heavily as the U.S. system on benefits tied to parental work. More generally as a result of these reforms, children are better buffered from the effects of their parents having reduced hours or periods out of work, whether because of a downturn in the economy or changes in family circumstances. Supporting family incomes—even if parents are not working—is costly, but it is also essential if child poverty is to be eliminated.

The investments in programs and services for children are also noteworthy. Increasingly, as inequality in the labor market has grown, attention within advanced industrialized countries has focused on the prospects for boosting social mobility so that children can have a future that is not determined by the income or occupation of their parents. If children from low-income families are to have more equal life chances, investments in proven early childhood programs and effective schools are critical. The British government is to be applauded for having made these investments.

Driving the British reforms is a remarkable commitment to end child poverty. This aspiration was first voiced by the Labour Party, when Tony Blair pledged in March 1999 to end child poverty and Gordon Brown then set specific targets to accomplish this, but is now widely shared by leaders across the political spectrum. It is my hope that this commitment and the policies it spurred will serve as an inspiration and a call to action for the United States and other countries to undertake their own war on poverty.

Appendices

APPENDIX 1: CHRONOLOGY OF THE BRITISH ANTIPOVERTY REFORMS, 1997 TO 2009

Key Dates for the Labour Party Government and the Antipoverty Initiative

May 1997 Labour Party elected; Tony Blair becomes prime minister, and Gordon Brown becomes chancellor of the Exchequer

March 1999 Blair delivers Beveridge speech, making a commitment to end child poverty in a generation

June 2001 Labour Party reelected; Blair continues as prime minister, and Brown as chancellor

May 2005 Labour Party reelected to a historic third term; Blair continues as prime minister, and Brown as chancellor

June 2007 Blair steps down after a decade in office; Brown becomes prime minister

March 2008 The government begins a review of its child poverty strategy with the publication of *Ending Child Poverty: Everybody's Business*

January 2009 Government consults with poverty experts on proposals for legislation on the child poverty target (*Ending Child Poverty: Making It Happen*)

Key Dates for Measures to Promote Work and Make Work Pay

July 1997 New Deal for Lone Parents (NDLP) is piloted in eight areas; Low Pay Commission is appointed

October 1998 NDLP is implemented nationwide; Family Credit rates for children ages zero to ten are raised

April 1999 National Minimum Wage is introduced

October 1999 Working Families Tax Credit (WFTC) replaces Family Credit (in place since 1988). New credit is more generous, particularly for children ages zero to ten, and includes a child care credit; pilot program combines Benefits Agency and Employment Service offices

April 2000 WFTC rates for children ages zero to ten are raised to eliminate differential with older children

April 2001 Rollout of work-focused interviews in NDLP

March 2002 Jobcentre Plus offices (combining Benefits and Employment) open; new Income Support (IS) claimants are required to attend work-focused interviews

April 2003 Working Tax Credit (WTC) replaces WFTC

October 2003 Pilot of Employment Retention and Advancement (ERA) program

April 2004 Requirement to participate in work-focused interviews is extended to IS claimants with children under age five; New Deal for Partners requires mandatory interviews for new and existing claimants

October 2004 Lone-parent IS claimants are required to come in for quarterly interviews

October 2005 Special child care assistance grant for lone parents starting work

October 2006 New Deal Plus for Lone Parents introduced

November 2006 Lisa Harker completes an independent report calling for measures to increase employment but also to reduce poverty among working parents and vulnerable groups

March 2007 David Freud completes an independent report calling for measures to increase the share of working parents; publication of *Working for Children*, which sets out the government strategy to tackle child poverty by getting more parents into work

July 2007 Publication of a green paper on welfare reform, *In Work, Better Off*, which proposes measures to get more parents into work, including a requirement that lone parents work when their youngest child reaches age eleven

December 2007 Publication of *Ready for Work: Full Employment in Our Generation*, which sets out the government strategy to provide more active support for employment

July 2008 A review of the tax credit system is announced

December 2008 Paul Gregg completes an independent report calling for the benefit system to provide personalized support for claimants to move into work; publication of a white paper on welfare reform, *Raising Expectations and Increasing Support: Reforming Welfare for the Future*, which sets out new expectations and supports to help welfare recipients move into work

Key Dates for Measures to Increase Financial Support for Families with Children

October 1997 Lone Parent Benefit is eliminated

April 1999 Sure Start Maternity Payment of £200 replaces £100 Maternity Payment; Child Benefit rate for the first child is raised 20 percent; IS rate for children ages zero to ten is raised

April 2000 Child Benefit rate is raised again

April 2001 Launching of Children's Tax Credit, which is worth up to £10 per week and paid to families on low incomes, regardless of whether the parents work (payment goes to the parent with the highest income)

April 2002 Sure Start Maternity Payment is raised to £500; Children's Tax Credit amount is doubled for children under age one

April 2003 Child Tax Credit replaces Children's Tax Credit, integrating benefits for children across programs and making payment to the parent who is the main carer; Maternity Allowance (paid maternity leave) extended from eighteen weeks to six months; two weeks of paid paternity leave for fathers is introduced

September 2003 Child Trust Funds are introduced, providing every child with a government-funded savings account of £250 at birth (£500 for children in the poorest one-third of families)

April 2004 Healthy Start program replaces Welfare Foods program

April 2007 Maternity Allowance is extended from six months to nine months

April 2008 Health in Pregnancy Grant is introduced

Key Dates for Investments in Children

May 1997 First national child care strategy is announced in the green paper, *Meeting the Childcare Challenge*

July 1998 Sure Start, with £540 million in funding over three years, is announced

September 1998 Universal, free, part-time early education for four-year-olds is introduced; National Literacy Strategy (piloted in 1996–1997 and 1997–1998) is rolled out nationwide

April 1999 First twenty-one Sure Start projects are announced

September 1999 Educational Maintenance Allowance is piloted

October 1999 Sixty-six trailblazer Sure Start projects are announced

December 1999 Right to parental leave (three months, unpaid) is introduced

July 2000 Sure Start funding is raised to £500 million to cover 500 local programs by 2003–2004 and to reach one-third of poor children

July 2002 Employment Act of 2002 provides six months of unpaid maternity leave (in addition to six months of paid maternity leave and two weeks of paid paternity leave) and introduces the right of parents with children under age six to request part-time or flexible work, effective April 2003; Education Act of 2002 gives local authorities extra powers in preparation for their provision of extended schools (providing child care from 8:00 AM to 6:00 PM)

October 2002 Extended schools are set up in twenty-five pathfinder local authorities

June 2003 First thirty-two Children's Centers, meant to serve as hubs for early education, child care, health, family support, and help into employment, are established; first minister for children is appointed

September 2003 *Every Child Matters* green paper is released; London Challenge (to improve secondary schools) is introduced

March 2004 £669 million in additional funding for Sure Start by 2007–2008, to fund 1,700 Children's Centers by 2008 (one each in 20 percent most-disadvantaged areas), is announced; pilot of free, part-time early education for 6,000 two-year-olds in disadvantaged areas is announced

April 2004 Universal, free, part-time early education is extended to three-year-olds

July 2004 Additional funding for Sure Start, to fund 2,500 Children's Centers by 2008, is announced; pilot of free, part-time early education for two-year-olds is extended to 12,000 locations

November 2004 Children's Act of 2004 assigns responsibility for inspecting child care and other children's programs to the Office for Standards in Education (Ofsted)

December 2004 Ten-year child care strategy (*Choice for Parents, the Best Start for Children: A Ten-Year Strategy for Childcare*), including a target of 3,500 Children's Centers by 2010, is announced

January 2005 188 Children's Centers are established; Sure Start programs start being folded into Children's Centers

March 2005 First national children's commissioner is appointed

July 2005 Extended schools prospectus is published, setting target of all schools to be extended schools by 2010

November 2005 Early results from National Evaluation of Sure Start (NESS) find few overall effects of the program and some adverse effects for disadvantaged groups

September 2006 Child Care Act of 2006 places new duties on local authorities, including duty to provide adequate child care for all working parents who want it; ten pilots of intensive home visiting for at-risk first-time mothers (modeled on the Nurse-Family Partnership) are announced; 1,000 Children's Centers (500 former Sure Start programs, 430 former Neighborhood Nurseries, and 70 former Early Excellence Centers) are in place

November 2006 £7 million in funding is announced for intensive home visiting pilots, to start April 2007

January 2007 Targeted youth support program begins (to be in place nationwide by 2008), and local authorities are required to ensure access to "positive activities" for young people (as set out in Education and Inspections Act 2006)

March 2007 Publication of *Every Parent Matters*, which sets out government policy on parents and parenting

November 2007 Review of how to extend the right to request part-time or flexible work to parents of older children

December 2007 Ten-year Children's Plan sets out government's plan to improve children and young people's lives

January 2008 Government announces intention to raise school-leaving age

March 2008 NESS releases new report, finding positive effects of Sure Start on seven of fourteen outcomes assessed

May 2008 Imelda Walsh completes an independent report calling for extension of the right to request flexible working to parents of older children

June 2008 National Challenge program (to improve secondary schools nationwide) is launched

January 2009 Publication of *Next Steps for Early Learning and Childcare: Building on the Ten-Year Strategy*, which sets out the next steps for the child care strategy; publication of white paper on social mobility, *New Opportunities: Fair Chances for the Future*

February 2009 Child Health Strategy is released

April 2009 Right to request flexible working is extended to parents of older children

APPENDIX 2: GAIN FROM WORK FOR A LONE-PARENT FAMILY WITH TWO CHILDREN UNDER AGE ELEVEN

	Gross Pay (1)	Tax and NIC (2)	Net Pay (3)	WFTC (or FC) (4)	CTC (5)	HB and CTB (6)
1998						
Sixteen hours per week	£52.00	—	£52.00	£73.50	—	£54.41
Thirty hours per week	108.00	£4.58	92.92	84.30	—	54.41
Forty hours per week	130.00	12.26	117.74	84.30	—	54.41
1999						
Sixteen hours per week	57.60	—	57.60	80.10	—	56.67
Thirty hours per week	108.00	4.20	103.80	91.15	—	56.67
Forty hours per week	144.00	12.89	131.11	91.15	—	56.24
2000						
Sixteen hours per week	60.00	—	60.00	139.35	—	20.48
Thirty hours per week	110.00	5.97	104.03	178.68	—	—
Forty hours per week	150.00	18.34	131.66	163.48	—	—
2001						
Sixteen hours per week	65.50	—	65.60	146.00	—	21.31
Thirty hours per week	123.00	3.30	119.70	179.36	—	—
Forty hours per week	164.00	10.58	153.43	147.16	—	—
2002						
Sixteen hours per week	67.20	—	67.20	150.40	—	20.48
Thirty hours per week	126.00	3.60	122.40	182.25	—	15.91
Forty hours per week	168.00	11.37	156.63	161.78	—	—
2003						
Sixteen hours per week	72.00	—	72.00	92.70	£65.73	36.71
Thirty hours per week	130.00	10.71	124.29	113.37	65.73	17.20
Forty hours per week	180.00	25.56	154.44	96.72	65.73	6.58
2004						
Sixteen hours per week	77.60	—	77.60	84.76	72.94	6.82
Thirty hours per week	145.50	13.10	132.40	124.24	72.94	—
Forty hours per week	194.00	29.60	164.40	105.74	72.94	—
2005						
Sixteen hours per week	80.80	—	80.80	96.58	75.46	45.29
Thirty hours per week	151.50	13.63	137.87	125.69	75.46	26.58
Forty hours per week	202.00	30.13	171.87	107.19	75.46	13.83
2006						
Sixteen hours per week	85.60	—	85.60	103.39	78.26	40.82
Thirty hours per week	160.50	15.87	144.63	134.21	78.26	18.50
Forty hours per week	214.00	32.37	181.63	115.71	78.26	5.83
2007						
Sixteen hours per week	88.32	—	88.32	105.45	81.13	42.51
Thirty hours per week	165.60	16.20	149.40	134.63	81.13	20.28
Forty hours per week	220.82	34.35	186.25	114.28	81.13	6.52
2008						
Sixteen hours per week	91.68	—	91.68	108.32	90.58	51.31
Thirty hours per week	172.00	17.94	154.06	144.18	90.58	15.49
Forty hours per week	230.00	36.54	193.46	120.78	90.58	2.93

Source: Author's compilation based on Department for Work and Pensions (2008e), *Tax Benefit Model Tables* (2001 to 2008); Department of Social Security (2000), *Tax Benefit Model Tables* (1998 to 2000).

Notes: (1) Gross weekly pay is calculated by multiplying hours per week by the applicable minimum wage rate (for that year); (2) tax and NIC combine income tax and national insurance contributions; (3) net weekly pay is gross pay minus tax and NIC; (4) Working Families Tax Credit (WFTC) includes child care payments for families using child care (FC refers to the Family Credit program, which preceded WFTC); (5) Child Tax Credit (CTC); (6) Housing Benefit (NB) and Council Tax Benefit (CTB); (7) Child Benefit (CB); (8) Council Tax (CT); (9) Child Care (CC) shows total child care costs (families working sixteen hours per week are assumed to have £50 per week in child care costs; families working thirty or forty

CB (7)	CT (8)	CC (9)	Net Income (10)	Income/ Poverty Line (11)	Income on IS (12)	IS/ Poverty Line (13)	Gain from Work (14)
£20.75	£9.40	£50.00	£161.41	100%	£147.82	91%	£13.59
20.75	9.40	100.00	163.73	101	147.82	91	15.91
20.75	9.40	100.00	188.55	116	147.82	91	40.73
24.00	10.10	50.00	181.67	106	159.09	93	22.58
24.00	10.10	100.00	189.62	111	159.09	93	30.53
24.00	11.10	100.00	216.40	127	159.09	93	57.31
25.00	11.10	50.00	208.73	119	172.34	98	36.39
25.00	11.10	100.00	221.61	126	172.34	98	49.27
25.00	11.10	100.00	234.06	134	172.34	98	61.72
25.85	11.40	50.00	223.21	119	187.30	100	35.91
25.85	11.10	100.00	224.91	120	187.30	100	27.61
25.85	11.10	100.00	252.34	134	187.30	100	65.04
26.30	12.60	50.00	244.25	122	195.07	98	49.18
26.30	12.50	100.00	248.91	124	195.07	98	53.84
26.30	11.10	100.00	250.70	125	195.07	98	55.63
26.80	13.40	50.00	257.34	124	207.52	100	49.82
26.80	13.40	100.00	260.79	126	207.52	100	53.27
26.80	13.40	100.00	263.67	127	207.52	100	56.15
27.55	14.60	50.00	242.62	112	201.69	93	40.93
27.55	14.60	100.00	270.08	125	201.69	93	68.39
27.55	14.60	100.00	283.58	131	201.69	93	81.89
28.40	15.40	50.00	289.53	129	208.97	93	80.56
28.40	15.40	100.00	307.00	137	208.97	93	98.03
28.40	15.40	100.00	309.75	138	208.97	93	100.78
29.15	16.50	50.00	299.88	115	215.19	83	84.69
29.15	16.50	100.00	317.41	122	215.91	83	101.50
29.15	16.50	100.00	323.24	124	215.91	83	107.33
30.20	17.10	50.00	310.71	115	242.71	90	68.00
30.20	17.10	100.00	328.74	121	242.71	90	86.03
30.20	17.10	100.00	331.68	122	242.71	90	88.97
31.35	17.00	50.00	337.59	119	259.34	92	78.25
31.35	17.00	100.00	348.04	123	259.34	92	88.70
31.35	17.00	100.00	353.45	125	259.34	92	94.11

hours per week are assumed to have £100 per week in child care costs); (10) net income is the sum of net pay plus WFTC plus CTC plus HB and CTB plus CB minus CT minus CC; (11) income/poverty line is net income as a percentage of the applicable relative poverty threshold (for that year; see appendix 5); (12) income on Income Support (IS) is the weekly amount a family would receive from Income Support (or other means-tested benefits) plus CB minus CT if the parent did not work or worked less than sixteen hours per week; (13) IS/poverty line is the ratio of the income from IS to the applicable relative poverty threshold (for that year); (14) gain from work is the weekly difference in net income from work and income that would be received from IS.

APPENDIX 3: GAIN FROM WORK FOR A COUPLE-PARENT FAMILY WITH TWO CHILDREN UNDER AGE ELEVEN

	Gross Pay (1)	Tax and NIC (2)	Net Pay (3)	WFTC (or FC) (4)	CTC (5)	HB and CTB (6)
1998						
Thirty hours per week	£97.50	£4.58	£92.92	£74.91	—	£21.37
Thirty hours per week	97.50	4.58	92.92	84.30	—	21.37
Sixty hours per week	195.00	34.36	160.64	45.10	—	3.03
1999						
Thirty hours per week	108.00	4.20	103.80	74.95	—	20.24
Thirty hours per week	108.00	4.20	103.80	91.15	—	20.24
Sixty hours per week	216.00	39.29	176.71	63.60	—	1.19
2000						
Thirty hours per week	110.00	5.97	104.03	108.68	—	4.87
Thirty hours per week	110.00	5.97	104.03	143.68	—	4.87
Sixty hours per week	220.00	40.74	179.26	137.30	—	—
2001						
Thirty hours per week	123.00	3.60	119.40	107.88	—	4.99
Thirty hours per week	123.00	3.60	119.40	142.88	—	4.99
Sixty hours per week	246.00	37.78	208.23	126.82	—	—
2002						
Thirty hours per week	126.00	3.70	122.30	111.76	—	7.21
Thirty hours per week	126.00	3.70	122.30	146.76	—	7.21
Sixty hours per week	252.00	36.97	215.03	131.87	—	—
2003						
Thirty hours per week	135.00	10.71	124.29	55.65	£65.73	9.57
Thirty hours per week	135.00	10.71	124.29	90.65	65.73	9.57
Sixty hours per week	270.00	55.26	214.74	75.70	65.73	—
2004						
Thirty hours per week	145.50	13.10	132.40	54.43	72.94	—
Thirty hours per week	145.50	13.10	132.40	89.43	72.94	—
Sixty hours per week	291.00	60.95	230.05	70.78	72.94	—
2005						
Thirty hours per week	151.50	14.13	137.38	55.33	75.46	9.68
Thirty hours per week	151.50	14.13	137.38	90.33	75.46	9.68
Sixty hours per week	303.00	63.13	239.87	70.38	75.46	—
2006						
Thirty hours per week	160.50	16.04	144.47	54.24	78.26	10.77
Thirty hours per week	160.50	16.04	144.47	94.24	78.26	10.77
Sixty hours per week	321.00	68.67	252.33	80.00	78.26	—
2007						
Thirty hours per week	165.60	16.40	149.20	54.84	81.13	15.02
Thirty hours per week	165.60	16.40	149.20	94.84	81.13	15.02
Sixty hours per week	331.20	70.65	260.55	80.00	75.14	—
2008						
Thirty hours per week	171.90	18.51	153.37	63.65	90.58	10.18
Thirty hours per week	171.90	18.51	153.37	103.65	90.58	10.18
Sixty hours per week	343.80	70.64	273.16	80.00	88.67	—

Source: See source information for appendix 2.

Notes: (1) Gross weekly pay is calculated by multiplying hours per week by the applicable minimum wage rate (for that year); (2) tax and NIC combines income tax and national insurance contributions; (3) net weekly pay is gross pay minus tax and NIC; (4) Working Families Tax Credit (WFTC) includes child care payments for families using child care (FC refers to the Family Credit program, which preceded WFTC); (5) Child Tax Credit (CTC); (6) Housing Benefit (NB) and Council Tax Benefit (CTB); (7) Child Benefit (CB); (8) Council Tax (CT); (9) Child Care (CC) shows total child care costs (for couple families working thirty hours per week, both no costs and £50 per week costs are modeled; families working sixty hours per

CB (7)	CT (8)	CC (9)	Net Income (10)	Income/ Poverty Line (11)	Income on IS (12)	IS/ Poverty Line (13)	Gain from Work (14)
£20.75	£12.60	—	£218.10	98%	£176.47	79%	£41.63
20.75	12.60	£50.00	177.49	80	176.47	79	1.02
20.75	12.60	100.00	137.67	62	176.47	79	−38.80
24.00	13.40	—	233.58	100	188.34	81	45.24
24.00	13.40	50.00	199.78	86	188.34	81	11.44
24.00	13.40	100.00	176.10	76	188.34	81	−12.24
25.00	14.50	—	253.08	105	202.09	84	50.99
25.00	14.50	50.00	238.08	99	202.09	84	35.99
25.00	14.50	100.00	252.06	105	202.09	84	49.97
25.85	15.50	—	268.46	104	217.50	85	50.96
25.85	15.50	50.00	253.46	99	217.50	85	35.96
25.85	15.50	100.00	271.95	106	217.50	85	54.45
26.30	16.40	—	277.47	102	227.21	83	50.26
26.30	16.40	50.00	262.47	96	227.21	83	35.26
26.30	16.40	100.00	283.09	104	227.21	83	55.88
26.80	17.90	—	290.93	103	238.62	84	52.31
26.80	17.90	50.00	275.93	98	238.62	84	37.31
26.80	17.90	100.00	291.87	103	238.62	84	53.25
27.55	19.50	—	294.87	100	233.55	79	61.32
27.55	19.50	50.00	279.87	95	233.55	79	46.32
27.55	19.50	100.00	309.37	105	233.55	79	75.82
28.40	20.90	—	313.74	103	240.92	79	72.82
28.40	20.90	50.00	298.74	98	240.92	79	57.82
28.40	20.90	100.00	321.61	105	240.92	79	80.69
29.15	22.20	—	323.84	98	247.84	75	76.00
29.15	22.20	50.00	313.84	95	247.84	75	66.00
29.15	22.20	100.00	341.91	103	247.84	75	94.07
30.20	25.00	—	335.60	97	276.36	80	59.24
30.20	25.00	50.00	325.60	94	276.36	80	49.24
30.20	25.00	100.00	351.09	101	276.36	80	74.73
31.35	24.80	—	355.67	99	293.79	81	61.88
31.35	24.80	50.00	345.67	96	293.79	81	51.88
31.35	24.80	100.00	379.73	105	293.79	81	85.94

week are assumed tohave £100 per week in child care costs); (10) net income is the sum of net pay plus WFTC plus CTC plus HB and CTB plus CB minus CT minus CC; (11) income/poverty line is net income as a percentage of the applicable relative poverty threshold (for that year; see appendix 5); (12) income on IS is the weekly amount a family would receive from Income Support (or other means-tested benefits) plus CB minus CT if the parent did not work or worked less than sixteen hours per week; (13) IS/poverty line is the ratio of the income from IS to the applicable relative poverty threshold (for that year); (14) gain from work is the weekly difference in net income from work and income that would be received from IS (or other means-tested benefits).

APPENDIX 4: GAIN FROM WORK FOR A COUPLE-PARENT FAMILY WITH THREE CHILDREN UNDER AGE FOURTEEN

	Gross Pay (1)	Tax and NIC (2)	Net Pay (3)	WFTC (or FC) (4)	CTC (5)	HB and CTB (6)
1998						
Thirty hours per week	£97.50	£4.58	£92.92	£95.36	—	£17.63
Thirty hours per week	97.50	4.58	92.92	104.75	—	17.63
Sixty hours per week	195.00	34.36	160.64	61.95	—	—
1999						
Thirty hours per week	108.00	4.20	103.80	95.85	—	16.33
Thirty hours per week	108.00	4.20	103.80	112.05	—	16.33
Sixty hours per week	216.00	39.29	176.71	66.40	—	1.19
2000						
Thirty hours per week	110.00	5.97	104.03	134.28	—	—
Thirty hours per week	110.00	5.97	104.03	169.28	—	—
Sixty hours per week	220.00	40.74	179.26	162.90	—	—
2001						
Thirty hours per week	123.00	3.60	119.40	133.88	—	0.82
Thirty hours per week	123.00	3.60	119.40	168.88	—	0.82
Sixty hours per week	246.00	37.78	208.23	152.82	—	—
2002						
Thirty hours per week	126.00	3.70	122.30	138.21	—	4.23
Thirty hours per week	126.00	3.70	122.30	173.21	—	4.23
Sixty hours per week	252.00	36.97	215.03	158.31	—	—
2003						
Thirty hours per week	135.00	10.71	124.29	55.65	£93.38	9.65
Thirty hours per week	135.00	10.71	124.29	90.65	93.38	9.65
Sixty hours per week	270.00	55.26	214.74	75.70	93.38	—
2004						
Thirty hours per week	145.50	13.10	132.40	54.43	104.16	—
Thirty hours per week	145.50	13.10	132.40	89.43	104.16	—
Sixty hours per week	291.00	60.95	230.05	70.78	104.16	—
2005						
Thirty hours per week	151.50	14.13	137.38	55.33	107.94	9.68
Thirty hours per week	151.50	14.13	137.38	90.33	107.94	9.68
Sixty hours per week	303.00	63.13	239.87	70.38	107.94	—
2006						
Thirty hours per week	160.50	16.04	144.47	54.24	112.14	10.77
Thirty hours per week	160.50	16.04	144.47	94.24	112.14	10.77
Sixty hours per week	321.00	68.67	252.33	80.00	107.36	—
2007						
Thirty hours per week	165.60	16.40	149.20	54.84	116.48	15.02
Thirty hours per week	165.60	16.40	149.20	94.84	116.48	15.02
Sixty hours per week	331.20	70.65	260.55	80.00	110.49	—
2008						
Thirty hours per week	171.90	18.53	153.37	63.65	130.62	10.18
Thirty hours per week	171.90	18.53	153.37	103.65	130.62	10.18
Sixty hours per week	343.80	70.64	273.16	80.00	128.71	—

Source: See source information for appendix 2.

Notes: (1) Gross weekly pay is calculated by multiplying hours per week by the applicable minimum wage rate (for that year); (2) tax and NIC combines income tax and national insurance contributions; (3) net weekly pay is gross pay minus tax and NIC; (4) Working Families Tax Credit (WFTC) includes child care payments for families using child care (FC refers to the Family Credit program, which preceded WFTC); (5) Child Tax Credit (CTC); (6) Housing Benefit (NB) and Council Tax Benefit (CTB); (7) Child Benefit (CB); (8) Council Tax (CT); (9) Child Care (CC) shows total child care costs (for families working thirty hours per week, both no costs and £50 per week are modeled; families working sixty hours per week

CB (7)	CT (8)	CC (9)	Net Income (10)	Income/ Poverty Line (11)	Income on IS (12)	IS/ Poverty Line (13)	Gain from Work (14)
£30.05	£12.60	—	£253.41	100%	£205.97	81%	£47.44
30.05	12.60	£50.00	212.80	84	205.97	81	6.83
30.05	12.60	100.00	170.09	67	205.97	81	−35.88
33.60	13.40	—	269.77	101	218.40	82	51.37
33.60	13.40	50.00	235.97	89	218.40	82	17.57
33.60	13.40	100.00	196.91	74	218.40	82	−21.49
35.00	14.50	—	293.81	107	232.73	85	61.08
35.00	14.50	50.00	278.81	102	232.73	85	46.08
35.00	14.50	100.00	297.66	109	232.73	85	64.93
36.20	15.50	—	311.00	106	253.14	86	57.86
36.20	15.50	50.00	296.00	101	253.14	86	42.86
36.20	15.50	100.00	317.95	109	253.14	86	64.81
36.85	16.40	—	322.04	104	264.98	85	57.06
36.85	16.40	50.00	307.04	99	264.98	85	42.06
36.85	16.40	100.00	330.64	106	264.98	85	65.66
37.55	17.90	—	340.16	105	281.40	87	58.76
37.55	17.90	50.00	325.16	101	281.40	87	43.76
37.55	17.90	100.00	341.02	106	281.40	87	59.62
38.60	19.50	—	348.69	104	248.93	74	99.76
38.60	19.50	50.00	333.69	100	248.93	74	84.76
36.20	15.50	100.00	362.69	112	248.93	74	113.76
39.80	20.90	—	369.02	106	256.69	74	112.33
39.80	20.90	50.00	354.02	101	256.69	74	97.33
39.80	20.90	100.00	376.89	108	256.69	74	120.20
40.85	22.20	—	381.12	102	263.92	70	117.20
40.85	22.20	50.00	371.12	98	263.92	70	107.20
40.85	22.20	100.00	399.19	106	263.92	70	135.27
42.30	25.00	—	395.15	100	328.45	83	66.70
42.30	25.00	50.00	385.15	98	328.45	83	56.70
42.30	25.00	100.00	410.64	104	328.45	83	82.19
43.90	24.80	—	420.81	102	351.34	85	69.47
43.90	24.80	50.00	410.81	100	351.34	85	59.47
43.90	24.80	100.00	444.87	108	351.34	85	93.53

are assumed to have £100 per week in costs); (10) net income is the sum of net pay plus WFTC plus CTC plus HB and CTB plus CB minus CT minus CC; (11) income/poverty line is net income as a percentage of the applicable relative poverty threshold (for that year; see appendix 5); (12) income on IS is the weekly amount a family would receive from Income Support (or other means-tested benefits) plus CB minus CT if the parent did not work or worked less than sixteen hours per week; (13) IS/poverty line is the ratio of the income from IS to the applicable relative poverty threshold (for that year); (14) gain from work is the weekly difference in net income from work and income that would be received from IS (or other means-tested benefits).

APPENDIX 5: RELATIVE POVERTY THRESHOLDS (60 PERCENT OF MEDIAN INCOME) FOR LONE-PARENT AND COUPLE FAMILIES WITH CHILDREN: BEFORE HOUSING COSTS

	1997	1998	1999	2000
Thresholds in nominal pounds				
Lone parent (two children)	£154	£162	£171	£175
Couple (two children)	211	222	233	240
Couple (three children)	241	253	266	274
Thresholds in 2007–2008 pounds				
Lone parent (two children)	216	222	227	227
Couple (two children)	300	305	310	320
Couple (three children)	342	348	353	364

Source: Author's compilation based on data from sources listed in notes.
Note: Thresholds are the amount of income a family of this type would need to have family income at 60 percent of median equivalized income for all families in that year. Values for thresholds in nominal pounds for families with two children between 2001 and 2008 are taken from Department for Work and Pensions, *Households Below Average Incomes* (2004, 2005, 2007a, 2008a, 2009a) and are then con-

APPENDIX 6: RELATIVE POVERTY THRESHOLDS (60 PERCENT OF MEDIAN INCOME) FOR LONE-PARENT AND COUPLE FAMILIES WITH CHILDREN: AFTER HOUSING COSTS

	1997	1998	1999	2000
Thresholds in nominal pounds				
Lone parent (two children)	£128	£135	£143	£150
Couple (two children)	176	185	196	206
Couple (three children)	201	211	223	235
Thresholds in 2007–2008 pounds				
Lone parent (two children)	182	185	189	196
Couple (two children)	250	254	260	271
Couple (three children)	285	290	296	309

Source: Author's compilation based on data from sources listed in notes.
Note: Thresholds are the amount of income a family of this type would need to have family income at 60 percent of median equivalized income for all families in that year. Values for thresholds in nominal pounds for families with two children between 2001 and 2008 are taken from Department for Works and Pensions, *Households Below Average Incomes* (2004, 2005, 2007a, 2008a, 2009a) and are then con-

2001	2002	2003	2004	2005	2006	2007	2008
£188	£200	£207	£216	£224	£260	£271	£283
257	273	283	294	306	332	346	361
293	311	323	335	349	378	394	412
239	254	257	259	260	279	282	283
327	346	351	353	355	357	360	361
373	394	400	402	405	407	410	412

verted to 2007–2008 pounds using the Retail Price Index. Values for thresholds for families with two children between 1997 and 2000 are provided in 2007–2008 pounds in Department for Works and Pensions (2009a) and are then deflated to nominal pounds using the Retail Price Index. Thresholds for couple families with three children were calculated using the OECD equivalence scale.

2001	2002	2003	2004	2005	2006	2007	2008
£156	£168	£175	£182	£186	£223	£231	£239
225	242	253	262	268	301	312	322
256	276	288	299	306	343	356	367
198	207	212	217	218	239	237	239
286	297	307	313	314	323	320	322
326	339	350	357	358	368	365	368

verted to 2007–2008 pounds using the Retail Price Index. Values for thresholds for families with two children between 1997 and 2000 are provided in 2007–2008 pounds in Department for Work and Pensions (2009a) and are then deflated to nominal pounds using the Retail Price Index. Thresholds for couple families with three children were calculated using the OECD equivalence scale.

Notes

INTRODUCTION

1. Blair (1999, 8–9).
2. Figures for Britain—taken from Brewer, Muriel, et al. (2009, tables 4.2 and 4.5)—consider income before housing costs are taken into account.
3. Clinton (1996, 66).
4. Figures for the United States from Dickens and Ellwood (2003a, table 4).
5. Haskey (1998).
6. Millar and Ridge (2001).
7. Blair (1999, 7).
8. The studies carried out by the Manpower Demonstration Research Corporation (MDRC) were particularly influential (see Gueron 2003).
9. Department for Work and Pensions (2007e).
10. Hills and Waldfogel (2004).
11. Gregg and Harkness (2003); Blundell, Brewer, and Shephard (2005); Francesconi and van der Klaauw (2007).
12. Hasluck, McKnight, and Elias (2000).
13. HM Treasury, Department for Work and Pensions, and Department for Children, Schools, and Families (2008).
14. HM Treasury (2001).
15. Waldfogel (2006a, 2006b).
16. Waldfogel (2006b).
17. Walsh (2008); Department for Children, Schools and Families, Department for Work and Pensions, HM Treasury, and Cabinet Office (2009).
18. HM Treasury (2002b).
19. Stannard and Huxley (2007).
20. Machin and McNally (2008b).
21. Lupton, Heath, and Salter (2009).
22. Emmerson, McNally, and Meghir (2005).
23. Cabinet Office (2009).
24. Cabinet Office (2009).
25. Department for Communities and Local Government (2007).
26. Hills (2003); see also HM Treasury (2002a).
27. Hills (2003, 157).
28. Estimate from Waldfogel (2007b).
29. According to Nicholas Timmins (2001), the windfall profits tax yielded £5.2 billion for Gordon Brown's first budget, in July 1997, which was allocated to

the New Deal employment program, spending on schools, and the start of the child care strategy.

30. See, for example, MacAskill and Bowcott (2001); Parker (2001).

31. As discussed earlier, Britain calculates its poverty measures both before and after taking housing costs into account. For simplicity, I use only the numbers before housing costs unless otherwise noted.

32. The reverse is also true. In fact, a common criticism of relative poverty rates by American scholars is that relative poverty can fall during a recession if the incomes of the median family falls more than the income of poor families.

33. Brewer, Muriel, et al. (2009).

34. Mike Brewer (2007, 2008) shows that while relative poverty was falling for families with children, it was rising for other groups not targeted by government policy over this period.

35. See Smeeding and Waldfogel (2010).

36. Vegeris and Perry (2003); Lyon, Barnes, and Sweiry (2006); Conolly and Kerr (2008).

37. See chapter 6 for details.

38. See Short and Shea (1995); Bauman (2003); Rogers and Ryan (2007); U.S. Bureau of the Census (2009b).

39. Commission for Economic Opportunity (2006); Center for Economic Opportunity (2009).

40. Commission for Economic Opportunity (2006); Center for Economic Opportunity (2009).

41. Center for American Progress (2007).

CHAPTER 1

1. This chapter draws extensively on Hills and Waldfogel (2004), who provide a detailed discussion of the background to the reforms.

2. Hills (2004, table 2.5).

3. Stewart and Hills (2005, figure 1.2).

4. In Britain, poverty statistics are calculated in two ways—before housing costs or after housing costs (that is, taking housing costs into account). Since housing costs are not usually factored into U.S. measures, I present statistics before housing costs unless otherwise noted.

5. If housing costs are subtracted from family income, child poverty rates are even higher (see Hills and Waldfogel 2004).

6. For instance, if poverty is defined as income below a fixed real line of 50 percent of mean income in 1996–1997 (the data refer to a period spanning the two years), the child poverty rate was lower in 1997–1998 than it had been in 1979 (24 percent versus 34 percent). These absolute child poverty rates are calculated using an absolute poverty line of 50 percent of mean income in

1996–1997, adjusted only for inflation; see Department for Work and Pensions (2003a, table H6).

7. Smeeding, Rainwater, and Burtless (2001, figure 5.1); see also Bradbury and Jantti (2001, table 2).

8. This is a lower poverty line than the half-of-average-income amount used in figures 1.1 and 1.2 because, unlike average income, the median is not pulled up by extremely high incomes.

9. The U.S. poverty line is commonly seen as not very generous. However, as John Hills and I explain (Hills and Waldfogel 2004), because U.S. incomes were so much higher than those in Britain in the mid-1990s, the U.S. poverty line translates, in purchasing power parity (PPP) terms, to a higher level than the absolute British measure referred to earlier, so somewhat more children fall below it.

10. Hills (1995).

11. See Gregg and Wadsworth (1996); see also Gregg, Hansen, and Wadsworth (1999).

12. Gregg, Hansen, and Wadsworth (1999).

13. Gregg, Hansen, and Wadsworth (1999).

14. National Statistics (2009b, table 3 [iii]). See also Alliance (2009).

15. Organisation for Economic Cooperation and Development (1998, tables 1.6 and 1.7).

16. Gregg, Hansen, and Wadsworth (1999).

17. Stewart and Swaffield (1997).

18. Haskey (1998).

19. Millar and Ridge (2001).

20. Hills and Waldfogel (2004).

21. U.S. Bureau of the Census (2009).

22. Department for Work and Pensions (2008d).

23. National Statistics (2004); Department for Work and Pensions (2009b).

24. *When Work Disappears* is the title of a book by the U.S. sociologist William Julius Wilson (1996), who argues that a host of disadvantages arise when work disappears from a community.

25. Social Exclusion Unit (2001b).

26. Centre for Analysis of Social Exclusion and HM Treasury (1999).

27. See, for example, Department for Social Security (1999a).

28. Social Exclusion Unit (2001a).

29. See, for instance, a key Treasury document, *Tackling Child Poverty and Extending Opportunity* (HM Treasury 1999a); see also *Tackling Child Poverty: Giving Every Child the Best Possible Start in Life* (HM Treasury 2001), which quotes a range of research evidence on the impact of child poverty on long-run outcomes.

30. Centre for Analysis of Social Exclusion and HM Treasury (1999).

31. Centre for Analysis of Social Exclusion and HM Treasury (1999, i).
32. Karoly et al. (1998); Waldfogel (1999); for evidence on Head Start, see Currie and Thomas (1995, 1999); Garces, Thomas, and Currie (2002).
33. Hills (2002).
34. Hills and Lelkes (1999, 3).
35. Hills and Lelkes (1999, 5).
36. Hills and Lelkes (1999).
37. Hills (2001, table 1.10).
38. For U.S. data, see Hayghe (1997); for British data, see Duffield (2002).
39. Organization for Economic Cooperation and Development (1997, table F).
40. Hills and Lelkes (1999); Hills (2002).
41. Blair (1999, 7).
42. Blair (1999, 7).
43. The major consultation documents were published in a volume edited by Robert Walker (1999a), who notes in his commentary that there are many points of agreement between these documents and the ideas in Blair's speech, but "none, however, proposes the policy goal of eradicating child poverty, let alone sets a date by which this should be achieved" (Walker 1999b, 153).
44. Atkinson (1998, 63).
45. Atkinson first presented this proposal in a lecture at the University of Glasgow in 1993; see Atkinson (1998).
46. Quoted in Atkinson (1998, 61).
47. Carey Oppenheim, personal communication, July 29, 2009.
48. Toynbee (2009).
49. In 1992 an overwhelming majority (83 percent) of the British electorate thought that the Labour Party would increase taxes and spend more, and only 43 percent felt that Labour's position was consistent with their own view. By 1997, with New Labour's pledge to stick to the Conservatives' spending limits, the share of the electorate believing that Labour would increase taxes and spend more, while still a majority, had declined (to 69 percent), while the share who felt that Labour's position was consistent with their own rose to 58 percent. By 2001 the majority view had shifted, with over half of the electorate saying that Labour would neither cut taxes nor spend more and with half the electorate saying that Labour's position on this was consistent with their own (see Sefton 2009, tables 11.1 and 11.4).
50. Bradshaw (2001); Deacon (2003); Stewart and Hills (2005).
51. Lisa Harker, personal communication, August 7, 2007.
52. Blair (1999, 8–9).
53. Quoted in Blair (1999, 10–11).
54. Brown, as quoted by Blair in his Beveridge Lecture; see Blair (1999, 9).
55. Brown, as quoted in Smith (1999, 204).

56. Giddens (1998, 2000).
57. Commission on Social Justice (1994).
58. Blair (1999, 12).
59. Blair (1999, 13).
60. Esping-Anderson (1990).
61. The second group identified by Esping-Anderson (1990), the Continental European countries (such as France, Germany, and Italy), are quite diverse but tend to follow a "corporatist" welfare state model, with both employers and the government playing an active role in social welfare provision; these countries also tend to have lower levels of income inequality than the Anglo-American group. The third group, the Nordic or Scandinavian countries (such as Denmark, Norway, and Sweden), are distinct in having the most active role for government in social welfare provision and in having the strongest commitment to reducing income inequality; this commitment is reflected in high progressive tax rates and low levels of wage inequality. There are, of course, some industrialized nations that do not fit into these groups— for instance, Asian countries such as Japan and South Korea; transition economies such as the Czech Republic, Poland, and Slovakia; and other newly industrializing countries, such as Mexico.
62. Michael Katz (1996) provides an overview of the Poor Laws and their influence on U.S. welfare policy, and Jose Harris (2007) provides an overview of the Poor Laws and their influence on British social policy.
63. See, for example, Katz (1996).
64. See, for example, Kamerman and Kahn (1991, 1995). An important exception is support for public education, an area in which the United States has led for many years (see Garfinkel, Smeeding, and Rainwater, forthcoming; Goldin and Katz 2008).
65. The social welfare expenditure data shown in table 1.1 include spending on social insurance (universal programs such as pensions and national health insurance) as well as social assistance (means-tested programs such as welfare). However, they do not include private social welfare expenditures (such as spending on health insurance by individuals and employers) or tax expenditures (such as the Earned Income Tax Credit, child care tax credits, and tax deductions for mortgage interest and property tax payments). If these expenditures were included, the American social welfare system would look larger (see Waldfogel 2008; Garfinkel, Smeeding, and Rainwater, forthcoming).
66. See Glennerster (2000).
67. There are many biographies of Beveridge and accounts of his reforms. Among the best are Jose Harris's 1977 biography (Harris 1977) and Nicholas Timmins's book, *The Five Giants* (2001).
68. Beveridge (1942).
69. Beveridge (1942).

70. See Glennerster (2000).
71. See discussion in Glennerster (2000).
72. See, for instance, Katz (1996, 2001).
73. Waldfogel (2008).

CHAPTER 2

1. The studies carried out by the Manpower Demonstration Research Corporation (MDRC) were particularly influential; for an overview of those studies, see Gueron (2003).
2. The British Social Attitudes Survey data for later years are not strictly comparable. But according to Geoff Dench (2009), a sizable share of British men and women were still expressing fairly traditional attitudes toward maternal employment as late as 2007. Most striking is the continued preference for mothers to be working part-time. For instance, that year fewer than one-third of men and women thought that a woman should work full-time after her youngest child starts school, while more than one-third of parents in couples thought that family life suffers if a mother works full-time.
3. Ekechuku (2003).
4. See, for instance, Ellwood (1998); Gais et al. (2001). The focus in Britain on personal advising had begun with the Job Seekers Allowance program, which replaced the traditional unemployment benefit program in 1996, but this focus was greatly increased under the New Deal.
5. This discussion follows the overview of the chronology of these reforms in HM Treasury (2004).
6. See, for example, Stewart and Swaffield (1997).
7. Department for Work and Pensions (2007a).
8. Quote from Harker (2006), as cited in Department for Work and Pensions (2007d, 20); see also DWP (2007b).
9. See, for example, Department for Work and Pensions (2006a, 2008b, 2008c).
10. Paul Gregg, personal communication, August 13, 2009.
11. Department for Work and Pensions (2007e, 6).
12. Data compiled by the author from 2000 and 2003 British Social Attitude Surveys (Economic and Social Data Service 2010a, 2010b).
13. HM Treasury (2000). EU data for 2005 showed that a higher share of women without children were working in Britain than in any other of the twenty-seven European countries, but this was not the case for women with children; as a result, there was a wider gap between mothers' and nonmothers' employment rates in Britain than in almost any other of the twenty-seven European countries—the exceptions being Germany, Ireland, Hungary, and Malta (see European Commission 2008).
14. Gregg (2008).

15. See Herr, Wagner, and Halpern (1996).

16. Low Pay Commission (1998). See also Department for Business Enterprise and Regulatory Reform (2007).

17. See chronology in Department for Business Enterprise and Regulatory Reform (2007).

18. In particular, the Low Pay Commission drew on studies reviewed in Fernie and Metcalf (1996), as well as on work by Dickens, Machin, and Manning (1994a, 1994b, 1994c).

19. See Card and Krueger (1994, 1995).

20. This discussion refers to the federally legislated minimum wage in effect in the United States. Individual states may set higher minimum wages (see Economic Policy Institute 2008).

21. See also estimates for 2005 by Graeme Cooke and Kayte Lawton (2008) from IPPR showing that a single minimum-wage earner supporting a couple family with two children would have to work almost eighty hours per week—or both parents would have to work about forty hours per week—to earn enough to move their family out of poverty through wages alone.

22. Author's calculations based on data on Strickland (1998).

23. Gregg, Waldfogel, and Washbrook (2006, figure 1).

24. See, for example, Ellwood (1988). The most significant expansions were enacted under the Omnibus Reconciliation Act of 1993, part of the Clinton administration's effort to promote work and make work pay. For families with two children, these expansions, implemented from 1994 to 1996, doubled the phase-in credit rate from 19.5 percent of earnings to 40 percent, increased the maximum credit from $1,511 to $3,556, and increased the phase-out credit rate from 14 percent to 21 percent. For families with one child, the expansions increased the phase-in credit rate from 18.5 percent to 34 percent, the maximum credit from $1,434 to $2,152, and the phase-out credit rate from 13 percent to 16 percent (for details, see Blank 2002, 2006; Hotz, Mullin, and Scholz 2006).

25. Blank and Card (2000).

26. Blank and Schmidt (2001); see also Blank (2002, 2006).

27. Blank and Schmidt (2001).

28. Danziger et al. (2002).

29. On the successful targeting, see, for example, Blank (2006) and Hotz et al. (2006). Studies of the employment effects include Eissa and Liebman (1996), Eissa and Nichols (2005), Grogger (2003), Hotz and Scholz (2003), Meyer and Rosenbaum (2000, 2001a, 2001b), and Neumark and Wascher (2007).

30. See Romich and Weisner (2000); Smeeding, Phillips, and O'Connor (2000); see also Barrow and McGranahan (2000); Gao, Kaushal, and Waldfogel (forthcoming).

31. HM Treasury (2002c).

32. For data on the number of recipients in 2009, see HM Revenue and Customs (2009); for data on the number of families with children, see National Statistics (2009c).
33. McKnight (2005).
34. Department for Work and Pensions (2007e).
35. See Hills and Waldfogel (2004).
36. Gregg and Harkness (2003).
37. Blundell, Brewer, and Shephard (2005); Francesconi and van der Klaauw (2007).
38. Hasluck, McKnight, and Elias (2000). Related evidence on the largest New Deal program—the New Deal for Young People—concluded that, between 1998 and 2001, it reduced the number of young people claiming unemployment by 35,000 to 40,000 and increased the number in employment by about 17,000 (see Blundell et al. 2003).
39. These studies are reviewed in Brewer, Ratcliffe, and Smith (2007) and Dickens and McKnight (2008).
40. Reflecting these differential employment effects, studies have found that the effects of the reforms on fertility and family formation varied by group. Thus, lone mothers affected by the reforms not only were more likely to work but also had fewer subsequent children and were less likely to marry (Francesconi and van der Klaauw 2007). For women in couples (the group for whom weak or no employment effects were found), in contrast, the reforms led to increased fertility, with the strongest effects for first births (Brewer, Ratcliffe, and Smith 2007); one study, however, also found an increased risk of divorce among women in low-income households between 1999 and 2002 (see Francesconi, Rainer, and van der Klaauw (2009). Thus, although Britain, like most of Europe, saw a big increase in the proportion of out-of-wedlock births over the decade, this increase probably reflects Europe-wide trends rather than the effect of the reforms. Data on Europe-wide trends show that the share of British births to nonmarried parents rose from 37 percent in 1997 to 44 percent in 2006, but they also show that this share rose even faster in other countries: in 1997 Britain ranked sixth-highest among thirty-three countries in the proportion of births to unmarried parents, but its position improved to ninth-highest of thirty-three in 2006 (see Eurostat 2008a).
41. Brewer, Clark, and Goodman (2003).
42. Department for Work and Pensions (2007e).
43. Shaw (2007).
44. Dickens and McKnight (2008).
45. Millar and Ridge (2001).
46. Department for Work and Pensions (2007a, 5).
47. Gordon Brown, in foreword to Department of Work and Pensions (2008d).

CHAPTER 3

1. HM Treasury (1999b, 35).
2. HM Treasury (2001, 15).
3. Quoted in Greener and Cracknell (1998, 13).
4. Studies include Korenman, Miller, and Sjaastad (1995); Duncan and Brooks-Gunn (1997); Dearing, McCartney, and Taylor (2001); Aughinbaugh and Gittleman (2003); Taylor, Dearing, and McCartney (2004); Berger, Paxson, and Waldfogel (2009).
5. See Mayer (1997).
6. See, for example, Blau (1999); Shea (2000).
7. The U.S. welfare-to-work reforms provide some experimental evidence but are difficult to interpret as purely income effects since they raised income along with employment. But see Morris and Gennetian (2003) and Morris, Duncan, and Rodriguez (2004), who take advantage of variation across the reforms to estimate instrumental variable models.
8. See, for example, Costello et al. (2003); Duyme, Dumaret, and Tomkiewicz (1999); Oreopoulos, Page, and Stevens (2005).
9. Morris and Gennetian (2003); Morris, Duncan, and Rodriguez (2004); see also review in Waldfogel (2006a).
10. See Dahl and Lochner (2008).
11. See Milligan and Stabile (2008).
12. HM Treasury (1999b).
13. One frequently cited study, in focusing on the shift in payment from the man's wallet (under Family Allowance) to the woman's purse (under Child Benefit), found that when benefits were paid to fathers, families spent more on men's clothing, whereas when benefits went to mothers, spending increased on women's and children's clothing; see Lundberg, Pollak, and Wales (1997).
14. For data on child benefit rates, see National Statistics (2009a).
15. Gregg, Waldfogel, and Washbrook (2006, figure 1 and appendix 1); see also Greener and Cracknell (1998).
16. HM Treasury (1999a).
17. HM Treasury (1999a, 35).
18. HM Treasury (1999b). See also HM Treasury (2002c).
19. HM Treasury (1999b).
20. HM Treasury (1999b, charts 3 and 4).
21. HM Treasury (2004, 33).
22. Statistics from HM Revenue and Customs (2009) show that 5.7 million families with children (2.3 million lone-parent families and 3.4 million couple families) received the CTC in 2009, out of a total of 7 million families overall; of these, 1.8 million received both the CTC and the WTC, while 3.9 million

received only the CTC (because they had no earnings or because their earnings were too high to quality for the WTC).

23. See HM Treasury (1999a).
24. See Harker and Kendall (2003); Waldfogel (2002, 2004).
25. See HM Treasury (1999b); Harker and Kendall (2003).
26. HM Treasury (2008).
27. HM Treasury (2001, 2009).
28. Sherraden (1991); Bennett et al. (2008).
29. For a more detailed discussion, see Waldfogel (2007a).
30. All statistics in this paragraph are from Women's Legal Defense and Education Fund (2009).
31. Total spending on Food Stamps was $30.4 billion in 2007 as compared to $31 billion in 1995, while total spending on WIC was $5.5 billion in 2007 versus $4.7 billion in 1995; all figures in constant 2007 dollars; see Scholz, Moffitt, and Cowan 2009.
32. David Harris, personal communication, September 13, 2009.
33. Ron Haskins, personal communication, September 25, 2009.
34. Expenditure data from Kaiser Family Foundation (2009a, 2009b); for enrollment data see U.S. Department of Health and Human Services (2009).
35. Swartz (2009).
36. Swartz (2009).
37. U.S. Department of Health and Human Services (2009).
38. Adam and Brewer 2004; Hills and Waldfogel (2004).
39. HM Treasury (2004).
40. Department for Work and Pensions (2006b).
41. HM Treasury, Department for Work and Pensions, and Department for Children, Schools, and Families (2008).

CHAPTER 4

1. For an overview of the U.S. war on poverty, see Danziger (2007).
2. Shonkoff and Phillips (2000).
3. See, for instance, Phillips, Crouse, and Ralph (1998).
4. Quote from Heckman and Lochner (2000, 78).
5. Quote from Heckman and Wax (2004, A14).
6. See Feinstein (2003).
7. See, for instance, Esping-Anderson (2005).
8. See Waldfogel (2006a, 2006b).
9. See Bainbridge et al. (2005).
10. Stratford, Finch, and Pethick (1997).
11. See Waldfogel and Garnham (2008).
12. Kazimirski et al. (2008).
13. Childcare use statistics from Kazimirski et al. (2008). See also Bell et al. (2005).

14. See review in Waldfogel (2002, 2004).
15. See review in Waldfogel (2002, 2004).
16. See Waldfogel (2006b).
17. See Waldfogel (2001).
18. See Ruhm (2000); Tanaka (2005).
19. See Berger, Hill, and Waldfogel (2005); Chatterji and Markowitz (2004).
20. See Waldfogel (2006a).
21. See Walsh (2008); Department for Children, Schools, and Families, Department for Work and Pensions, HM Treasury, and Cabinet Office (2009).
22. For an overview of the process leading up to Sure Start, see Glass (1999).
23. Belsky, Barnes, and Melhuish (2007). Although there was some discussion of randomly assigning poor areas to receive Sure Start (so that the program could be experimentally evaluated), the decision was made to roll the program out starting with the poorest areas, where the need for the program was presumably the greatest. This decision made it difficult later for evaluators to identify a control group, as we shall see later in the chapter.
24. For more detailed descriptions of Sure Start, see Anning and Ball (2008); Belsky, Barnes, and Melhuish (2007).
25. See Glass (2005).
26. Glass (2005, 2).
27. Stewart (2009a, 67).
28. The Ten-Year Child Care Strategy, published in 2004, was co-authored by HM Treasury, the Department for Education and Skills, the Department for Work and Pensions, and the Department for Trade and Industry. For a review of the evidence leading up to the strategy, see Waldfogel (2004); see also Alakeson (2004) and Esping-Anderson (2005).
29. For more details, see Waldfogel (2004).
30. The extension to fifteen hours per week was made available first to the most-deprived children in each local authority. It will be a universal entitlement starting in September 2010.
31. Hodge (2005, 1).
32. Department for Children, Schools, and Families (2009f).
33. For a report on the EPPE research, see Sammons et al. (2002, 2003); for a summary of funding for the Graduate Leader Fund, see Department of Children, Schools, and Families (2009f).
34. Department for Children, Schools, and Families, Department for Work and Pensions, HM Treasury, and Cabinet Office (2009).
35. See National Evaluation of Sure Start (2005).
36. These issues are discussed at length in Belsky, Barnes, and Melhuish (2007); see in particular the foreword by Naomi Eisenstadt (2007).
37. See Barnes et al. (2008).
38. See National Evaluation of Sure Start (2008).
39. See Power (2007).

40. Merrell, Tymms, and Jones (2007). See also Frean (2007).
41. The most recent release of Foundation Stage results at this writing is Department for Children, Schools, and Families (2008a). For more detailed data on children's scores in 2007–2008, see Department for Children, Schools, and Families (2009e).
42. Beginning in 2006, the government reported the share of children working at the expected level in both social and emotional development and communication, language, and literacy, for the country as a whole as well as for children in the 30 percent most deprived areas and in more affluent areas (see DCSF 2008a). These figures were 44, 33, and 50 percent respectively in 2006 and rose to 49, 38, and 54 percent respectively in 2008. Thus, it appears that children overall are making some progress in the Foundation Stage and that progress may be slightly faster for children in the more deprived areas than the others (a 5 percentage point gain over the two year period, as compared to a 4 percentage point gain in the more affluent areas). But we do not know what children's performance on these kinds of measures was in the 1990s.
43. Cabinet Office (2009, 6).
44. Waldfogel and Garnham (2008). See also Stanley, Bellamy, and Cooke (2006); Butt et al. (2007); and Stewart (2009a).

CHAPTER 5

1. Quoted by BBC News (2007b).
2. Tony Blair, speech to Labour Party conference, October 1, 1996, as quoted in MacAskill (1996). It is not clear which education results Blair was referring to. In the math tests administered in 1995 to seventh- and eighth-graders by the Third International Math and Science Study (TIMSS), England ranked twenty-fifth, a poor showing, but not thirty-fifth (see TIMSS International Study Center 2007).
3. An explosion of studies by labor economists in the 1990s documented the role that educational differentials were playing in the growth in inequality; see, for example, Machin (1999). Stephen Machin and Anna Vignoles (2005) and Claudia Goldin and Lawrence Katz (2008) provide excellent current overviews of this research.
4. Glennerster (2001).
5. Coughlan (2007).
6. Cabinet Office (2009).
7. Cabinet Office (2009).
8. Coughlan (2007).
9. Coughlan (2007).
10. For an overview of the National Literacy Strategy, see Stannard and Huxley (2007).
11. See Machin and McNally (2004, 2005, 2008a, and 2008b).

12. See Machin and McNally (2008b).
13. For an extensive discussion of both the literacy and numeracy strategies, see Barber (2007).
14. See parent interviews in Power (2007).
15. See discussion in Lupton, Heath, and Salter (2009).
16. See Department for Education and Employment (1999).
17. Machin (2003). For data on how British enrollment rates compared to those in other countries, see National Statistics (1996).
18. For a detailed description of the EMA, see Emmerson, McNally, and Meghir (2005).
19. See Emmerson, McNally, and Meghir (2005).
20. The later evaluation (using administrative data) found slightly (but not significantly) smaller effects on participation, but also documented positive effects on educational attainment; see Chowdry, Dearden, and Emmerson (2007).
21. Department for Children, Schools, and Families (2009g).
22. Department for Education and Skills (2005).
23. Cabinet Office (2009).
24. For details, see Lupton, Heath, and Salter (2009).
25. See Glennerster (2001).
26. Cabinet Office (2009).
27. See Glennerster (2001).
28. See Lipsett (2008); Frean (2009); Department for Children, Schools, and Families (2009a). A set of papers in a special issue of the *Oxford Review of Education* offers a generally negative perspective on Blair's educational legacy, but as Geoff Whitty (2009), director of the Institute of Education at the University of London, points out, these papers stress the failings and neglect some positive achievements (for a twenty-year perspective, see Whitty 2008). Ruth Lupton (from CASE at the London School of Economics) and her co-authors offer a more positive assessment in their review (see Lupton, Heath, and Salter 2009); see also two reports that draw on international as well as national data by Alan Smithers (2004, 2007), from the University of Buckingham, for the Sutton Trust.
29. See Barber (2007).
30. See Department for Work and Pensions (2007c).
31. See Department for Education and Skills (2006).
32. Holmlund, McNally, and Viarengo (2009).
33. Barber (2007, 186).
34. Barber (2007, 39).
35. Department for Work and Pensions (2007c).
36. All statistics in this paragraph are from Department for Children, Schools, and Families (2009b).
37. See, for example, the evidence presented at a summit on social mobility and

education held June 1–3, 2008, and sponsored by the Carnegie Corporation and the Sutton Trust (Sutton Trust 2009).

38. Barber (2004).
39. This point is emphasized by Barber and Mourshed (2007).
40. Daniel Koretz (2009) provides a very useful discussion of the challenges of using these international data to assess an individual country's performance.
41. For information on the TIMSS, see Martin et al. (2000); Mullis et al. (1998a, 1998b, 2004); Mullis, Martin, and Fay (2008a, 2008b).
42. Other international data sets provide information over a shorter time period. In the Progress in International Reading Literacy Study (PIRLS) test administered in 2001 and 2006, English fourth-graders scored well relative to children in other countries, although their average reading scores declined over the period (author's tabulations of data from PIRLS 2001 and 2006 scores, available in Mullis et al. (2003) and Mullis et al. (2007); Scotland, which did not participate in the national literacy and numeracy strategies, appears separately in the PIRLS and displays average scores that are lower and flat over the period). In the Program for International Student Assessment (PISA) tests for fifteen-year-olds from OECD countries, average math scores for children in Britain did not change much from 2003 to 2006 (a relatively good performance over a period when the mean country in the data set saw declining scores), and average science scores declined from 2000 to 2006 (a relatively poor performance over a period when the mean country in the data set saw flat scores) (author's tabulations from PISA 2000, 2003, and 2006 scores, available in OECD [2001b, 2004, 2007]).
43. Author's tabulations from the European Quality of Life Survey data, available from European Foundation for the Improvement of Living and Working Conditions (2003, 2007).
44. These gaps were the subject of two reports by Department for Children, School, and Families in 2009 (see DCSF 2009c, 2009d).
45. See, for instance, discussion in HM Treasury (2008).
46. On the London Challenge, see Brighouse (2007). On the National Challenge, see Department for Children, School, and Families (2009c).
47. See Major (2008). See also Brooks and Tough (2006).
48. Burgess, Wilson, and Worth (2009); Wilson, Burgess, and Briggs (forthcoming). See also Burgess et al. (2008).
49. See, for instance, discussion in Department for Education and Skills (2006).
50. Gregg and Macmillan (2008).
51. All statistics in this paragraph are from Gilby et al. (2005).
52. Cummings et al. (2007); see also discussion in Gray and Whitty (2007); Whitty (2008).
53. For an overview of the child protection and foster care systems, see Waldfogel (1998).

54. Cabinet Office (2009).
55. HM Treasury (2008).
56. Department for Children, Schools, and Families and Department of Health (2009).
57. National Health Service (2009a).
58. National Health Service (2009b).
59. Belot and James (2009).
60. See Department for Children, School, and Families (2007c); see also the one-year progress report in DCSF (2008c).

CHAPTER 6

1. Quote from Department for Social Security (1998).
2. Figure for 2006 from Freud (2007).
3. See Department for Work and Pensions (2007d).
4. See Gregg and Harkness (2003); Brewer et al. (2006).
5. For overviews of the U.S. welfare reforms, see Blank (2002, 2009a); Grogger and Karoly (2005); Moffitt (2003, 2007).
6. See, for example, Meyer (2007).
7. See Meyer and Rosenbaum (2000, 2001a, 2001b).
8. Figures on welfare caseloads from Haskins (2006); figures on share of population on welfare from Grogger and Karoly (2005).
9. Grogger and Karoly (2005).
10. All figures in this paragraph from Scholz, Moffitt, and Cowan (2009).
11. U.S. House of Representatives, Ways and Means Committee (2004).
12. See Blank (2009b).
13. As discussed earlier, Britain calculates its poverty measures both before and after taking housing costs into account. For simplicity, I use only the before housing cost numbers unless otherwise noted.
14. Elliott (2003).
15. Department for Work and Pensions (2005).
16. The reverse is also true. In fact, a common criticism of relative poverty rates by American scholars is that relative poverty can fall during a recession if the incomes of the median family falls more than the income of poor families.
17. Brewer et al. (2008).
18. Brewer et al. (2008).
19. See Smeeding and Waldfogel (2010).
20. See Dickens and Ellwood (2003a, 2003b); Hills and Waldfogel (2004); Smeeding (2007); Waldfogel (2007a); Schwalb and Wiseman (2008).
21. These studies include Bennett, Lu, and Song (2005), Blank (2009a), Haskins (2001), and Primus et al. (1999). Analyses of the Three-City Study show that some families have relied on support from other family members or on other

types of benefit programs, such as disability; see Frogner, Moffitt, and Ribar (2007) and Cherlin et al. (2007); see also Slack et al. (2007), who provide results from five non-experimental studies.

22. See Blank (2007, 2009a, 2009b); see also Acs and Loprest (2004); Turner, Danziger, and Seefeldt (2006); Zedlewski and Nelson (2003).

23. See Reichman, Teitler, and Curtis (2005); Seefeldt and Orzol (2005).

24. For concerns about how much living standards have increased at the bottom of the income distribution, see, for instance, Besharov and McCall (2008).

25. See Brewer, O'Dea, et al. (2009).

26. Dickens and Ellwood (2003a, 2003b); Hills and Waldfogel (2004); Smeeding (2007); Waldfogel (2007a).

27. Brewer (2007, 2008) shows that while relative poverty was falling for families with children, it was rising for other groups not targeted by government policy over this period.

28. Department for Children, Schools, and Families (2009f).

29. See Department for Work and Pensions (2003a). In addition to the three official measures, there are various other measures that researchers and advocates have put forward. For instance, Jonathan Bradshaw and his colleagues (2008) have developed a "minimum income standard," with input from families and experts.

30. See discussion in Willitts (2006).

31. This cutoff is somewhat arbitrary, and some analysts instead examine families' raw deprivation scores.

32. See discussion in Brewer, Muriel, et al. (2008).

33. Vegeris and Perry (2003); Lyon, Barnes, and Sweiry (2006); Conolly and Kerr (2008).

34. There was an increase in both measures of food insecurity in 1998, but this seems to have been due to a change in the month when the survey was administered as well as to some changes in screening questions. The survey month alternated during the period from 1995 to 1999: the survey was administered in April in 1995, 1997, and 1999, in September in 1996, and in August in 1998. Rates of food insecurity may have been higher in 1998 because August is a summer month when children are not in school, and thus are not benefiting from school meals. Additionally, although the questions used to measure food insecurity did not change over time, there was a change in screening for the questions in 1998, which may also have affected the percentage identified as food-insecure; see Bickel, Carlson, and Nord (1999).

35. Analyses of current and former welfare recipients in the Women's Employment Study confirm this pattern: food insufficiency in that sample fell from 25 percent in 1997 to 17 percent in 2001, before rising to 19 percent in 2003 (see Sullivan, Turner, and Danziger 2008).

36. The statistics in this paragraph are from Short and Shea (1995), Bauman (1999, 2003), and Rogers and Ryan (2007).

37. See, for example, Meyer and Sullivan (2003, 2008).
38. Families with low incomes do not always have correspondingly low expenditures, in part because low incomes are often measured with a lot of error. However, the opposite is more generally true: families with low expenditures tend to have correspondingly low incomes. As a result, if we track trends in family economic well-being using aggregate expenditure data rather than income data, the picture is not always the same. Analyses conducted at the Institute for Fiscal Studies in Britain, for instance, show that trends in poverty and expenditures over the past thirty years have differed (Brewer, Goodman, and Leicester 2006). They find that between 1996–1997 and 2002–2003, while relative child poverty was falling if measured by family incomes, it was rising if measured by family expenditures. Although some have interpreted this result as indicating that the antipoverty reforms in Britain may not have reduced expenditure poverty among children (see, for example, Field and Cackett 2007), we need to be careful in drawing such conclusions, since this study does not specifically address the period of the antipoverty reforms, nor does it explicitly focus on the low-income families most affected by the reforms. For this reason, I place more weight on the two studies of expenditures conducted by Gregg, Waldfogel, and Washbrook (2005, 2006), discussed later in this section. Income and expenditure trends also differ in the United States (see, for instance, Meyer and Sullivan 2008; but see also Bavier 2008). For useful discussions of and evidence on the distinction between income, expenditure, consumption, and material hardship, see Mayer and Jencks (1989, 1993), Jencks, Mayer, and Swingle (2004a, 2004b), Mayer (2004), Iceland and Bauman (2007), and Sullivan, Turner, and Danziger (2008).
39. See discussion in Burgess et al. (2004); Duncan and Brooks-Gunn (1997); Gregg, Harkness, and Machin (1999).
40. See Meyer and Sullivan (2004, 2006, 2008).
41. Also relevant is research in Britain by Christopher Farrell and William O'Connor (2003), who find that as families move from benefits to work they spend more money on food and clothing. In the United States, Greg Duncan, Aletha Huston, and Thomas Weisner (2007) document how families in the New Hope experiment used their additional income to purchase child care and after-school activities for their children.
42. Gregg, Waldfogel, and Washbrook (2005).
43. The FES was merged with the National Food Survey in 2001–2002 and now forms the combined Expenditure and Food Survey.
44. Gregg, Waldfogel, and Washbrook (2006).
45. A potential concern with using income to identify treatment and control groups is that the benefit changes may have moved some families from one income group to another. My colleagues and I (Gregg, Waldfogel, and Washbrook 2006) also estimated some models that divide families by educational

level rather than income, but this division is crude: half of all families fall into the lower education group (adults who left school at age sixteen).

46. For details on how income and expenditure figures are equivalized see Gregg, Waldfogel, and Washbrook (2006).

47. Although one might worry that families underreport their spending on alcohol and tobacco, the DDD methodology would control for this.

48. Kaushal, Gao, and Waldfogel (2007).

49. See also Gao, Kaushal, and Waldfogel (forthcoming), who examine the effect of the EITC and find that expenditures do increase in families headed by mothers with a moderate level of education (at least high school but less than college) when EITC benefits are higher, but that these expenditure gains are focused primarily on housing, with smaller increases in items such as child care and car ownership.

50. See, for example, Middleton, Ashworth, and Braithwaite (1997); Shropshire and Middleton (1999).

51. See, for example, Duncan and Brooks-Gunn (1997).

52. See Duncan and Chase-Lansdale (2004); Dunifon, Kalil, and Bajracharya (2005); Han (2005, 2008); Han and Waldfogel (2007); Parcel and Menaghan (1994); Smolensky and Gootman (2003); Waldfogel (2006a).

53. These programs include Wisconsin's New Hope, the Minnesota Family Investment Program, and several others. Only New Hope offers long-run follow-up data.

54. For an overview of how the effects of parental employment and nonparental child care vary by child age, see Waldfogel (2006a). Few of the MDRC studies included data on infants or toddlers. The limited evidence that is available suggests that welfare-to-work reforms may have had negative effects on later achievement for children who were age zero or one at the time their mothers were exposed to the reforms, although the sample sizes are small and the effects are mostly not statistically significant; see Morris, Duncan, and Clark-Kauffman (2005).

55. Morris et al. (2001).

56. Morris et al. (2001); see also Morris, Duncan, and Clark-Kauffman (2005).

57. Morris, Duncan, and Clark-Kauffman (2005).

58. Gennetian et al. (2002).

59. Chase-Lansdale et al. (2003). See also Coley et al. (2007); Li-Grining et al. (2006).

60. Marianne Bitler and Hilary Hoynes (2006) review studies of the effects of welfare reforms on health. Surprisingly little attention has been paid thus far to the long-run effects of the reforms on other child outcomes. Amalia Miller and Lei Zhang (2007) look at the school performance of fourth- and eighth-graders and find gains in 2003 and 2005 for children in low-income families; for school attainment, see also Miller and Zhang (2008). Two studies examine

the effects of the welfare reforms on child abuse and neglect, finding some adverse effects; see Paxson and Waldfogel (2002, 2003).

61. For details, see Brady-Smith et al. (2001).

62. See review in Waldfogel (2006a).

63. On the timing of employment, see Hill (2006); on breast-feeding, see Haider, Jacknowitz, and Schoeni (2003).

64. The British government for several years has tracked progress on a set of key indicators through its annual "Opportunity for All" reports. As shown in table 6.5, over the period 1997 to 2007, Britain saw improvements in fourteen of the twenty-one indicators for which data are available; there was no detectable progress on three others and declines in well-being on only four. The last such report (see Department for Work and Pensions 2007c) reported on a set of twenty-four specific indicators of child health and development, organized into seventeen main categories and various subcategories. Although data are not available for all indicators (and although one might quarrel with whether these twenty-four items are the right ones for the government to have been tracking), the report card on these indicators suggests a fairly positive record of achievement on items identified early on by the Labour government as targets for improvement.

65. Gregg, Harkness, and Smith (2009).

66. National Evaluation of Sure Start (2008). See also Melhuish et al. (2008).

67. Machin and McNally (2008a, 2008b); see also Stannard and Huxley (2007).

68. Department for Work and Pensions (2003a).

69. In principle, one could also compare countries' performance using absolute poverty rates, as is customary in the United States. See, for example, Notten and de Neubourg (2007, 2008), who do this for Europe and the United States over the period 1994 to 2000. However, such calculations have not been done for the post-2000 period, owing to data limitations.

70. For instance, a thirty-country study found that the U.S. child poverty rate (on a relative measure defined as below 60 percent of median income) in 2004— when Britain's rate stood at 24 percent—was 30 percent, higher than in any other country except Mexico; see Caminada and Goudswaard (2009).

71. The statistics in this paragraph are from the author's calculations using data from Eurostat (2008b). See figure 6.2 note for information about data sources. The poverty rate is defined as the percentage of children with an equivalized disposable income below a poverty threshold set at 60 percent of the national median equivalized disposable income (after transfers).

72. Ideally, we would like to know not just whether child poverty was falling in Britain, relative to its European peers, but also whether the position of the poor was improving. However, consistent European data are not available over time. Data from the British Family Resources Survey indicate that in 1999–2000, when 26 percent of children were poor (their families had in-

comes below 60 percent of median income, before housing costs), half of that group (13 percent of children) had incomes below 50 percent of the median, while the other half had incomes between 50 and 59 percent of the median. Similarly, in 2005–2006, when 22 percent of children were poor (their families had incomes below 60 percent of the median), half of the group (11 percent of children) had incomes below 50 percent of the median, while the other half had incomes between 50 and 59 percent of the median (Department for Work and Pensions 2008a). These figures suggest that the incomes of poor children did not deteriorate over the period.

73. Typically, these studies rate child well-being using an array of available data on different types of items. As such, they have been criticized for sometimes placing too much weight on items that are relatively unimportant but are included because the data are available, while ignoring items that theoretically would be more important but are left out because data on them are lacking; see Aaronovitch (2009).

74. *BBC News* (2007a). See also Sarah Boseley (2007), who reported in *The Guardian* that British children were "poorer, at greater risk and more insecure.".

75. UNICEF Innocenti Research Centre (2007).

76. Associated Press, "UNICEF ranks well-being of British, U.S. children last in industrialized world," *USA Today*, February 14, 2007. Available at: http://www.usatoday.com/news/world/2007-02-14-unicef-child-wellbeing_x.htm (accessed February 16, 2010).

77. *BBC News* (2007a).

78. Stewart (2009b, 285).

79. There is a good deal of interest in measuring happiness and life satisfaction across countries; see, for example, Marlier, Atkinson, and Nolan (2007). However, happiness and satisfaction are not always consistently defined, and often what analysts really have in mind is mental health or other specific health and well-being outcomes.

80. See Stewart (2009b) for details.

81. A 2009 report on child well-being in OECD countries also pointed to high levels of drunkenness among British youth, along with high levels of teen pregnancy and unemployment (see Organization for Economic Cooperation and Development 2009).

82. A recent report by Jonathan Bradshaw and Dominic Richardson (2009) compares child well-being in Britain and other European countries and finds that Britain generally compares poorly. However, as the authors note, the index used in this report, drawing mostly on data from 2006, is not strictly comparable to indices used in earlier reports, when Britain also compared poorly, and thus cannot tell us how child well-being in Britain has changed over time.

83. As noted earlier, many analysts argue that if we want to measure well-being, what we should be assessing is people's happiness. However, comparative data on happiness are fairly limited. The European Quality of Life Survey

does include two relevant measures—one is a question about how happy the respondent is these days (on a scale from 1 to 10), and the other is a question about how satisfied the respondent is with his or her life these days (again on a scale from 1 to 10)—but only for the 2003 to 2007 period.

84. Elliott and Ungoed-Thomas (2004).

CHAPTER 7

1. HM Treasury, Department for Work and Pensions, and Department for Children, Schools, and Families (2008).
2. Hills (2001); Sefton (2003, 2009); Taylor-Gooby (2005).
3. Sefton (2009).
4. Sefton (2009).
5. Statistics in this paragraph compiled by the author from the British Social Attitudes Survey (Economic and Social Data Service 2010a, 2010b).
6. Timmins (2007).
7. For details, see Tower Hamlets Partnership (2009).
8. Percival (2008).
9. Brown (2008).
10. See Brewer, Browne, et al. (2009); see also Brewer and Browne (2007); Brewer, Muriel, et al. (2009).
11. House of Commons (2009).
12. House of Commons (2009).
13. House of Commons (2009).
14. House of Commons (2009).
15. Cameron (2009).
16. Quote from Centre for Social Justice (2007, 7). See also Cameron (2009).
17. Letwin (2006); Centre for Social Justice (2007); Cameron (2009).
18. Cameron (2009, 6–7).
19. The Conservatives' proposals for reform are summarized in Centre for Social Justice (2009).
20. See two 2008 reports on the early years prepared for the Conservative Party; Allen and Smith (2008); Callan (2008). See also, for example, the speech given by Michael Gove, shadow secretary for Children, Schools, and Families, at the Institute for Public Policy Research, on August 4, 2008 (Gove 2008).
21. Cameron (2009, 7).
22. Cameron (2009); Stratton (2009).
23. Unless otherwise noted, the statistics on the distribution of poor children by family type are from Department for Work and Pensions (2009a). The statistics on poverty risk by parental disability, family size, and race and ethnic group are from Department for Work and Pensions (2008a).
24. Unless otherwise noted, all statistics in this paragraph are from Department for Work and Pensions (2009a).

25. One might ask whether the increase in lone parenthood is related to the anti-poverty reforms, since these provided more assistance to low-income families and might therefore have increased the incentives to have children. However, the reforms also increased lone-parent employment, which would tend to discourage having children. Mike Brewer, Anita Ratcliffe, and Sarah Smith (2007) examine the period 1995 to 2003 and find no evidence that the reforms increased lone parenthood or fertility in lone-parent families; however, it appears that the reforms did lead to a small (approximately 10 percent) increase in fertility in *two-parent* families, who were also entitled to the benefit increases but did not see a substantial increase in mothers' employment. See also Francesconi and van der Klaauw (2007), who examine an earlier period (1991 to 2001) and find a decrease in single-mother fertility, and Francesconi, Rainer, and van der Klaauw (2009), who find an increase in divorce from 1999 to 2003.

26. Having a child in the family with a disability, in contrast, is not strongly associated with an elevated risk of poverty, perhaps because of the more generous supports for families with children with disabilities.

27. Details on the share of adults with a disability by family type are provided in HM Treasury (2004).

28. It would be useful to know more about the extent to which the share of families with a parent with a disability and their risk of poverty have increased over time.

29. All figures in this paragraph are from Department for Work and Pensions (2008a, table 4.5). Estimates refer to 2006–2007, but owing to small sample sizes for some ethnic groups, they are calculated as three-year averages and therefore reflect data from 2004–2005, 2005–2006, and 2006–2007.

30. Lucinda Platt (2009) finds that comparing three-year rolling averages from the period 2001–2002 to 2003–2004 to the period 2004–2005 to 2006–2007, the poverty rate for Bangladeshi children fell from 72 percent to 58 percent, and the poverty rate for Pakistani children fell from 59 percent to 54 percent, while the poverty rate for white British children was constant at 20 percent (poverty defined in relative terms, before housing costs).

31. Comparable data from 1994–1995 to 1997–1998 show poverty rates of about 75 percent for Pakistani and Bangladeshi children, over 50 percent for black children or children from other groups, and over 40 percent for Indian children, compared to 30 percent for white children (HM Treasury 1999a, chart 1.11; see also Berthoud 1997, 1998; Department for Social Security 1999b).

32. Employment statistics from Kenway and Palmer (2007).

33. Employment statistics from Kenway and Palmer (2007).

34. Platt (2007).

35. Platt (2007).

36. Platt (2009).

37. Platt (2009).

38. Platt (2009).
39. Platt (2007).
40. National Statistics (2007).
41. National Statistics (2008).
42. The statistics on numbers of immigrants in this paragraph come from National Statistics (2008).
43. Dickens and McKnight (2008).
44. There are, of course, other challenges. Particularly prominent at the time of this writing is the challenge posed by the economic downturn and financial crisis, as I discuss in the introduction. And as John Hills (2009) notes, any future reforms will also have to confront the challenges posed by an aging population as well as the need to address other global issues, such as climate change.
45. Bamfield and Horton (2009).
46. Gordon Brown, in foreword to Department of Work and Pensions (2008d).
47. House of Commons (2009).
48. Cameron (2009).
49. Stanley and McNeil (2009).
50. For more in-depth discussions of this issue, see Bell, Brewer, and Phillips (2007); Waldfogel and Garnham (2008).
51. Garfinkel et al. (1998).
52. For a brief overview of U.S. child support policies and the role of child support in anti-poverty policy, see Waldfogel (2009). For a more detailed discussion, see Garfinkel et al. (1998).
53. At the same time, concern has been raised about trends in intergenerational mobility, although these are hard to assess since the mobility of the current generation of children—that is, how independent their adult position is from their family background—will not be observed until they are adults themselves. This concern has been raised in headlines such as "Children Who Cannot Escape the Poverty Trap: Inequality in Britain Is Worse Than in the 1970s Warns a New Study on Childhood" (Asthana 2007). But the research evidence is not clear on this point. Studies that compare children's occupations to their parents' find that social mobility is about the same now as it was for the previous generation, while studies that compare children's incomes to their parents' find that social mobility may have declined. Analyses for the most recent cohort of young people suggest that social mobility may now be increasing (Gregg and Macmillan 2009). See the review in Cabinet Office (2008), and see also Hills (2009) and Hills, Sefton, and Stewart (2009).
54. Timmins (2007).
55. Cabinet Office (2008).
56. Cabinet Office (2009). A related review considered ways to ensure fair access to professional jobs; see Panel on Fair Access to the Professions (2009).
57. House of Commons (2009).

58. All figures are from Park et al. (2008, appendix III); see also the discussion in Sefton (2009).

59. Blake et al. (2009, 48).

CHAPTER 8

1. For an overview of the War on Poverty and subsequent approaches to poverty in the United States, see Danziger (2007); Danziger and Haveman (2001).

2. Barack Obama endorsed this goal during an interview on April 13, 2008 (CNN 2008).

3. See, for example, Campaign 2000 (2009) for Canada, Lunn (2009) for Australia, and Fletcher and Dwyer (2008) for New Zealand.

4. See, for example, European Commission (2008).

5. Cancian and Danziger (2009).

6. White House (2009).

7. Sherman (2009).

8. U.S. Bureau of the Census (2009a).

9. DeParle (2009).

10. The parallels between the commitment to put a man on the moon and the commitment to end child poverty were noted by Labour member of Parliament Jamie Reed during the second reading of the Child Poverty Bill (House of Commons 2009). For an earlier use of the moon metaphor, see *The Moon and the Ghetto* by Richard Nelson (1977).

11. Commission for Economic Opportunity (2006).

12. Center for Economic Opportunity (2009).

13. See Bosman (2009); Center for Economic Opportunity (2009).

14. Center for American Progress (2007).

15. Matthews (2008).

16. Matthews (2009).

17. Bruce Bradbury, personal communication, September 27, 2009.

18. Australia Senate, Community Affairs References Committee (2004).

19. Fletcher and Dwyer (2008).

20. Frazer and Marlier (2007, 59).

21. Organization for Economic Cooperation and Development (2008).

22. Danziger and Ratner (forthcoming).

23. David Harris, personal communication, September 23, 2009.

24. *Households Below Average Income* (HBAI) data show that the child poverty rate for families with children under age five is only slightly higher than the rate for families with children overall, which was not the case before reform. Detailed analyses by Sosthenes Ketende and Heather Joshi (2008) of the Millennium Cohort Study children, born in 2001, find that 30 percent were in poverty—a higher poverty rate than in the HBAI data for that year, but still

much lower than the 40 percent rate for families with newborns before reform (as we saw in chapter 1).

25. Dahl and Lochner (2008); Gregg, Waldfogel, and Washbrook (2005, 2006); Kaushal, Magnuson, and Waldfogel (2009); Milligan and Stabile (2008); Waldfogel and Washbrook (2009).

26. For a review of this evidence, see Smolensky and Gootman (2003); Waldfogel (2004, 2006a).

27. For details on state laws, see Han, Ruhm, and Waldfogel (2009); Waldfogel (2009).

28. Naomi Eisenstadt, quoted in Gentleman (2009, 3–4).

29. This evidence is reviewed in Smolensky and Gootman (2003); Waldfogel (2004, 2006a).

30. Sammons et al. (2002).

31. See Kirp (2007); Waldfogel (2006a).

32. Rothstein, Jacobsen, and Wilder (2008).

33. For a discussion of the role that evidence played in this initiative, see Haskins, Paxson, and Brooks-Gunn (2009).

34. House of Commons (2009).

35. See, for example, Beer (2008).

36. For the National Academies report, see Citro and Michael (1995).

37. Center for Economic Opportunity (2008).

38. Center for Economic Opportunity (2009).

39. See the discussion in Toynbee (2009); see also the report of Margaret Blake and her colleagues (2009) about their qualitative interviews (although with a very small sample).

40. See Sefton (2009).

41. Bamfield and Horton (2009).

42. Major (2009).

43. House of Commons (2009).

44. Labour member of Parliament Karen Buck, in the debate on the Child Poverty Bill (see House of Commons 2009).

45. See discussion in Hills and Waldfogel (2004).

References

Aaronovitch, David. 2009. "Happiness Schmappiness." *The Times*, August 8, p.4.

Acs, Gregory, and Pamela Loprest. 2004. *Leaving Welfare: Employment and Well-Being of Families That Left Welfare in the Post-Entitlement Era*. Kalamazoo, Mich.: W. E. Upjohn Institute.

Adam, Stuart, and Mike Brewer. 2004. *Supporting Families: The Financial Costs and Benefits of Children Since 1975*. Bristol, U.K.: Policy Press.

Alakeson, Vidhya. 2004. *A 2020 Vision for Early Years: Extending Choice; Improving Life Chances*. London: Social Market Foundation.

Allen, Graham, and Iain Duncan Smith. 2008. *Early Intervention: Good Parents, Great Kids, Better Citizens*. London: Centre for Social Justice & Smith Institute.

The Alliance. 2009. *The Other Half of Britain: Problems and Issues in the Traditional Industrial Areas of England, Scotland, and Wales*. Available at: http://www.doverdc.co.uk/pdf/otherhalf.pdf (accessed August 18, 2009).

Anning, Angela, and Mog Ball, eds. 2008. *Improving Services for Young Children: From Sure Start to Children's Centers*. London: Sage Publications.

Asthana, Anushka. 2007. "Children Who Cannot Escape the Poverty Trap: Inequality in Britain Is Worse Than in the 1970s Warns a New Study on Childhood." *The Observer*, September 2, p.20.

Atkinson, Anthony B. 1998. "The Case for an Official Poverty Target." In *An Inclusive Society: Strategies for Tackling Poverty*, edited by Carey Oppenheim. London: Institute for Public Policy Research.

Aughinbaugh, Alison, and Maury Gittleman. 2003. "Does Money Matter? A Comparison of the Effect of Income on Child Development in the United States and Great Britain." *Journal of Human Resources* 28(2): 416–40.

Australia Senate. Community Affairs References Committee. 2004. *A Hand Up Not a Hand Out: Renewing the Fight Against Poverty*. Available at: http://www.aph.gov.au/senate/committee/clac_ctte/completed_inquiries/2002-04/poverty/report/report.pdf (accessed September 27, 2009).

Bainbridge, Jay, Marcia K. Meyers, Sakiko Tanaka, and Jane Waldfogel. 2005. "Who Gets an Early Education? Family Income and the Enrollment of Three- to Five-Year-Olds from 1968 to 2000." *Social Science Quarterly* 86(3): 724–45.

Bamfield, Louise, and Tim Horton. 2009. *Understanding Attitudes to Tackling Economic Inequality*. York: Joseph Rowntree Foundation. Available at: www.jrf.org.uk/publications/attitudes_economic_inequality (accessed August 18, 2009).

Barber, Michael. 2004. "The Virtue of Accountability: System Redesign, Inspection, and Incentives in the Era of Informed Professionalism." *Journal of Education* 185(1): 7–38.

———. 2007. *Instruction to Deliver: Fighting to Transform Britain's Public Services.* London: Methuen.

Barber, Michael, and Mona Mourshed. 2007. *How the World's Best-Performing School Systems Come Out on Top.* Washington, D.C.: McKinsey & Co.

Barnes, Jacqueline, Mog Ball, Pamela Meadows, Jenny McLeish, Jay Belsky, and the Family Nurse Partnership (FNP) Implementation Research Team. 2008. *Nurse-Family Partnership Program: The First-Year Pilot Sites Implementation in England.* Research report DCSF-RW051. London: Department for Children, Schools, and Families.

Barrow, Lisa, and Leslie McGranahan. 2000. "The Effects of the Earned Income Credit on the Seasonality of Household Expenditures." *National Tax Journal* 53(4): 1211–43.

Bauman, Kurt. 1999. "Extended Measures of Well-Being: Meeting Basic Needs." Current Population Reports P70-67. Washington: U.S. Bureau of the Census.

———. 2003. "Extended Measures of Well-Being: Living Conditions in the United States: 1998." Current Population Reports P79-87. Washington: U.S. Bureau of the Census.

Bavier, Richard. 2008. "Reconciliation of Income and Consumption Data in Poverty Measurement." *Journal of Policy Analysis and Management* 27(1): 44–62.

BBC News. 2007a. "U.K. Is Accused of Failing Children." *BBC News,* February 14. Available at: http://newsvote.bbc.co.uk (accessed February 17, 2010).

———. 2007b. "Blair: In His Own Words." *BBC News,* May 11. Available at: http://news.bbc.co.uk/2/hi/uk_news/politics/3750847.stm (accessed February 17, 2010).

Beer, Alex. 2008. "The U.K. Poverty Measure Triptych: Absolute, Relative, and Material Deprivation." Paper presented to the thirtieth annual research conference of the Association for Public Policy Analysis and Management (APPAM). Los Angeles (November 7).

Bell, Alice, Caroline Bryson, Matt Barnes, and Ruth O'Shea. 2005. *Use of Childcare Among Families from Minority Ethnic Backgrounds.* London: National Centre for Social Research.

Bell, Kate, Mike Brewer, and David Phillips. 2007. *Lone Parents and "Mini-Jobs."* York, U.K.: Joseph Rowntree Foundation.

Belot, Michele, and Jonathan James. 2009. "Healthy School Meals and Educational Outcomes." Working paper 2009-01. University of Essex, Institute for Social and Economic Research (ISER).

Belsky, Jay, Jacqueline Barnes, and Edward Melhuish, eds. 2007. *The National Evaluation of Sure Start: Does Area-Based Early Intervention Work?* Bristol, U.K.: Policy Press.

Bennett, Jim, Elena Chavez Quezada, Kayte Lawton, and Pamela Perun. 2008. "The U.K. Child Trust Fund: A Successful Launch." Available at: http://www

.ippr.org/publicationsandreports/publication.asp?id=618 (accessed April 10, 2009).

Bennett, Neil, Hsien-Hen Lu, and Younghwan Song. 2005. "Welfare Reform and Changes in the Economic Well-Being of Children." *Population Research and Policy Review* 23(5–6): 671–99.

Berger, Lawrence, Jennifer Hill, and Jane Waldfogel. 2005. "Maternity Leave, Early Maternal Employment, and Child Outcomes in the U.S." *Economic Journal* 115: F29–47.

Berger, Lawrence, Christina Paxson, and Jane Waldfogel. 2009. "Income and Child Development." *Children and Youth Services Review* 31(9): 978–89.

Berthoud, Richard. 1997. "Income and Standards of Living." In *Ethnic Minorities in Britain: Diversity and Disadvantage*, edited by Tariq Madood, Richard Berthoud, Jane Lakey, James Nazroo, Patton Smith, Satnam Virdee, and Sharon Beishon. London: Policy Studies Institute.

———. 1998. "Incomes of Ethnic Minorities." Colchester, U.K.: University of Essex, Institute for Social and Economic Research.

Besharov, Douglas, and Douglas McCall. 2008. "Income Transfers Won't Eradicate Poverty." Unpublished paper. College Park: University of Maryland.

Beveridge, William. 1942. *Social Insurance and Allied Services*. London: Her Majesty's Stationery Office.

Bickel, Gary, Steven Carlson, and Mark Nord. 1999. *Household Food Security in the United States, 1995–1998: Advance Report*. Available at: http://www.fns.usda.gov/oane/MENU/Published/FoodSecurity/fsecsum.htm (accessed December 17, 2009).

Bitler, Marianne, and Hilary Hoynes. 2006. "Welfare Reform and Indirect Impacts on Health." Working paper 12642. Cambridge, Mass.: National Bureau of Economic Research.

Blair, Tony. 1999. "Beveridge Revisited: A Welfare State for the Twenty-First Century." Lecture delivered at Toynbee Hall, London (March 18).

Blake, Margaret, Elizabeth Clery, Joanna d'Ardenne, and Robin Legard. 2009. *Cognitive Testing: British Social Attitudes Child Poverty Questions*. Department for Work and Pensions research report 574. London: DWP.

Blank, Rebecca M. 2002. "Evaluating Welfare Reform in the United States." *Journal of Economic Literature* 40(4): 1105–66.

———. 2006. "What Did the 1990s Welfare Reforms Accomplish?" In *Public Policy and the Income Distribution*, edited by Alan Auerbach, David Card, and John Quigley. New York: Russell Sage Foundation.

———. 2007. "Improving the Safety Net for Single Mothers Who Face Serious Barriers to Work." *Future of Children* 17(2): 183–97.

———. 2009a. "What We Know, What We Don't Know, and What We Need to Know." In *Welfare Reform and Its Long-Term Consequences for America's Poor*, edited by James Ziliak. New York: Cambridge University Press.

———. 2009b. "Economic Change and the Structure of Opportunity for Low-

Skilled Workers." In *Changing Poverty and Changing Antipoverty Policies*, edited by Maria Cancian and Sheldon Danziger. New York: Russell Sage Foundation.

Blank, Rebecca, and David Card. 2000. "The Labor Market and Welfare Reform." In *Finding Jobs: Work and Welfare Reform*, edited by David Card and Rebecca Blank. New York: Russell Sage Foundation.

Blank, Rebecca, and Lucie Schmidt. 2001. "Work, Wages, and Welfare." In *The New World of Welfare*, edited by Rebecca Blank and Ron Haskins. Washington, D.C.: Brookings Institution Press.

Blau, David. 1999. "The Effect of Income on Child Development." *Review of Economics and Statistics* 81(2): 261–76.

Blundell, Richard, Mike Brewer, and Andrew Shephard. 2005. "Evaluating the Labor Market Impact of the Working Families Tax Credit Using Difference in Differences." HM Revenue and Customs working paper 4. Available at: http://eprints.ucl.ac.uk/18451 (accessed December 17, 2009).

Blundell, Richard, Howard Reed, John Van Reenen, and Andrew Shephard. 2003. "The Impact of the New Deal for Young People on the Labor Market: A Four-Year Assessment." In *The Labor Market Under New Labour: The State of Working Britain*, edited by Richard Dickens, Paul Gregg, and Jonathan Wadsworth. Basingstoke, U.K.: Palgrave Macmillan.

Boseley, Sarah. 2007. "British Children: Poorer, at Greater Risk and More Pressure." *The Guardian*, February 14.

Bosman, Julie. 2009. "Cash Incentive Program for Poor Families Is Renewed." *New York Times*, September 23.

Bradbury, Bruce, and Markus Jantti. 2001. "Child Poverty Across Twenty-Five Countries." In *The Dynamics of Child Poverty in Industrialized Countries*, edited by Bruce Bradbury, Stephen Jenkins, and John Micklewright. Cambridge: Cambridge University Press.

Bradshaw, Jonathan. 2001. "Child Poverty Under Labour." In *An End in Sight?* edited by Geoff Fimister. London: Child Poverty Action Group.

Bradshaw, Jonathan, Sue Middleton, Abigail Davis, Nina Oldfield, Noel Smith, Linda Cusworth, and Julie Williams. 2008. *A Minimum Income Standard for Britain: What People Think*. York, U.K.: Joseph Rowntree Foundation.

Bradshaw, Jonathan, and Dominic Richardson. 2009. "An Index of Child Well-Being in Europe." *Child Indicators Research*. Available at: http://www.springer link.com/content/r5kq13v750q53782/fulltext.pdf (accessed August 17, 2009).

Brady-Smith, Christy, Jeanne Brooks-Gunn, Jane Waldfogel, and Rebecca Fauth. 2001. "Work or Welfare? Assessing the Impact of Recent Employment and Policy Changes on Very Young Children." *Evaluation and Program Planning* 24(4): 409–25.

Brewer, Mike. 2007. "Welfare Reform in the U.K.: 1997–2007." Paper presented to the Economic Council of Sweden conference "From Welfare to Work." Stockholm (May 7).

———. 2008. "A Decade of Personal Tax and Transfer Reforms in the U.K.: In Search of Equity or Efficiency?" Presentation given at NZAE/ESAM conference, Wellington (July 2008). Available at: http://www.ifs.org.uk/publications/4293 (accessed February 17, 2010).

Brewer, Mike, and James Browne. 2007. "Memorandum on Estimates of the Costs of Meeting the Government's Child Poverty Target in 2010–2011." Available at: http://www.ifs.org.uk/docs/tsc_note.pdf (accessed September 18, 2009).

Brewer, Mike, James Browne, Robert Joyce, and Holly Sutherland. 2009. *Micro-Simulating Child Poverty in 2010 and 2020*. Available at: http://www.ifs.org.uk/publications/4434 (accessed September 18, 2009).

Brewer, Mike, Tom Clark, and Alissa Goodman. 2003. "What Really Happened to Child Poverty in the U.K. Under Labour's First Term?" *Economic Journal* 113(488): F240–57.

Brewer, Mike, Alan Duncan, Andrew Shephard, and Maria Jose Suarez. 2006. "Did Working Families Tax Credit Work? The Impact of In-Work Support on Labor Supply in Great Britain." *Labor Economics* 13(6): 699–720.

Brewer, Mike, Alissa Goodman, and Andrew Leicester. 2006. *Household Spending in Britain: What Can It Teach Us About Poverty?* Bristol, U.K.: Policy Press.

Brewer, Mike, Alistair Muriel, David Phillips, and Luke Sibieta. 2008. "Poverty and Inequality in the U.K.: 2008." *IFS Commentary 105*. London: Institute for Fiscal Studies. Available at: www.ifs.org.uk/comms/comm105.pdf (accessed February 17, 2010).

———. 2009. "Poverty and Inequality in the U.K.: 2009." *IFS Commentary C109*. London: Institute for Fiscal Studies. Available at: http://www.ifs.org.uk/comms/c109.pdf (accessed September 18, 2009).

Brewer, Mike, Cormac O'Dea, Gillian Paull, and Luke Sibieta. 2009. *The Living Standards of Families with Children Reporting Low Incomes*. Department for Work and Pensions research report 577. Available at: http://research.dwp.gov.uk/asd/asd5/rports2009-2010/rrep577.pdf (accessed July 29, 2009).

Brewer, Mike, Anita Ratcliffe, and Sarah Smith. 2007. "Does Welfare Reform Affect Fertility? Evidence from the U.K." Working paper 7-177. Bristol, U.K.: University of Bristol, Centre for Market and Public Organization.

Brighouse, Tim. 2007. "The London Challenge—A Personal View." In *Education in a Global City: Essays from London*, edited by Tim Brighouse and Leisha Fullick. London: University of London, Institute of Education.

Brooks, Richard, and Sarah Tough. 2006. *Pupil Attainment: Time for a Three Rs Guarantee*. London: Institute for Public Policy Research. Available at: http://www.ippr.org/publicationsandreports/publication.asp?id=517 (accessed September 16, 2008).

Brown, Gordon. 2008. Speech to Specialist Schools and Academies Trust. Available at: http://www.number10.gov.uk/Page18045 (accessed September 18, 2009).

Burgess, Simon, Paul Gregg, Emma Hall, Sara Meadows, Carol Propper, and Elizabeth Washbrook. 2004. *Up to Five: Report to Department for Employment and Skills*. Bristol, U.K.: University of Bristol, Center for Market and Public Organization (CMPO).

229

Burgess, Simon, Deborah Wilson, Adam Briggs, and Anete Piebalga. 2008. *Segregation and the Attainment of Minority Ethnic Pupils in England.* Working paper 08-204. Bristol, U.K.: University of Bristol, Centre for Market and Public Organization (CMPO). Available at: http://www.bris.ac.uk /cmpo/publications/ papers/2008/wp204.pdf (accessed August 17, 2009).

Burgess, Simon, Deborah Wilson, and Jack Worth. 2009. *Passing Through School: The Evolution of Attainment of England's Ethnic Minorities.* Bristol, U.K.: University of Bristol, Centre for Market and Public Organization (CMPO).

Butt, Sarah, Kate Goddard, Ivana La Valle, and Maxine Hill. 2007. *Childcare Nation? Progress on the Childcare Strategy and Priorities for the Future.* London: Daycare Trust and National Centre for Social Research.

Cabinet Office. 2008. *Getting On, Getting Ahead.* London: Cabinet Office.

———. 2009. *New Opportunities: Fair Chances for the Future.* London: Cabinet Office.

Callan, Samantha. 2008. *Breakthrough Britain: The Next Generation. A Policy Report from the Early Years Commission.* London: Centre for Social Justice.

Cameron, David. 2009. "Speech to Conservative Party Conference." Available at: http://www.guardian.co.uk/politics/2009/oct/08/david-cameron-speech-in-full (accessed October 27, 2009).

Caminada, Koen, and Kees Goudswaard. 2009. "Effectiveness of Poverty Reduction in the EU: A Descriptive Analysis." *Poverty and Public Policy.* Manuscript 1023. Available at: http://media.leidenuniv.nl/legacy/effectiveness-of-poverty-reduction-in-the-eu.pdf (accessed August 17, 2009).

Campaign 2000. 2009. *2009 Report Card on Child and Family Poverty in Canada.* Available at: http://www.campaign2000.ca/reportCards/national/2009EnglishC 2000NationalReportCard.pdf (accessed December 17, 2009).

Cancian, Maria, and Sheldon Danziger, eds. 2009. *Changing Poverty, Changing Policies.* New York: Russell Sage Foundation.

Card, David, and Alan Krueger. 1994. "Minimum Wages and Employment: A Case Study of the Fast Food Industry." *American Economic Review* 84(4): 772–93.

———. 1995. *Myth and Measurement: The New Economics of the Minimum Wage.* Princeton, N.J.: Princeton University Press.

Center for American Progress. 2007. *From Poverty to Prosperity: A National Strategy to Cut Poverty in Half.* Report and recommendations of the Center for American Progress Task Force on Poverty (April). Available at: http://www.american progress.org/issues/2007/04/pdf/poverty_report.pdf (accessed September 18, 2009).

Center for Economic Opportunity. 2008. *The CEO Poverty Measure.* Available at: http://www.nyc.gov/html/ceo/downloads/pdf/final_poverty_report.pdf (accessed September 27, 2009).

———. 2009. *Early Achievements and Lessons Learned.* Available at: http://www .nyc.gov/html/ceo/downloads/pdf/early_achievement_report_2008.pdf (accessed September 18, 2009).

Centre for Analysis of Social Exclusion (CASE) and HM Treasury, eds. 1999. *Per-*

sistent Poverty and Lifetime Inequality: The Evidence. CASE report 5 and HM Treasury occasional paper 10. London: London School of Economics/CASE and HM Treasury.

Centre for Social Justice. 2007. *Breakthrough Britain: Ending the Costs of Social Breakdown: Executive Summary.* Available at: http://www.centreforsocialjustice.org .uk/client/downloads/overview.pdf (accessed September 18, 2009).

———. 2009. *Dynamic Benefits: Towards Welfare That Works: Executive Summary.* Available at: http://www.centreforsocialjustice.org.uk/client/downloads/CSJ DynamicBenefitsExecWEB.pdf (accessed September 18, 2009).

Chase-Lansdale, Lindsay P., Robert Moffitt, Brenda Lohman, Andrew Cherlin, Rebekah Levine Coley, Laura Pittman, Jennifer Roff, and Elizabeth Votruba-Drzal. 2003. "Mothers' Transitions from Welfare to Work and the Well-Being of Preschoolers and Adolescents." *Science* 299(March 7): 1548–52.

Chatterji, Pinka, and Sara Markowitz. 2004. "Does the Length of Maternity Leave Affect Maternal Health?" Working paper 10206. Cambridge, Mass.: National Bureau of Economic Research.

Cherlin, Andrew, Bianca Frogner, David Ribar, and Robert Moffitt. 2007. "Welfare Reform in the Mid-2000s: How African-American and Hispanic Families in Three Cities Are Faring." Working paper 07-01. Baltimore: Johns Hopkins University.

Chowdry, Haroon, Lorraine Dearden, and Carol Emmerson. 2007. *Education Maintenance Allowance: Evaluation with Administrative Data.* London: Institute for Fiscal Studies.

Citro, Constance, and Robert Michael. 1995. *Measuring Poverty: A New Approach.* Washington: National Academies Press.

Clinton, William Jefferson. 1996. *Between Hope and History.* New York: Random House.

CNN. 2008. Transcript of Democratic Candidates Compassion Forum (April 13). Available at: http://transcripts.cnn.com/TRANSCRIPTS/0804/13/se.01.html (accessed November 17, 2008).

Cohen, Barbara, James Parry, and Kenneth Yang. 2000. *Household Food Security in the United States, 1998 and 1999: Detailed Statistical Report.* Available at: http:// www.ers.usda.gov/ (accessed January 21, 2009).

Coley, Rebekah Levine, Brenda Lohman, Elizabeth Votruba-Drzal, Laura Pittman, and P. Lindsay Chase-Lansdale. 2007. "Maternal Functioning, Time, and Money: The World of Work and Welfare." *Children and Youth Services Review* 29(6): 721–41.

Commission for Economic Opportunity. 2006. *Increasing Opportunity and Reducing Poverty in New York City.* Report to Mayor Michael R. Bloomberg (September). Available at: http://www.nyc.gov/html/om/pdf/ceo_report2006.pdf (accessed September 18, 2009).

Commission on Social Justice. 1994. *Social Justice: Strategies for National Renewal.* London: Institute for Public Policy Research.

Conolly, Anne, and Anne Kerr. 2008. *Families with Children in Britain: Findings from the 2006 Families and Children Study (FACS)*. Department for Work and Pensions research report 486. London: The Stationery Office.

Cooke, Graeme, and Kayte Lawton. 2008. *Working Out of Poverty: A Study of the Low-Paid and "Working Poor."* London: Institute for Public Policy Research. Available at: http://www.ippr.org/publicationsandreports/publication.asp ? id=581 (accessed December 17, 2008).

Costello, E. Jane, Scott Compton, Gordon Keeler, and Adrian Angold. 2003. "Relationship Between Poverty and Psychopathology: A Natural Experiment." *Journal of the American Medical Association* 290(15): 2023–29.

Coughlan, Sean. 2007. "Education, Education, Education." *BBC News*, December 9. Available at: http://news.bbc.co.uk/2/hi/uk_news/education /6564933.stm (accessed February 17, 2010).

Crompton, Rosemary, Michaela Brockmann, and Richard D. Wiggins. 2003. "A Woman's Place . . . Employment and Family Life for Men and Women." In *British Social Attitudes: The Twentieth Report—Continuity and Change over Two Decades*, edited by Alison Park, John Curtice, Katarina Thomson, Lindsey Jarvis, and Catherine Bromley. London: Sage Publications.

Cummings, Colleen, Alan Dyson, Daniel Muijs, Ivy Papps, Diana Pearson, Carla Raffo, Lucy Tiplady, and Liz Todd, with Deanne Crowther. 2007. *Evaluation of the Full-Service Extended Schools Initiative: Final Report*. Department for Education and Skills research brief RB852. Available at: http://www.dcsf.gov.uk/research/data/uploadfiles/RB852.pdf (accessed July 29, 2009).

Currie, Janet, and Duncan Thomas. 1995. "Does Head Start Make a Difference?" *American Economic Review* 85(3): 341–64.

——. 1999. "Does Head Start Help Hispanic Children?" *Journal of Public Economics* 74(2): 235–62.

Dahl, Gordon, and Lance Lochner. 2008. "The Impact of Family Income on Child Achievement: Evidence from the Earned Income Tax Credit." Working paper 14599. Cambridge, Mass.: National Bureau of Economic Research.

Danziger, Sheldon. 2007. "Fighting Poverty Revisited: What Did Researchers Know Forty Years Ago? What Do We Know Today?" *Institute for Research on Poverty Focus* 25(1): 3–11.

Danziger, Sheldon, and Robert Haveman. 2001. "The Evolution of Poverty and Antipoverty Policy." In *Understanding Poverty*, edited by Sheldon Danziger and Robert Haveman. New York and Cambridge, Mass.: Russell Sage Foundation Press and Harvard University Press.

Danziger, Sheldon, Colleen Heflin, Mary Corcoran, Elizabeth Oltmans, and Hui-Chen Wang. 2002. "Does It Pay to Move from Welfare to Work?" *Journal of Policy Analysis and Management* 21(4): 671–92.

Danziger, Sheldon, and David Ratner. Forthcoming. "Labor Market Outcomes and the Transition to Adulthood." *Future of Children*.

Deacon, Alan. 2003. "Leveling the Playing Field, Activating the Players: New Labour and the Cycle of Disadvantage." *Policy and Politics* 31(2): 123–37.

Dearing, Eric, Kathleen McCartney, and Beck Taylor. 2001. "Change in Family Income-to-Needs Matters More for Children with Less." *Child Development* 72(6): 1779–93.

Dench, Geoff. 2009. "Exploring Parents' Views." In *British Social Attitudes: The Twenty-Fifth Report*, edited by Alison Park, John Curtice, Katarina Thomson, Miranda Phillips, and Elizabeth Clery. London: National Centre for Social Research.

DeParle, Jason. 2009. "Hunger in U.S. at a 14-Year High." *New York Times*, November 17, 2009. Available at: http://www.nytimes.com/2009/11/17/us/17hunger .html?_r=1&pagewanted=print (accessed November 19, 2009).

Department for Business Enterprise and Regulatory Reform. 2007. *History of the Minimum Wage*. Available at: http://www.dti.gov.uk/employment/pay/ national-minimum-wage/History-National-Minimum-Wage/page12572.html (accessed August 15, 2007).

Department for Children, Schools, and Families (DCSF). 2004. "National Curriculum Assessment and GCSE/GNVQ Attainment by Pupil Characteristics in England 2002 (Final) and 2003 (Provisional)." Statistical First Release 04/2004. Available at: http://www.dcsf.gov.uk/rsgateway/DB/SFR (accessed January 30, 2009).

———. 2005. "National Curriculum Assessments, GCSE and Equivalent Attainment, and Post-16 Attainment by Pupil Characteristics in England 2004." Statistical First Release 08/2005. Available at: http://www.dcsf.gov.uk/rsgateway/DB/ SFR (accessed January 30, 2009).

———. 2006. "National Curriculum Assessments, GCSE and Equivalent Attainment, and Post-16 Attainment by Pupil Characteristics in England 2005." Statistical First Release 09/2006. Available at: http://www.dcsf.gov.uk/rsgateway/DB/ SFR (accessed January 30, 2009).

———. 2007a. "National Curriculum Assessments, GCSE and Equivalent Attainment, and Post-16 Attainment by Pupil Characteristics in England 2005/06 (Revised)." Statistical First Release 04/2007. Available at: http://www.dcsf.gov .uk/rsgateway/DB/SFR (accessed January 30, 2009).

———. 2007b. "National Curriculum Assessments, GCSE and Equivalent Attainment, and Post-16 Attainment by Pupil Characteristics in England 2006/07." Statistical First Release 38/2007. Available at: http://www.dcsf.gov.uk/rsgate way/DB/SFR (accessed January 30, 2009).

———. 2007c. *The Children's Plan*. London: DCSF.

———. 2008a. "Foundation Stage Profile Results in England, 2007/08." Statistical First Release 25/2008. Available at: http://www.dcsf.gov.uk/rsgateway/DB/SFR (accessed January 30, 2009).

———. 2008b. "Attainment by Pupil Characteristics, in England 2007/08." Statistical First Release 32/2008. Available at: http://www.dcsf.gov.uk/rsgateway/DB/ SFR/ (accessed January 30, 2009).

———. 2008c. *The Children's Plan One Year On: A Progress Report.* London: DCSF.

———. 2009a. "Record Investment Pays Dividends as Achievement Gap Narrows." Available at: http://www.dcsf.gov.uk/pns/DisplayPN.cgi?pn_id=2009_0008.

———. 2009b. "GCSE and Equivalent Results in England, 2007/08 (Revised)." Statistical First Release 02/2009. Available at: http://www.dcsf.gov.uk/rsgate way/DB/SFR/ (accessed January 30, 2009).

———. 2009c. *Deprivation and Education: The Evidence on Pupils in England, Foundation Stage to Key Stage 4.* Available at: http://www.dcsf.gov.uk/research/data/ uploadfiles/DCSF-RTP-09-01.pdf (accessed July 29, 2009).

———. 2009d. *Breaking the Link Between Disadvantage and Low Attainment: The Way Forward.* Available at: http://publications.dcsf.gov.uk/eOrderingDownload/ 00357-2009.pdf (accessed July 29, 2009).

———. 2009e. *Individual Scale Point Results for the Foundation Stage Profile in England, 2007/08.* Experimental Statistical Release. Available at: http://www.dcsf.gov .uk/rsgateway/DB/SFR/s000812/sfr_25_2008.pdf (accessed August 14, 2009).

———. 2009f. "Child Poverty." London: DCSF.

———. 2009g. "Participation in Education, Training, and Employment by Sixteen–Eighteen-Year-Olds in England." Statistical First Release 12/2009. Available at: http://www.dcsf.gov.uk/rsgateway/DB/SFR/s000849/index.shtml (accessed September 14, 2009).

Department for Children, Schools, and Families (DCSF) and Department of Health (DH). 2009. *Healthy Lives, Brighter Futures: The Strategy for Children and Young People's Health.* Available at: http://publications.everychildmatters.gov.uk/ default.aspx?PageFunction=productdetails&PageMode=publications&Product Id=285374a (accessed April 8, 2009).

Department for Children, Schools and Families (DCSF), Department for Work and Pensions (DWP), HM Treasury, and Cabinet Office. 2009. *Next Steps for Early Learning and Childcare: Building on the Ten-Year Strategy.* Available at: http:// www.dcsf.gov.uk/everychildmatters/resources-and-practice/IG00356 (accessed February 17, 2010).

Department for Communities and Local Government (DCLG). 2007. Neighborhood Renewal Unit. 2007. "New Deal for Communities." Available at: http:// www.neighbourhood.gov.uk/page.asp?id=617 (accessed September 15, 2008).

Department for Education and Employment (DfEE). 1999. *Improving Literacy and Numeracy: A Fresh Start.* Report of the Great Britain Working Group on Post-School Basic Skills, chaired by Sir Claus Moser. London: DfEE.

Department for Education and Skills (DfES). 2005. *14-19 Education and Skills.* Annesley, U.K.: DfES Publications.

———. 2006. *Statistics of Education: Trends in Attainment Gaps: 2005.* London: National Statistics.

Department for Social Security (DSS). 1998. *New Ambitions for Our Country: A New Contract for Welfare*. London: The Stationery Office.

———. 1999a. *Opportunity for All: Tackling Poverty and Social Exclusion*. London: The Stationery Office.

———. 1999b. *Households Below Average Income, 1994/95–1997/98*. London: DSS.

———. 2000. *Tax Benefit Model Tables: June 2000*. Available at: http://research.dwp .gov.uk/asd/tbmt.asp (accessed August 12, 2009).

———. Various years. *Social Security Statistics*. London: Department for Social Security.

Department for Work and Pensions (DWP). 2003a. *Measuring Child Poverty*. London: DWP.

———. 2003b. *Income Support Quarterly Enquiry*. February, 2002. London: DWP.

———. 2004. *Households Below Average Income: An Analysis of the Income Distribution 1994/95–2002/03*. Leeds: Corporate Document Services.

———. 2005. *Households Below Average Income: An Analysis of the Income Distribution 1994/95–2003/04*. London: DWP.

———. 2006a. *A New Deal for Welfare: Empowering People to Work*. London: DWP.

———. 2006b. *Opportunity for All: Eighth Annual Report 2006: Indicators Document*. London: DWP.

———. 2007a. *Households Below Average Income: An Analysis of the Income Distribution 1994/95–2005/06*. London: DWP.

———. 2007b. *Working for Children*. London: DWP.

———. 2007c. *Opportunity for All: Indicators Update 2007*. London: DWP. Available at: http://www.dwp.gov.uk/docs/opportunityforall2007.pdf (accessed January 30, 2009).

———. 2007d. *In Work, Better Off: Next Steps to Full Employment*. London: The Stationery Office.

———. 2007e. *Ready for Work: Full Employment in Our Generation*. London: The Stationery Office.

———. 2008a. *Households Below Average Income: An Analysis of the Income Distribution 1994/95–2006/07*. London: DWP.

———. 2008b. *No One Written Off: Reforming Welfare to Reward Responsibility: Public Consultation*. London: DWP.

———. 2008c. *Raising Expectations and Increasing Support: Reforming Welfare for the Future*. London: DWP.

———. 2008d. *Transforming Britain's Labor Market: Ten Years of the New Deal*. London: DWP.

———. 2008e. *Tax Benefit Model Tables: April 2008*. Available at: http://research .dwp.gov.uk/asd/tbmt.asp (accessed August 12, 2009).

———. 2009a. *Households Below Average Income: An Analysis of the Income Distribution 1994/95–2007/08*. Available at: http://research.dwp.gov.uk/asd/hbai/ hbai2008/pdf_files/full_hbai09.pdf (accessed September 18, 2009).

——. 2009b. *Benefit Expenditure Tables*. Available at: http://research.dwp.gov
.uk/asd/asd4/medium_term.asp (accessed August 11, 2009).

Dickens, Richard, and David Ellwood. 2003a. "Child Poverty in Britain and the
United States." In *The Labor Market under New Labour: The State of Working Britain*, edited by Richard Dickens, Paul Gregg, and Jonathan Wadsworth. Basingstoke, U.K.: Palgrave Macmillan.

——. 2003b. "Child Poverty in Britain and the United States." *Economic Journal*
113(488): F219–39.

Dickens, Richard, Stephen Machin, and Alan Manning. 1994a. "The Effects of
Minimum Wages on Employment: Theory and Evidence from the U.S." Working paper 4742. Cambridge, Mass.: National Bureau of Economic Research.

——. 1994b. "The Effects of Minimum Wages on Employment: Theory and Evidence from Britain." Discussion paper 0183. London: London School of Economics, Centre for Economic Performance.

——. 1994c. "Estimating the Effect of Minimum Wages on Employment from the
Distribution of Wages: A Critical View." Discussion paper 0203. London: London School of Economics, Centre for Economic Performance.

Dickens, Richard, and Abigail McKnight. 2008. "Assimilation of Migrants into the
British Labor Market." Centre for Analysis of Social Exclusion (CASE) paper
133 (October). Available at: http://sticerd.lse.ac.uk/case (accessed August 25,
2009).

Duncan, Greg, and Jeanne Brooks-Gunn, eds. 1997. *The Consequences of Growing
Up Poor*. New York: Russell Sage Foundation.

Duncan, Greg, and P. Lindsay Chase-Lansdale, eds. 2004. *For Better and for Worse:
Welfare Reform and the Well-Being of Children and Families*. New York: Russell
Sage Foundation.

Duncan, Greg, Aletha Huston, and Thomas Weisner. 2007. *Higher Ground: New
Hope for the Working Poor and Their Children*. New York: Russell Sage Foundation.

Dunifon, Rachel, Ariel Kalil, and Ashish Bajracharya. 2005. "Maternal Working
Conditions and Child Well-Being in Welfare-Leaving Families." *Developmental
Psychology* 41(6): 851–59.

Duyme, Michael, Annick-Camille Dumaret, and Stanislaw Tomkiewicz. 1999.
"How Can We Boost the IQs of 'Dull Children'? A Late Adoption Study." *Pro-
ceedings of the National Academy of Sciences* 96(15): 8790–94.

Economic and Social Data Service. 2010a. *British Social Attitudes Survey 2000*. Available at: http://www.esds.ac.uk/findingdata/sndescription.asp?sn=4486 (accessed February 17, 2010).

——. 2010b. *British Social Attitudes Survey 2003*. Available at: http://www.esds.
ac.uk/findingdata/sndescription.asp?sn=5235 (accessed February 17, 2010).

Economic Policy Institute. 2008. "Minimum Wage: EPI Issue Guide." Available
at: http://www.epi.org/publications/entry/issue_guide_on_minimum_wage (accessed December 17, 2009).

Eisenstadt, Naomi. 2007. "Foreword." In *The National Evaluation of Sure Start: Does Area-Based Early Intervention Work?* edited by Jay Belsky, Jacqueline Barnes, and Edward Melhuish. Bristol, U.K.: Policy Press.

Eissa, Nada, and Jeffrey Liebman. 1996. "Labor Supply Response to the Earned Income Tax Credit." *Quarterly Journal of Economics* 111(2): 605–37.

Eissa, Nada, and Austin Nichols. 2005. "Tax-Transfer Policy and Labor Market Outcomes." Urban Institute and Brookings Institution Tax Policy Center (October 7). Available at: http://www.taxpolicycenter.org/publications/url.cfm?ID =411237 (accessed March 15, 2009).

Ekechuku, Godwin U. 2003. "Maternal Employment and Attitudes Toward Women Participating in the Workforce." Available at: http://www.lima.ohio -state.edu/academics/sociology/paper%2022.pdf (accessed July 14, 2009).

Elliott, John, and Jon Ungoed-Thomas. 2004. "British Take Lead on Good Parenting." *Sunday Times,* July 25.

Elliott, Larry. 2003. "Brown on Course to Hit Child Poverty Target." *The Guardian,* December 12, 2003.

Ellwood, David. 1988. *Poor Support.* New York: Basic Books.

———. 1998. "Dynamic Policy-Making: An Insider's Account of Reforming U.S. Welfare." In *The Dynamics of Modern Society,* edited by Lutz Leisering and Robert Walker. Bristol, U.K.: Policy Press.

Emmerson, Carol, Sandra McNally, and Costas Meghir. 2005. "Economic Evaluation of Education Initiatives." In *What's the Good of Education: The Economics of Education in the U.K.,* edited by Stephen Machin and Anna Vignoles. Princeton, N.J.: Princeton University Press.

Esping-Anderson, Gøsta. 1990. *Three Worlds of Welfare Capitalism.* Princeton, N.J.: Princeton University Press.

———. 2005. "Social Inheritance and Equal Opportunities Policies." In *Maintaining Momentum: Promoting Social Mobility and Life Chances from Early Years to Adulthood,* edited by Simone Delorenzi, Jodie Reed, and Peter Robinson. London: Institute for Public Policy Research.

European Commission. 2008. *Child Poverty and Well-Being in the EU: Current Status and Way Forward.* Available at: http://ec.europa.eu/employment_social/ spsi/docs/social_inclusion/2008/child_poverty_en.pdf (accessed September 18, 2009).

European Foundation for the Improvement of Living and Working Conditions. 2003. *European Quality of Life Survey 2003.* Available at: http://www.euro found.europa.eu/areas/qualityoflife/eqls/2003/eqls.htm (accessed February 5, 2009).

———. 2007. *European Quality of Life Survey 2007.* Available at: http://www.euro found.europa.eu/areas/qualityoflife/eqls/2007/index.htm (accessed February 5, 2009).

Eurostat. 2008a. "Live Births Outside Marriage and Crude Birth Rate, EU-27." Available at: http://epp.eurostat.ec.europa.eu/statistics_explained/index.php

?title=File:Live_births_outside_marriage_and_crude_birth_rate,_EU-27.PNG &filetimestamp=20090430100105 (accessed December 17, 2009).

———. 2008b. "At-Risk-of-Poverty Rate by Age Group, After Social Transfers." Available at: http://epp.eurostat.ec.europa.eu/portal/page/portal/product _details/dataset?p_product_code=TSDSC230 (accessed November 10, 2008).

Farrell, Christopher, and William O'Connor. 2003. *Low-Income Families and House-hold Spending*. Department for Work and Pensions research report 192. London: The Stationery Office.

Feinstein, Leon. 2003. "Inequality in the Early Cognitive Development of British Children in the 1970 Cohort." *Economica* 70(277): 73–97.

Fernie, Sue, and David Metcalf. 1996. "Low Pay and Minimum Wages: The British Evidence." Unpublished paper. London: London School of Economics, Centre for Economic Performance.

Field, Frank, and Ben Cackett. 2007. "Welfare Isn't Working: Child Poverty." London: Reform.

Fletcher, Michael, and Maire Dwyer. 2008. *A Fair Go for All Children: Actions to Address Child Poverty in New Zealand*. Available at: http://www.occ.org.nz/ __data/assets/pdf_file/0018/4932/OCC_ChildPoverty_070808.pdf (accessed November 1, 2009).

Francesconi, Marco, Helmut Rainer, and Wilbert van der Klaauw. 2009. "The Effects of In-Work Benefit Reform in Britain on Couples: Theory and Evidence." *Economic Journal* 119(February): F66–100.

Francesconi, Marco, and Wilbert van der Klaauw. 2007. "The Socioeconomic Consequences of In-Work Benefit Reform for British Lone Mothers." *Journal of Human Resources* 42(1): 1–31.

Frazer, Hugh, and Eric Marlier. 2007. *Tackling Child Poverty and Promoting the Social Inclusion of Children in the EU*. Available at: http://www.peer-review -social-inclusion.eu/network-of-independent-experts/2007/reports/first-semes ter-2007/synthesis-report-2007-1 (accessed November 12, 2008).

Frean, Alexandra. 2007. "£3bn Scheme to Help Pre-School Children Learn 'Has Had No Effect.'" *The Times*, August 28.

———. 2009. "Poor Pupils Are Falling Further Behind, Say Tories." *The Times*, January 5.

Freud, David. 2007. *Reducing Dependency, Increasing Opportunity: Options for the Future of Welfare to Work*. An independent report to the Department for Work and Pensions. London: DWP.

Frogner, Bianca, Robert Moffitt, and David Ribar. 2007. "How Families Are Doing Nine Years After Welfare Reform: 2005 Evidence from the Three-City Study." Working paper 07-03. Baltimore: Johns Hopkins University.

Gais, Thomas, Richard Nathan, Irene Lurie, and Thomas Kaplan. 2001. "Implementation of the Personal Responsibility Act of 1996." In *The New World of Welfare: An Agenda for Reauthorization and Beyond*, edited by Rebecca M. Blank and Ron Haskins. Washington, D.C.: Brookings Institution Press.

Gao, Qin, Neeraj Kaushal, and Jane Waldfogel. Forthcoming. "How Have Expansions in the Earned Income Tax Credit Affected Family Expenditures?" In *Welfare Reform and Its Long-Term Consequences for America's Poor*, edited by James Ziliak. New York: Cambridge University Press.

Garces, Eliana, Duncan Thomas, and Janet Currie. 2002. "Longer-Term Effects of Head Start." *American Economic Review* 92(4): 999–1012.

Garfinkel, Irwin, Sara McLanahan, Daniel Meyer, and Judith Seltzer, eds. 1998. *Fathers Under Fire: The Revolution in Child Support Enforcement*. New York: Russell Sage Foundation.

Garfinkel, Irwin, Timothy Smeeding, and Lee Rainwater. Forthcoming. *The American Welfare State: Laggard or Leader?* New York: Oxford University Press.

Gennetian, Lisa, Greg Duncan, Virginia Knox, Wanda Vargas, Elizabeth Clark-Kauffman, and Andrew London. 2002. *How Welfare and Work Policies for Parents Affect Adolescents: A Synthesis of Research*. New York: MDRC.

Gentleman, Amelia. 2009. "Bar None." *The Guardian*, October 14. Available at: http://www.guardian.co.uk/society/2009/oct/14/naomi-eisenstadt-social (accessed October 14, 2009).

Giddens, Anthony. 1998. *The Third Way: The Renewal of Social Democracy*. Cambridge: Polity Press.

——. 2000. *The Third Way and Its Critics*. Cambridge: Polity Press.

Gilby, Nicholas, Tara Mackey, Jo Mason, Anna Ullman, and Sam Clemens. 2005. *Extended Services in Primary Schools*. Department for Education and Skills research brief RB809. London: DfES.

Glass, Norman. 1999. "Sure Start: The Development of an Early Intervention Program for Young Children in the United Kingdom." *Children and Society* 13(4): 257–64.

——. 2005. "Surely Some Mistake?" *The Guardian*, January 5.

Glennerster, Howard. 2000. *British Social Policy Since 1945*. 2d ed. Malden, Mass.: Blackwell.

——. 2001. "United Kingdom Education: 1997–2001." Centre for Analysis of Social Exclusion (CASE) paper 50. Available at: http://sticerd.lse.ac.uk/dps/case/cp/CASEpaper50.pdf (accessed February 15, 2009).

Goldin, Claudia, and Lawrence Katz. 2008. *The Race Between Education and Technology*. Cambridge, Mass.: Harvard University Press.

Goodman, Alissa, and Steven Webb. 1994. "For Richer, for Poorer: The Changing Distribution of Income in the United Kingdom 1961/9." *IFS Commentary 42*. London: Institute for Fiscal Studies.

Gove, Michael. 2008. "Liberty, Equality, Family? Why Conservative Social Policy Delivers Progressive Ends." Speech delivered at the Institute for Public Policy Research. (London, August 4).

Gray, Sandra Leaton, and Geoff Whitty. 2007. "Comprehensive Schooling and Social Inequality in London: Past, Present, and Possible Future." In *Education in a*

Global City: Essays from London, edited by Tim Brighouse and Leisha Fullick. London: University of London, Institute of Education.

Greener, Kim, and Richard Cracknell. 1998. *Child Benefit*. House of Commons research paper 98/79 (July 29). Available at: http://www.parliament.uk/Commons/lib/research/rp98/rp98-079.pdf (accessed November 13, 2008).

Gregg, Paul. 2008. *Realizing Potential: A Vision for Personalized Conditionality and Support*. An independent report to the Department for Work and Pensions. London: DWP.

Gregg, Paul, Kirsten Hansen, and Jonathan Wadsworth. 1999. "The Rise of the Workless Household." In *The State of Working Britain*, edited by Paul Gregg and Jonathan Wadsworth. Manchester: Manchester University Press.

Gregg, Paul, and Susan Harkness. 2003. "Welfare Reform and the Employment of Lone Parents." In *Labor Under New Labour*, edited by Richard Dickens, Paul Gregg, and Jonathan Wadsworth. Oxford: Oxford University Press.

Gregg, Paul, Susan Harkness, and Stephen Machin. 1999. *Child Development and Family Income*. York, U.K.: Joseph Rowntree Foundation.

Gregg, Paul, Susan Harkness, and Sarah Smith. 2009. "Welfare Reform and Lone Parents in the U.K." *Economic Journal* 119(February): F38–65.

Gregg, Paul, and Lindsay Macmillan. 2009. "Intergenerational Mobility and Education in the Next Generation: Forecasting Intergenerational Mobility for the Current Cohorts of Youths." Paper presented to the Intergenerational Mobility Conference. London School of Economics (June 23).

Gregg, Paul, and Jonathan Wadsworth. 1996. "More Work in Fewer Households." In *New Inequalities*, edited by John Hills. Cambridge: Cambridge University Press.

Gregg, Paul, Jane Waldfogel, and Elizabeth Washbrook. 2005. "That's the Way the Money Goes: Expenditure Patterns as Real Incomes Rise for the Poorest Families with Children." In *A More Equal Society? New Labour, Poverty, Inequality, and Exclusion*, edited by John Hills and Kitty Stewart. Bristol, U.K.: Policy Press.

———. 2006. "Tackling Child Poverty in the U.K.: Are Low-Income Families with Children Starting to Catch Up?" *Labor Economics* 13(6): 721–46.

Grogger, Jeffrey. 2003. "The Effects of Time Limits, the EITC, and Other Policy Changes on Welfare Use, Work, and Income Among Female-Head Families." *Review of Economics and Statistics* 85(2): 394–408.

Grogger, Jeffrey, and Lynn Karoly. 2005. *Welfare Reform: Effects of a Decade of Change*. Cambridge, Mass.: Harvard University Press.

Gueron, Judith. 2003. "Presidential Address: Fostering Research Excellence and Impacting Policy and Practice: The Welfare Reform Story." *Journal of Policy Analysis and Management* 22(2): 163–74.

Haider, Steven, Alison Jacknowitz, and Robert Schoeni. 2003. "Welfare Work Requirements and Child Well-Being: Evidence from the Effects on Breast-Feeding." *Demography* 40(3): 479–97.

Han, Wen-Jui. 2005. "Maternal Nonstandard Work Schedules and Child Cognitive Outcomes." *Child Development* 76(1): 137–54.

———. 2008. "Shift Work and Child Behavior." *Work, Employment, and Society* 22(1): 67–87.

Han, Wen-Jui, Christopher Ruhm, and Jane Waldfogel. 2009. "Parental Leave Policies and Parents' Employment and Leave-Taking." *Journal of Policy Analysis and Management* 26(1): 29–54.

Han, Wen-Jui, and Jane Waldfogel. 2007. "Parental Work Schedules, Family Process, and Early Adolescents' Risky Behavior." *Children and Youth Services Review* 29(9): 1249–66.

Harker, Lisa. 2006. *Delivering on Child Poverty: What Would It Take?* Report for the Department for Work and Pensions. London: DWP.

Harker, Lisa, and Liz Kendall. 2003. *An Equal Start: Improving Support During Pregnancy and the First Twelve Months.* London: Institute for Public Policy Research.

Harris, Jose. 1977. *William Beveridge: A Biography.* Oxford: Oxford University Press.

———. 2007. "Principles, Poor Laws, and Welfare States." In *Making Social Policy Work*, edited by John Hills, Julian Le Grand, and David Piachaud. Bristol, U.K.: Policy Press.

Haskey, John. 1998. "One Parent Families and Their Dependent Children in Britain." In *Private Lives and Public Responses*, edited by Reuben Ford and Jane Millar. London: Policy Studies Institute.

Haskins, Ron. 2001. "Effects of Welfare Reform on Family Income and Poverty." In *The New World of Welfare*, edited by Rebecca M. Blank and Ron Haskins. Washington, D.C.: Brookings Institution Press.

———. 2006. *Work over Welfare: The Inside Story of the 1996 Welfare Reform Law.* Washington, D.C.: Brookings Institution Press.

Haskins, Ron, Christina Paxson, and Jeanne Brooks-Gunn. 2009. "Social Science Rising: A Tale of Evidence Shaping Public Policy." Available at: http://futureofchildren.org/futureofchildren/publications/docs/19_02_PolicyBrief.pdf (accessed September 30, 2009).

Hasluck, Chris, Abigail McKnight, and Peter Elias. 2000. *Evaluation of the New Deal for Lone Parents: Early Lessons from the Phase One Prototype.* Department for Social Security (DSS) research report 110. Leeds, U.K.: Corporate Document Services.

Hayghe, Howard. 1997. "Developments in Women's Labor Force Participation." *Monthly Labor Review* 120(September): 41–46.

Heckman, James J., and Lance Lochner. 2000. "Rethinking Education and Training Policy: Understanding the Sources of Skill Formation in a Modern Economy." In *Securing the Future: Investing in Children from Birth to College*, edited by Sheldon Danziger and Jane Waldfogel. New York: Russell Sage Foundation.

Heckman, James J., and Amy Wax. 2004. "Home Alone." *Wall Street Journal*, January 23.

Herr, Toby, Suzanne Wagner, and Robert Halpern. 1996. "Making the Shoe Fit: Creating a Work Preparation System for a Large and Diverse Welfare Population." Available at: http://www.familyimpactseminars.org/s_wifis09c02.pdf (accessed September 11, 2009).

Hill, Heather. 2006. "Maternity Leave for the Poor: Welfare-to-Work Exemptions and Employment Rates Among Single Mothers with Young Children." Paper presented to the annual meeting of the Association for Public Policy Analysis and Management. Madison, Wisconsin (November 2–4).

Hills, John. 1995. *Inquiry into Income and Wealth.* 2 vols. York, U.K.: Joseph Rowntree Foundation.

——. 2001. "Poverty and Social Security: What Rights? Whose Responsibilities?" In *British Social Attitudes: The Eighteenth Report—Public Policy, Social Ties,* edited by Alison Park, John Curtice, Katarina Thomson, Lindsey Jarvis, and Catherine Bromley. London: Sage Publications.

——. 2002. "Following or Leading Public Opinion? Social Security Policy and Public Attitudes Since 1997." *Fiscal Studies* 23(4): 539–58.

——. 2003. "The Blair Government and Child Poverty: An Extra One Percent for the Kids of the United Kingdom." In *One Percent for the Kids: New Policies, Brighter Futures for America's Children,* edited by Isabel Sawhill. Washington, D.C.: Brookings Institution Press.

——. 2004. *Inequality and the State.* Oxford: Oxford University Press.

——. 2009. "Future Pressures: Intergenerational Links, Wealth, Demography, and Sustainability." In *Towards a More Equal Society? Poverty, Inequality, and Policy Since 1997,* edited by John Hills, Tom Sefton, and Kitty Stewart. Bristol, U.K.: Policy Press.

Hills, John, and Orsolya Lelkes. 1999. "Social Security, Select Universalism, and Patchwork Redistribution." In *British Social Attitudes: The Sixteenth Report—Who Shares New Labour Values?*, edited by Richard Jowell, John Curtice, Alison Park, and Katarina Thomson. Aldershot, U.K.: Ashgate.

Hills, John, Tom Sefton, and Kitty Stewart. 2009. "Conclusions: Climbing Every Mountain or Retreating from the Foothills?" In *Towards a More Equal Society? Poverty, Inequality, and Policy Since 1997,* edited by John Hills, Tom Sefton, and Kitty Stewart. Bristol, U.K.: Policy Press.

Hills, John, and Jane Waldfogel. 2004. "A 'Third Way' in Welfare Reform? Evidence from the United Kingdom." *Journal of Policy Analysis and Management* 23(4): 765–88.

HM Revenue and Customs. 2009. *Child and Working Tax Credits Statistics: April 2009.* Available at: http://www.hmrc.gov.uk/stats/personal-tax-credits/cwtc-apr09.pdf (accessed September 24, 2009).

——. Various years. "Personal Tax Credits, Child and Working Tax Credit, Main Tables, Finalized Awards for Entitlement, Years 2003–2008." Available at: http://www.hmrc.gov.uk/stats/personal-tax-credits/menu.htm (accessed February 17, 2010).

HM Treasury. 1999a. *Tackling Child Poverty and Extending Opportunity*. The Modernization of Britain's Tax and Benefit System 4. London: HM Treasury.

———. 1999b. *Supporting Children Through the Tax and Benefit System*. The Modernization of Britain's Tax and Benefit System 5. London: HM Treasury.

———. 2000. "Brown Launches Pre-Budget Report Consultation Tour, Setting New Targets to Help Lone Parents Get into Work." Available at: http://web archive.nationalarchives.gov.uk/+/http://www.hm-treasury.gov.uk/newsroom _and_speeches/press/2000/press_110_00.cfm (accessed September 16, 2009).

———. 2001. *Tackling Child Poverty: Giving Every Child the Best Possible Start in Life*. Pre-budget report. London: HM Treasury.

———. 2002a. *Budget 2002*. London: HM Treasury.

———. 2002b. *2002 Spending Review: Opportunity and Security for All*. London: The Stationery Office.

———. 2002c. *The Child and Working Tax Credits*. The Modernization of Britain's Tax and Benefit System 10. London: HM Treasury.

———. 2004. *Child Poverty Review*. London: HM Treasury.

———. 2008. *Facing Global Challenges: Supporting People Through Difficult Times*. Pre-Budget Report. London: HM Treasury.

———. 2009. *Budget 2009: Building Britain's Future*. London: HM Treasury.

HM Treasury, Department for Education and Skills (DfES), Department for Work and Pensions (DWP), and Department for Trade and Industry (DTI). 2004. *Choice for Parents, the Best Start for Children: A Ten-Year Strategy for Childcare*. London: HM Treasury.

HM Treasury, Department for Work and Pensions (DWP), and Department for Children, Schools, and Families (DCSF). 2008. *Ending Child Poverty: Everybody's Business*. London: HM Treasury.

Hodge, Margaret. 2005. *Choice for Parents, the Best Start for Children: A Ten-Year Strategy for Child Care—Transmittal Memo*. London: Department for Education and Skills.

Holmlund, Helena, Sandra McNally, and Martina Viarengo. 2009. "Does Money Matter for Schools?" Centre for the Economics of Education discussion paper 105 (January). Available at: http://cee.lse.ac.uk/cee%20dps/ceedp105.pdf (accessed February 5, 2009).

Hotz, Joseph, Charles Mullin, and John Karl Scholz. 2006. "Examining the Effects of the Earned Income Tax Credit on the Labor Market Participation of Families on Welfare." Working paper 11968. Cambridge, Mass.: National Bureau of Economic Research.

Hotz, Joseph, and John Karl Scholz. 2003. "The Earned Income Tax Credit." In *Means-Tested Transfer Programs in the United States*, edited by Robert Moffitt. Chicago: University of Chicago Press.

House of Commons. 2009. "Child Poverty Bill Second Reading." *Hansard*, July 20.

Iceland, John, and Kurt Bauman. 2007. "Income Poverty and Material Hardship: How Strong Is the Association?" *Journal of Socioeconomics* 36(3): 376–96.

Institute for Fiscal Studies (IFS). 2009. "Inequality and Poverty Spreadsheet." Available at: http://www.ifs.org.uk/fiscalFacts/povertyStats (accessed July 28, 2009).

Jencks, Christopher, Susan Mayer, and Joseph Swingle. 2004a. "Who Has Benefited from Economic Growth in the United States Since 1969? The Case of Children." Faculty research working paper 04-047. Cambridge, Mass.: Harvard University, John F. Kennedy School of Government.

———. 2004b. "Can We Fix the Federal Poverty Measure So It Provides Reliable Information About Changes in Children's Living Conditions?" Unpublished paper. Cambridge, Mass.: Harvard University, John F. Kennedy School of Government.

Kaiser Family Foundation. 2009a. "Total CHIP Expenditures, FY2008." Available at: http://www.statehealthfacts.org/comparetable.jsp?cat=4&ind=235&print=1 (accessed September 30, 2009).

———. 2009b. "Federal CHIP Expenditures, FY1998–2007." Available at: http://www.statehealthfacts.org/comparetable.jsp?ind=234&cat=4&print=1 (accessed September 30, 2009).

Kamerman, Sheila, and Alfred Kahn. 1991. *Child Care, Parental Leave, and the Under Threes: Policy Innovation in Europe.* New York: Auburn House.

———. 1995. *Starting Right: How America Neglects Its Youngest Children and What We Can Do About It.* New York: Oxford University Press.

———. 1997. "Investing in Children: Government Expenditures for Children and Their Families in Western Industrialized Countries." In *Child Poverty and Deprivation in the Industrialized Countries, 1945–1995,* edited by Giovanni Andrea Cornia and Sheldon Danziger. Oxford: Oxford University Press.

Karoly, Lynn, Peter Greenwood, Susan Everingham, Jill Hoube, Rebecca Kilburn, Peter Rydell, Matthew Sanders, and James Chiesa. 1998. *Investing in Our Children: What We Know and Don't Know About the Costs of Early Childhood Interventions.* Santa Monica, Calif.: RAND.

Katz, Michael. 1996. *In the Shadow of the Poorhouse: A Social History of Welfare in America.* Rev. ed. New York: Basic Books.

———. 2001. *The Price of Citizenship: Redefining the American Welfare State.* New York: Metropolitan Books.

Kaushal, Neeraj, Gao Qin, and Jane Waldfogel. 2007. "Welfare Reform and Family Expenditures: How Are Single Mothers Adapting to the New Welfare and Work Regime?" *Social Service Review* 81(3): 369–96.

Kaushal, Neeraj, Katherine Magnuson, and Jane Waldfogel. 2009. "How Is Family Income Related to Investments in Children's Learning?" Unpublished paper. Columbia University and University of Wisconsin–Madison.

Kazimirski, Anne, Ruth Smith, Sarah Butt, Eleanor Ireland, and Eva Lloyd. 2008. *Childcare and Early Years Survey 2007: Parents' Use, Views, and Experiences.* Research report DCSF-RR025. London: National Centre for Social Research and Department for Children, Schools, and Families.

Kenway, Peter, and Guy Palmer. 2007. *Poverty Among Ethnic Groups: How and Why Does It Differ?* York, U.K.: Joseph Rowntree Foundation.

Ketende, Sosthenes, and Heather Joshi. 2008. "Income and Poverty." In *Millennium Cohort Study Third Survey: A User Guide to Initial Findings*, edited by Kirstine Hansen and Heather Joshi. London: University of London, Institute of Education, Centre for Longitudinal Studies.

Kirp, David. 2007. *The Sandbox Investment*. Cambridge, Mass.: Harvard University Press.

Korenman, Sanders, Jane Miller, and J. Sjaastad. 1995. "Long-Term Poverty and Child Development in the United States: Results from the NLSY." *Children and Youth Services Review* 17(1–2): 127–55.

Koretz, Daniel. 2009. "How Do American Students Measure Up? Making Sense of International Comparisons." *Future of Children* 19(1): 37–52.

Letwin, Oliver. 2006. "Why We Have Signed Up to Labour's Anti-Poverty Target." Available at: http://www.conservatives.com (accessed September 18, 2009).

Li-Grining, Christine, Elizabeth Votruba-Drzal, Heather Bachman, and P. Lindsay Chase-Lansdale. 2006. "Are Certain Preschoolers at Risk in the Era of Welfare Reform? The Moderating Role of Children's Temperament." *Children and Youth Services Review* 28(9): 1102–23.

Lipsett, Anthea. 2008. "Education Allowance Has Failed, Say Tories." *The Guardian*, August 4.

Low Pay Commission. 1998. *The National Minimum Wage: First Report of the Low Pay Commission*. London: The Stationery Office.

———. 2008. *The National Minimum Wage: Low Pay Commission Report 2008*. London: The Stationery Office.

Lundberg, Shelly, Robert Pollak, and Terence Wales. 1997. "Do Husbands and Wives Pool Their Resources? Evidence from the United Kingdom Child Benefit." *Journal of Human Resources* 32(3): 463–80.

Lunn, Stephen. 2009. "Spend More to Cut Child Poverty." *The Australian*, September 2. Available at: http://www.theaustralian.news.com.au/story/0,25197,26015239-5013404,00.html (accessed September 18, 2009).

Lupton, Ruth, Natalie Heath, and Emma Salter. 2009. "Education: New Labour's Top Priority." In *Towards a More Equal Society? New Labour, Poverty, Inequality, and Exclusion*, edited by John Hills, Tom Sefton, and Kitty Stewart. Bristol, U.K.: Policy Press.

Lyon, Nick, Matt Barnes, and Daniel Sweiry. 2006. *Families with Children in Britain: Findings from the 2004 Families and Children Study (FACS)*. Department for Work and Pensions research report 340. Leeds, U.K.: Corporate Document Services.

MacAskill, Ewen. 1996. "Blair's Promise—Everyone Can Be a Winner." *The Guardian*, October 2.

MacAskill, Ewen, and Owen Bowcott. 2001. "Furious NHS Protester Blocks Blair's Path." *The Guardian*, May 17. Available at: http://www.guardian.co.uk/politics/2001/may/17/uk.election200111 (accessed August 14, 2009).

Machin, Stephen. 1999. "Wage Inequality in the 1970s, 1980s, and 1990s." In *The State of Working Britain*, edited by Paul Gregg and Jonathan Wadsworth. Manchester: Manchester University Press.

——. 2003. "Unto Them That Hath. . . . " *CentrePiece* 8(1; winter): 5–9.

Machin, Stephen, and Sandra McNally. 2004. "Large Benefits, Low Cost." *CentrePiece* 9(1; spring): 2–7.

——. 2005. "Gender and Student Achievement in British Schools." *Oxford Review of Economic Policy* 21(3): 357–72.

——. 2008a. "The Literacy Hour." *Journal of Public Economics* 92(5–6): 1441–62.

——. 2008b. "The Three Rs: The Scope for Literacy and Numeracy Policies to Raise Achievement." Unpublished paper. London: London School of Economics, Center for the Economics of Education.

Machin, Stephen, and Anna Vignoles. 2005. "Education Policy and Evidence." In *What's the Good of Education: The Economics of Education in the U.K.*, edited by Stephen Machin and Anna Vignoles. Princeton, N.J.: Princeton University Press.

Major, Lee Elliot. 2008. "Educational Mobility, Attitudes, and Aspirations During the Primary School Years." In *Getting in Early: Primary Schools and Early Intervention*, edited by Jean Gross. London: Smith Institute.

——. 2009. "On Average, Our Schools Are Serving Up a Lesson in Failure." *The Times*, July 24.

Marlier, Eric, Anthony B. Atkinson, and Brian Nolan. 2007. *The EU and Social Inclusion: Facing the Challenges*. Bristol, U.K.: Policy Press.

Martin, Michael O., Ina V. S. Mullis, Eugenio J. Gonzales, Kelvin D. Gregory, Robert A. Garden, Kathleen M. O'Connor, Steven J. Chrostowski, and Teresa A. Smith. 2000. *TIMSS 1999 International Science Report: Findings from IEA's Repeat of the Third International Mathematics and Science Study at the Eighth Grade*. Chestnut Hill, Mass.: Boston College.

Matthews, Deb. 2008. *Breaking the Cycle: Ontario's Poverty Reduction Strategy*. Available at: http://www.growingstronger.ca/english/poverty_report_access.asp (accessed September 27, 2009).

——. 2009. *Poverty Reduction Act 2009*. Ontario: Legislative Assembly of Ontario.

Mayer, Susan. 1997. *What Money Can't Buy: The Effect of Parental Income on Children's Outcomes*. Cambridge, Mass.: Harvard University Press.

——. 2004. "Potential Policy-Related Uses of Measures of Consumption Among Low-Income Populations." Unpublished paper. Chicago: University of Chicago, Harris School.

Mayer, Susan, and Christopher Jencks. 1989. "Poverty and the Distribution of Material Hardship." *Journal of Human Resources* 24(1): 88–114.

——. 1993. "Recent Trends in Economic Inequality in the United States: Income Versus Expenditures Versus Material Well-Being." In *Poverty and Prosperity in the USA in the Late Twentieth Century*, edited by Edward Wolff. New York: St. Martin's Press.

McKnight, Abigail. 2005. "Employment: Tackling Poverty Through 'Work for Those Who Can.'" In *A More Equal Society? New Labour, Poverty, Inequality, and Exclusion*, edited by John Hills and Kitty Stewart. Bristol, U.K.: Policy Press.

Melhuish, Edward, Jay Belsky, Alistair Leyland, Jacqueline Barnes, and the National Evaluation of Sure Start Research Team. 2008. "Effects of Fully Established Sure Start Local Programs on Three-Year-Old Children and Their Families Living in England: A Quasi-Experimental Observational Study." *The Lancet* 372(9650): 1641–47.

Merrell, Christine, Peter Tymms, and Paul Jones. 2007. "Changes in Children's Cognitive Development at the Start of School in England 2000–2006." Unpublished paper. Durham, U.K.: Durham University, Curriculum, Evaluation and Management Centre.

Meyer, Bruce. 2007. "The U.S. Earned Income Tax Credit, Its Effects, and Possible Reforms." *Swedish Economic Policy Review* 14(2): 55–80.

Meyer, Bruce, and Dan Rosenbaum. 2000. "Making Single Mothers Work: Recent Tax and Welfare Policy and Its Effects." *National Tax Journal* 53(4): 1027–62.

———. 2001a. "Making Single Mothers Work: Recent Tax and Welfare Policy and Its Effects." In *Making Work Pay: The Earned Income Tax Credit and Its Impact on America's Families*, edited by Bruce Meyer and Douglas Holtz-Eakin. New York: Russell Sage Foundation.

———. 2001b. "Welfare, the Earned Income Tax Credit, and the Labor Supply of Single Mothers." *Quarterly Journal of Economics* 116(3): 1063–1114.

Meyer, Bruce, and James Sullivan. 2003. "Measuring the Well-Being of the Poor Using Income and Consumption." *Journal of Human Resources* 38(S): 1180–1220.

———. 2004. "The Effects of Welfare and Tax Reform: The Material Well-Being of Single Mothers in the 1980s and 1990s." *Journal of Public Economics* 88(7–8): 1387–1420.

———. 2006. "Consumption, Income, and Material Well-Being After Welfare Reform." Working paper 11976. Cambridge, Mass.: National Bureau of Economic Research.

———. 2008. "Three Decades of Consumption and Income Poverty." Unpublished paper. Chicago and South Bend, Ind.: University of Chicago and University of Notre Dame.

Middleton, Sue, Karl Ashworth, and Ian Braithwaite. 1997. *Small Fortunes: Spending on Children, Childhood Poverty, and Parental Sacrifice*. York, U.K.: Joseph Rowntree Foundation.

Millar, Jane, and Tess Ridge. 2001. *Families, Poverty, Work, and Care*. Research report 153. London: Department for Work and Pensions. Available at: http://research.dwp.gov.uk/asd/asd5/rrep153.pdf (accessed August 18, 2009).

Miller, Amalia, and Lei Zhang. 2007. "The Effects of Welfare Reform on the Academic Performance of Children in Low-Income Households." Unpublished paper. Charlottesville: University of Virginia.

————. 2008. "Intergenerational Effects of Welfare Reform." Unpublished paper. Charlottesville: University of Virginia.

Milligan, Kevin, and Mark Stabile. 2008. "Do Child Tax Benefits Affect the Well-Being of Children? Evidence from Canadian Child Benefit Expansions." Working paper 14624. Cambridge, Mass.: National Bureau of Economic Research (December). Available at: http://www.nber.org/papers/w14624 (accessed February 17, 2010).

Morris, Pamela, Greg Duncan, and Elizabeth Clark-Kauffman. 2005. "Child Well-Being in an Era of Welfare Reform: The Sensitivity of Transitions in Development to Policy Change." *Developmental Psychology* 41(6): 919–32.

Morris, Pamela, Greg Duncan, and Chris Rodriguez. 2004. "Using Welfare Reform Experiments to Estimate the Impact of Income on Child Achievement." Unpublished paper. Evanston, Ill.: Northwestern University.

Morris, Pamela, and Lisa Gennetian. 2003. "Identifying the Effects of Income on Children's Development Using Experimental Data." *Journal of Marriage and Family* 65(3): 716–29.

Morris, Pamela, Aletha Huston, Greg Duncan, Danielle Crosby, and Johannes Bos. 2001. *How Welfare and Work Policies Affect Children: A Synthesis of Research.* New York: MDRC.

Mullis, Iris V. S., Michael O. Martin, Albert E. Beaton, Eugenio J. Gonzalez, Dana L. Kelly, and Teresa A. Smith. 1998a. *Mathematics Achievement in the Primary School Years: IEA TIMSS.* Chestnut Hill, Mass.: Boston College.

————. 1998b. *Mathematics and Science Achievement in the Final Year of Secondary School: IEA's TIMSS.* Chestnut Hill, Mass.: Boston College.

Mullis, Iris V. S., Michael O. Martin, and Pierre Foy. 2008a. *TIMSS 2007 International Mathematics Report: Findings from IEA's Trends in International Mathematics and Science Study at the Fourth and Eight Grades.* Chestnut Hill, Mass.: IEA TIMSS and PIRLS International Study Center.

————. 2008b. *TIMSS 2007 International Science Report:. Findings from IEA's Trends in International Mathematics and Science Study at the Fourth and Eight Grades.* Chestnut Hill, Mass.: IEA TIMSS and PIRLS International Study Center.

Mullis, Iris V. S., Michael O. Martin, Eugenio J. Gonzalez, and Steven J. Chrostowski. 2004. *TIMSS 2003 International Mathematics Report: Findings from IEA's Trends in International Mathematics and Science Study at the Fourth and Eighth Grades.* Chestnut Hill, Mass.: Boston College.

Mullis, Iris V. S., Michael O. Martin, Eugenio J. Gonzalez, and Ann M. Kennedy. 2003. *PIRLS 2001 International Report: IEA's Study of Reading Literacy Achievement in Primary School.* Chestnut Hill, Mass.: Boston College.

Mullis, Iris V. S., Michael O. Martin, Ann M. Kennedy, and Pierre Foy. 2007. *PIRLS 2006 International Report: IEA's Progress in International Reading Literacy Study in Primary School on Forty Countries.* Chestnut Hill, Mass.: Boston College.

National Evaluation of Sure Start (NESS). 2005. *Early Impacts of Sure Start Local*

Programs on Children and Families. Report 13. London: Department for Education and Skills.

———. 2008. *The Impact of Sure Start on Three-Year-Olds and Their Families*. London: University of London, Institute for the Study of Children, Families, and Social Issues, Birkbeck College.

National Health Service (NHS). 2009a. *About Healthy Start*. Available at: http://www.healthystart.nhs.uk/en/fe/about_healthy_start.html (accessed February 5, 2009).

———. 2009b. *The School Fruit and Vegetable Scheme*. Available at: http://www.5aday.nhs.uk/sfvs/about/default.aspx (accessed February 5, 2009).

National Statistics. 1996. *Full-Time Participation Rates by Eighteen-Year-Olds in Secondary Education: EU Comparison, 1996*. Available at: http://www.statistics.gov.uk/STATBASE/xsdataset.asp?vlnk=188 (accessed February 4, 2009).

———. 2004. *Government Expenditures on Social Security Benefits, 1991/92 to 2001/02: Annual Abstract of Statistics*. London: National Statistics.

———. 2007. "Tables." *Population Trends* 130 (winter). London: National Statistics.

———. 2008. "Tables." *Population Trends* 132 (summer). London: National Statistics.

———. 2009a. "Child Benefit." Available at: http://www.dwp.gov.uk/asd/asd1/child_benefit/ChildBenefit.pdf (accessed March 15, 2009).

———. 2009b. "Work and Worklessness." Available at: http://www.statistics.gov.uk/statbase/Product.asp?vlnk=12859 (accessed July 14, 2009).

———. 2009c. *Social Trends*. Available at: http://www.statistics.gov.uk/socialtrends39/ (accessed September 24, 2009).

Nelson, Richard. 1977. *The Moon and the Ghetto*. New York: Norton.

Neumark, David, and William Wascher. 2007. "Minimum Wages, the Earned Income Tax Credit, and Employment: Evidence from the Post-Welfare Reform Era." Working paper 12915. Cambridge, Mass.: National Bureau of Economic Research.

Nord, Mark, Nader Kabbani, Laura Tiehen, Margaret Andrews, Gary Bickel, and Steven Carlson. 2001. *Household Food Security in the United States, 2000*. Available at: http://www.ers.usda.gov/ (accessed January 21, 2009).

———. 2002. *Household Food Security in the United States, 2001*. Food Assistance and Nutrition Research Report 29 (FANRR29). Available at: http://www.ers.usda.gov/ (accessed January 21, 2009).

———. 2003. *Household Food Security in the United States, 2002*. Food Assistance and Nutrition Research Report 35 (FANRR35). Available at: http://www.ers.usda.gov/ (accessed January 21, 2009).

———. 2004. *Household Food Security in the United States, 2003*. Food Assistance and Nutrition Research Report 42 (FANRR42). Available at: http://www.ers.usda.gov/ (accessed January 21, 2009).

———. 2005. *Household Food Security in the United States, 2004*. Economic Research Report 11 (ERR11). Available at: http://www.ers.usda.gov/ (accessed January 21, 2009).

———. 2006. *Household Food Security in the United States, 2005*. Economic Research Report 29 (ERR29). Available at: http://www.ers.usda.gov/ (accessed January 21, 2009).

———. 2007. *Household Food Security in the United States, 2006*. Economic Research Report 49 (ERR49). Available at: http://www.ers.usda.gov/ (accessed January 21, 2009).

Notten, Geranda, and Chris de Neubourg. 2007. "Relative or Absolute Poverty in the U.S. and EU? The Battle of Rates." Working paper MGsoG/207/WP001. Maastricht, the Netherlands: Maastricht University, Maastricht Graduate School of Governance.

———. 2008. "Monitoring Absolute and Relative Poverty: 'Not Enough' Is Not the Same as 'Much Less.'" Unpublished paper. Maastricht, The Netherlands: Maastricht University, Maastricht Graduate School of Governance.

Oreopoulos, Philip, Marianne Page, and Ann Huff Stevens. 2005. "The Intergenerational Effects of Worker Displacement." Working paper W11587. Cambridge, Mass.: National Bureau of Economic Research (August). Available at: http://papers.ssrn.com/sol3/papers.cfm?abstract_id=795271.

Organisation for Economic Cooperation and Development (OECD). 1997. *Employment Outlook 1997*. Paris: OECD. Available at: http://www.oecd.org/data oecd/19/15/2080479.pdf (accessed July 14, 2009).

———. 1998. *Employment Outlook 1998*. Paris: OECD.

———. 2001a. *Employment Outlook 2001*. Paris: OECD. Available at: http://www .oecd.org/document/18/0,3343,en_2649_33927_31693539_1_1_1_1,00.html (accessed July 14, 2009).

———. 2001b. *PISA 2000: Knowledge and Skills for Life*. Paris: OECD.

———. 2004. *PISA 2003: Learning for Tomorrow's World*. Paris: OECD.

———. 2007. *PISA 2006: Science Competencies for Tomorrow's World*. Paris: OECD.

———. 2008. *Growing Unequal: Income Distribution and Poverty in OECD Countries*. Paris: OECD.

———. 2009. *Doing Better for Children*. Paris: OECD.

Panel on Fair Access to the Professions. 2009. *Unleashing Aspiration: Summary and Recommendations of the Full Report*. London: Cabinet Office.

Parcel, Toby, and Elizabeth Menaghan. 1994. *Parents' Jobs and Children's Lives*. New York: Aldine de Gruyter.

Park, Alison, John Curtice, Katarina Thompson, Miranda Phillips, Mark Johnson, and Elizabeth Clery, eds. 2008. *British Social Attitudes: The Twenty-fourth Report*. London: Sage Publications.

Parker, Simon. 2001. "Blair Promises More Radical Reform of Public Services." *The Guardian*, May 16. Available at: http://www.guardian.co.uk/society/2001/may/16/7 (accessed August 14, 2009).

Paxson, Christina, and Jane Waldfogel. 2002. "Work, Welfare, and Child Maltreatment." *Journal of Labor Economics* 20(3): 435–74.

——. 2003. "Welfare Reforms, Family Resources, and Child Maltreatment." *Journal of Policy Analysis and Management* 22(1): 85–113.

Percival, Jenny. 2008. "Brown to Trial Child Development Grants." *The Guardian*, June 23.

Phillips, Meredith, James Crouse, and John Ralph. 1998. "Does the Black-White Test Score Gap Widen After Children Enter School?" In *The Black-White Test Score Gap*, edited by Christopher Jencks and Meredith Phillips. Washington, D.C.: Brookings Institution Press.

Platt, Lucinda. 2007. "Child Poverty, Employment, and Ethnicity in the U.K.: The Role and Limitations of Policy." *European Societies* 9(2): 175–99.

——. 2009. *Ethnicity and Child Poverty*. Research report 576. London: Department for Work and Pensions.

Poverty Site. 2009. "United Kingdom: Work and Lone Parents." Available at: http://www.poverty.org.uk/46/index.shtml (accessed February 17, 2010).

Power, Anne. 2007. *City Survivors: Bringing Up Children in Disadvantaged Neighborhoods*. Bristol, U.K.: Policy Press.

Primus, Wendell, Lynette Rawlings, Kathy Larin, and Kathryn Porter. 1999. *The Initial Impacts of Welfare Reform on the Incomes of Single-Mother Families*. Washington, D.C.: Center for Budget and Policy Priorities.

Reichman, Nancy, Julien Teitler, and Marah Curtis. 2005. "TANF Sanctioning and Hardship." *Social Service Review* 79(2): 215–36.

Rogers, Annette, and Camille Ryan. 2007. "Extended Measures of Well-Being: Living Conditions in the United States, 2003." Current Population Reports P70-110. Washington: U.S. Bureau of the Census.

Romich, Jennifer, and Thomas Weisner. 2000. "How Families View and Use the EITC: Advance Payment Versus Lump Sum Delivery." *National Tax Journal* 53(4): 1245–1265.

Rothstein, Richard, Rebecca Jacobsen, and Tamara Wilder. 2008. *Grading Education: Getting Accountability Right*. Washington, D.C.: Economic Policy Institute.

Ruhm, Christopher. 2000. "Parental Leave and Child Health." *Journal of Health Economics* 19(6): 931–60.

Sammons, Pam, Kathy Sylva, Edward Melhuish, Iram Siraj-Blatchford, Brenda Taggart, and Karen Elliott. 2002. *Measuring the Impact of Preschool on Children's Cognitive Development over the Preschool Period*. Effective Provision of Preschool Education (EPPE) Project technical paper 8a. London: University of London, Institute of Education.

——. 2003. *Measuring the Impact of Preschool on Children's Social/Behavioral Development over the Preschool Period*. EPPE Project technical paper 8b. London: University of London, Institute of Education.

Scholz, John Karl, Robert Moffitt, and Benjamin Cowan. 2009. "Trends in Income Support." In *Changing Poverty and Changing Antipoverty Policies*, edited by Maria Cancian and Sheldon Danziger. New York: Russell Sage Foundation.

Schwalb, Rebecca, and Mike Wiseman. 2008. "Poverty in the U.S. and the U.K.: Relative Measurement and Relative Achievement." Paper presented to the thirtieth annual Association for Public Policy Analysis and Management (APPAM) research conference. Los Angeles (November 7).

Seefeldt, Kristin, and Sean Orzol. 2005. "Watching the Clock Tick: Factors Associated with TANF Accumulation." *Social Work Research* 24(9): 215–29.

Sefton, Tom. 2003. "What We Want from the Welfare State." In *British Social Attitudes: The Twentieth Report: Continuity and Change over Two Decades*, edited by Alison R. Park, John Curtice, Katarina Thomson, Lindsey Jarvis, and Catherine Bromley. Aldershot, U.K.: Ashgate.

———. 2009. "Moving in the Right Direction? Public Attitudes to Poverty, Inequality, and Redistribution." In *Toward a More Equal Society? Poverty, Inequality, and Policy Since 1997*, edited by John Hills, Tom Sefton, and Kitty Stewart. Bristol, U.K.: Policy Press.

Shaw, Jonathan. 2007. "Eradicating Child Poverty." *Economic Review* 24(4): 4.

Shea, John. 2000. "Does Parents' Money Matter?" *Journal of Public Economics* 77(2): 155–84.

Sherman, Arloc. 2009. *Stimulus Keeping 6 Million Americans Out of Poverty in 2009, Estimates Show*. Washington, D.C.: Center for Budget and Policy Priorities. Available at: http://www.cbpp.org/files/9-9-09pov2.pdf (accessed November 19, 2009).

Sherraden, Michael. 1991. *Assets and the Poor: A New American Welfare Policy*. Armonk, N.Y.: M. E. Sharpe.

Shonkoff, Jack P., and Deborah A. Phillips, eds. 2000. *From Neurons to Neighborhoods: The Science of Early Childhood Development*. Washington, D.C.: National Academies Press.

Short, Kathleen, and Martina Shea. 1995. "Beyond Poverty, Extended Measures of Well-Being: 1992." Current Population Reports P70-50RV. Washington: U.S. Bureau of the Census.

Shropshire, Jules, and Sue Middleton. 1999. *Small Expectations: Learning to Be Poor?* York, U.K.: Joseph Rowntree Foundation.

Slack, Kristen Shook, Katherine Magnuson, Lawrence Berger, Joan Yoo, Rebekah Levine Coley, Rachel Dunifon, Amy Dworsky, Ariel Kalil, Jean Knab, Brenda Lohman, and Cynthia Osborne. 2007. "Family Economic Well-Being Following the 1996 Welfare Reform: Trend Data from Five Non-Experimental Panel Studies." *Children and Youth Services Review* 29(6): 698–720.

Smeeding, Timothy. 2007. "Poverty, Work, and Policy: The United States in Comparative Perspective." Testimony before the Subcommittee on Income Security and Family Support, House Committee on Ways and Means, Congress of the United States (February 13).

Smeeding, Timothy, Katherin Ross Phillips, and Michael O'Connor. 2000. "The EITC: Expectation, Knowledge, Use, and Economic and Social Mobility." *National Tax Journal* 53(4): 1187–1209.

Smeeding, Timothy, Lee Rainwater, and Gary Burtless. 2001. "U.S. Poverty in a Cross-National Context." In *Understanding Poverty*, edited by Sheldon Danziger and Gary Burtless. Cambridge, Mass.: Harvard University Press.

Smeeding, Timothy, and Jane Waldfogel. 2010. "Fighting Poverty: Policy Can Make a Huge Difference." *Journal of Policy Analysis and Management* 29(2): 401–07.

Smith, Richard. 1999. "Eradicating Child Poverty." *British Medical Journal* 319 (7204): 203–4.

Smithers, Alan. 2004. *England's Education*. Centre for Education and Employment Research, University of Liverpool.

——. 2007. "Blair's Education: An International Perspective." London: Sutton Trust. Available at: http://www.buckingham.ac.uk/education/research/ceer/pdfs/blairseducation.pdf (accessed September 11, 2009).

Smolensky, Eugene, and Jennifer Gootman, eds. 2003. *Working Families and Growing Kids: Caring for Children and Adolescents*. Washington, D.C.: National Academies Press.

Social Exclusion Unit (SEU). 2001a. *Preventing Social Exclusion: Report by the Social Exclusion Unit*. London: Cabinet Office.

——. 2001b. *A New Commitment to Neighborhood Renewal: National Strategy Action Plan*. London: Cabinet Office.

Stanley, Kate, Kate Bellamy, and Graeme Cooke. 2006. *Equal Access? Appropriate and Affordable Childcare for Every Child*. London: Institute for Public Policy Research.

Stanley, Kate, and Clare McNeil. 2009. "Picking Up the Benefits." London: IPPR. Available at: http://www.ippr.org/articles/id=3772 (accessed November 16, 2009).

Stannard, John, and Laura Huxley. 2007. *The Literacy Game: The Story of the National Literacy Strategy*. London: Routledge.

Stewart, Kitty. 2009a. "'A Scar on the Soul of Britain': Child Poverty and Disadvantage Under New Labour." In *Toward a More Equal Society? Poverty, Inequality, and Policy Since 1997*, edited by John Hills, Tom Sefton, and Kitty Stewart. Bristol, U.K.: Policy Press.

——. 2009b. "Poverty, Inequality, and Child Well-Being in International Context: Still Bottom of the Pack?" In *Toward a More Equal Society? Poverty, Inequality and Policy Since 1997*, edited by John Hills, Tom Sefton and Kitty Stewart. Bristol, U.K.: Policy Press.

Stewart, Kitty, and John Hills. 2005. "Introduction." In *A More Equal Society? New Labour, Poverty, Inequality, and Exclusion*, edited by John Hills and Kitty Stewart. Bristol, U.K.: Policy Press.

Stewart, Mark, and Joanna Swaffield. 1997. "The Dynamics of Low Pay in Britain." In *Jobs, Wages, and Poverty: Patterns of Persistence and Mobility in the New Flexible Labor Market*, edited by Paul Gregg. London: London School of Economics, Centre for Economic Performance.

REFERENCES

Stratford, Nina, Steven Finch, and Jane Pethick. 1997. *Survey of Parents of Three- and Four-Year-Old Children and Their Use of Early Years Services*. Research brief 31. London: Department for Education and Employment.

Stratton, Allegra. 2009. "Tory Bill Attempts to Water Down Minimum Wage." *The Guardian*, May 13. Available at: http://www.guardian.co.uk/politics/2009/may/13/minimum-wage-tory-bill/print (accessed September 18, 2009).

Strickland, Pat. 1998. "Working Families Tax Credit and Family Credit." House of Commons research paper 98-46. London: House of Commons Library (April 9). Available at: http://www.parliament.uk/commons/lib/research/rp98/rp98-046.pdf (accessed April 10, 2009).

Sullivan, James, Lesley Turner, and Sheldon Danziger. 2008. "The Relationship Between Income and Material Hardship." *Journal of Policy Analysis and Management* 27(1): 63–81.

Sutherland, Holly. 2001. "Five Labour Budgets (1997–2001): Impacts on the Distribution of Household Incomes and on Child Poverty." Available at: http://econpapers.repec.org/paper/esemsimrn/mu_2frn_2f41.htm (accessed December 17, 2009).

Sutton Trust. 2009. "Social Mobility and Education: Report of a High-Level Summit Sponsored by the Carnegie Corporation of New York and the Sutton Trust." Available at: http://www.suttontrust.com/reports/summit_report.pdf (accessed September 14, 2009).

Swartz, Katherine. 2009. "Health Care for the Poor: For Whom, What Care, and Whose Responsibility?" In *Changing Poverty and Changing Antipoverty Policies*, edited by Maria Cancian and Sheldon Danziger. New York: Russell Sage Foundation.

Tanaka, Sakiko. 2005. "Parental Leave and Child Health Across OECD Countries." *Economic Journal* 115(501): F7–28.

Taylor, Beck, Eric Dearing, and Kathleen McCartney. 2004. "Income and Outcomes in Early Childhood." *Journal of Human Resources* 34(4): 980–1007.

Taylor-Gooby, Peter. 2005. *Attitudes to Social Justice*. London: Institute for Public Policy Research.

Taylor-Gooby, Peter, and Rose Martin. 2008. "Trends in Sympathy for the Poor." In *British Social Attitudes: The Twenty-Fourth Report*, edited by Alison Park, John Curtice, Katarina Thompson, Miranda Phillips, Mark Johnson, and Elizabeth Clery. London: Sage Publications.

Timmins, Nicholas. 2001. *The Five Giants: A Biography of the Welfare State*. London: HarperCollins.

———. 2007. "Running to Stand Still: How Labour Struggles to Hold Back Rising Inequality in Britain." *Financial Times*, May 2.

TIMSS International Study Center. 2007. *Highlights of Results from TIMSS: Third International Mathematics and Science Study*. Available at: http://timss.bc.edu/timss1995i/TIMSSPDF/P2HiLite.pdf (accessed July 29, 2009).

TIMSS and PIRLS International Study Center. 2009a. *Third International Math and*

Science Study 1995. Available at: http://timss.bc.edu/timss1995.html (accessed February 17, 2010).

———. 2009b. *Trends in International Math and Science Study 1999*. Available at: http://timss.bc.edu/timss1999.html (accessed February 17, 2010).

———. 2009c. *Trends in International Math and Science Study 2003*. Available at: http://timss.bc.edu/timss2003.html (accessed February 17, 2010).

Tower Hamlets Partnership. 2009. *Child Poverty Strategy 2009–2012*. London: Tower Hamlets Partnership.

Toynbee, Polly. 2009. "This Is One Legacy Target That Labour Can't Afford to Miss." *The Guardian*, March 14.

Turner, Lesley, Sheldon Danziger, and Kristin Seefeldt. 2006. "Failing the Transition from Welfare to Work: Women Chronically Disconnected from Employment and Cash Welfare." *Social Science Quarterly* 87(2): 227–49.

UNICEF Innocenti Research Centre. 2000. *A League Table of Child Poverty in Rich Nations*. Innocenti Report Card 1 (June). Available at: http://www.unicef-irc.org/publications/pdf/repcard1e.pdf (accessed February 17, 2010).

———. 2007. *An Overview of Child Well-Being in Rich Countries*. Innocenti Report Card 7. Florence: UNICEF Innocenti Research Centre.

U.S. Bureau of the Census. 2009a. *Historical Poverty Tables*. Available at: http://www.census.gov/hhes/www/poverty/histpov/famindex.html (accessed September 16, 2009).

———. 2009b. *Extended Measures of Well-Being: Living Conditions in the Untied States, 2005*. Available at: http://www.census.gov/population/www/socdemo/extended-05.html (accessed February 17, 2010).

U.S. Department of Health and Human Services. Centers for Medicare and Medicaid Services. 2009. "National CHIP Policy." Available at: http://www.cms.hhs.gov/NationalCHIPPolicy/01_Overview.asp#TopOfPage (accessed September 20, 2009).

U.S. House of Representatives. Ways and Means Committee. 2004. *2004 Green Book*. Available at: http://www.gpoaccess.gov/wmprints/green/2004.html (accessed September 30, 2009).

Vegeris, Sandra, and Jane Perry. 2003. *Families and Children 2001: Living Standards and the Children*. Department for Work and Pensions research report 190. London: The Stationery Office.

Waldfogel, Jane. 1998. *The Future of Child Protection: How to Break the Cycle of Abuse and Neglect*. Cambridge, Mass.: Harvard University Press.

———. 1999. "Early Childhood Interventions and Outcomes." Centre for Analysis of Social Exclusion (CASE) paper 21 (February). Available at: http://sticerd.lse.ac.uk/dps/case/cp/Paper21.pdf (accessed March 15, 2009).

———. 2001. "What Other Nations Do: International Policies Toward Parental Leave and Child Care." *Future of Children* 11(1): 98–111.

———. 2002. "Child Care, Women's Employment, and Child Outcomes." *Journal of Population Economics* 15(3): 527–48.

——. 2004. "Social Mobility, Life Chances, and the Early Years." Centre for Analysis of Social Exclusion (CASE) paper 88. Available at: http://sticerd.lse.ac.uk/dps/case/CP/CASEPaper88.pdf (accessed January 29, 2009).

——. 2006a. *What Children Need*. Cambridge, Mass.: Harvard University Press.

——. 2006b. "Early Childhood Policy: A Comparative Perspective." In *Blackwell Handbook of Early Childhood Development*, edited by Kathleen McCartney and Deborah Phillips. Malden, Mass.: Wiley.

——. 2007a. "Welfare Reforms and Child Well-Being in the U.S. and U.K." *Swedish Economic Policy Review* 14(2): 137–68.

——. 2007b. "Investing in Our Children: The U.S. Can Learn from the U.K." Washington, D.C.: Center for American Progress. Available at: http://www.americanprogress.org/issues/2007/07/investing_in_children.html (accessed July 27, 2009).

——. 2008. "Economic Dimensions of Social Policy." In *The Handbook of Social Policy*, edited by James Midgely, Martin Tracy, and Michelle Livermore. Thousand Oaks, Calif.: Sage Publications.

——. 2009. "The Role of Family Policy in Antipoverty Policy." In *Changing Poverty and Changing Antipoverty Policies*, edited by Maria Cancian and Sheldon Danziger. New York: Russell Sage Foundation.

Waldfogel, Jane, and Alison Garnham. 2008. *Childcare and Child Poverty*. "Initiative on Eradicating Child Poverty: The Role of Key Policy Areas." Report prepared for the Joseph Rowntree Foundation (November 10). Available at: http://www.jrf.org.uk/publications/childcare-and-child-poverty (accessed April 28, 2009).

Waldfogel, Jane, and Elizabeth Washbrook. 2009. "Early Years Policy." Report. London: Sutton Trust.

Walker, Robert. 1999a. *Ending Child Poverty: Popular Welfare for the Twenty-First Century?* Bristol, U.K.: Policy Press.

——. 1999b. "Dimensions of the Debate: Reflections on the Beveridge Lecture." In *Ending Child Poverty: Popular Welfare for the Twenty-First Century?*, edited by Robert Walker. Bristol, U.K.: Policy Press.

Walsh, Imelda. 2008. *Flexible Working: A Review of How to Extend the Right to Request Flexible Working to Parents of Older Children*. London: Department for Business, Enterprise, and Regulatory Reform (BERR). Available at: http://www.berr.gov.uk/files/file46092.pdf (accessed January 29, 2009).

White House. 2009. "Poverty." Available at: http://www.whitehouse.gov/issues/poverty (accessed November 19, 2009).

Whitty, Geoff. 2008. "Twenty Years of Progress? Education Policy 1988 to the Present." *Educational Management Administration and Leadership* 36(2): 165–84.

——. 2009. "Evaluating 'Blair's Educational Legacy'? Some Comments on the Special Issue of *Oxford Review of Education*." *Oxford Review of Education* 35(2): 267–80.

Willitts, Maxine. 2006. *Measuring Child Poverty Using Material Deprivation: Possible*

Approaches. Department for Work and Pensions working paper 28. Available at: http://research.dwp.gov.uk/asd/asd5/WP28.pdf (accessed September 16, 2009).

Wilson, Deborah, Simon Burgess, and Adam Briggs. Forthcoming. "The Dynamics of School Attainment of England's Ethnic Minorities." *Journal of Population Economics*.

Wilson, William Julius. 1996. *When Work Disappears: The World of the New Urban Poor*. New York: Knopf.

Women's Legal Defense and Education Fund. 2009. "Meager and Diminishing Welfare Benefits Perpetuate Widespread Material Hardship for Poor Women and Children." Available at: http://www.legalmomentum.org/assets/pdfs/tanf-meager-benefits.pdf (accessed August 17, 2009).

World Health Organization (WHO). 2004. *Young People's Health in Context: Health Behavior in School-Aged Children (HBSC) Study: International Report from the 2001–2002 Survey*. Copenhagen: WHO.

———. 2008. *Inequalities in Young People's Health: Health Behavior in School-Aged Children (HBSC) Study: International Report from the 2005–2006 Survey*. Copenhagen: WHO.

Zedlewski, Sheila, and Sandi Nelson. 2003. *Families Coping Without Earnings or Government Cash Assistance*. Assessing the New Federalism occasional paper 64. Washington, D.C.: Urban Institute.

Index

Boldface numbers refer to figures and tables.